TRANSACTIONS OF THE

AMERICAN PHILOSOPHICAL SOCIETY

HELD AT PHILADELPHIA

FOR PROMOTING USEFUL KNOWLEDGE

———————

VOLUME 71, PART 2 · 1981

The Ox That Gored

J. J. FINKELSTEIN

LATE WILLIAM M. LAFFAN PROFESSOR OF ASSYRIOLOGY AND
BABYLONIAN LITERATURE AT YALE UNIVERSITY

(PREPARED FOR PUBLICATION BY MARIA DEJ. ELLIS
BABYLONIAN SECTION, UNIVERSITY MUSEUM,
UNIVERSITY OF PENNSYLVANIA)

THE AMERICAN PHILOSOPHICAL SOCIETY

INDEPENDENCE SQUARE: PHILADELPHIA

1981

Library of Congress Catalog
Card Number 80-65852
International Standard Book Number 0-87169-712-2
US ISSN 0065-9746

EDITORIAL PREFACE

The late J. J. Finkelstein spent many years collecting the material which forms the basis for *The Ox That Gored*. Much of that effort is reflected in preliminary studies that range from discussions of specific problems posed by ancient Mesopotamian texts to essays concerning the cosmological context into which these texts fit.[1] The present volume draws on those preliminary studies and adds much new material.

When Finkelstein died in November, 1974, he left a draft of a comprehensive work on the subject of the goring ox and related topics. His reasons for the manner in which he chose to approach the topic, and the ramifications into which he was led, are set forth below, in the Introduction. Finkelstein divided his presentation of the material into three parts. Of these, Part III was published in a preliminary form as "The Goring Ox: Some Historical Perspectives on Deodands, Forfeitures, Wrongful Death, and the Western Notion of Sovereignty," in the *Temple Law Quarterly*.[2] Since the third part had already been published in preliminary form, and since reprinting it even in a revised version would be prohibitively expensive,

the Publications Committee of the American Philosophical Society and I agreed that only the first two parts of the study would be published here. The third section does, of course, remain an integral part of Finkelstein's presentation, as he himself explains in the Introduction, but the interested reader will need to use it in its original form.

Of the two sections of the study which are published here, Part I was in fairly good shape, but needed considerable editorial work. Part II presented more serious problems; it was in the form of a very rough first draft, and needed extensive revision. I had to rearrange the material in that section into one chapter less than was originally intended by Finkelstein,[3] but apart from that the current text basically reflects Finkelstein's original. With one notable exception, discussed in the first note to chapter VII, I have made no significant additions to the manuscript, since to do so would have violated the personal nature of the work.

I should perhaps conclude by saying that, had Finkelstein lived to see this work through publication himself, he and I would undoubtedly have found many points of disagreement. Where such issues arose, I have tried to be faithful to his point of view. Apart from the adjustments I have mentioned I have left the work much as he wrote it, and I trust he would have approved of the changes I did need to make.

Philadelphia   Maria deJ. Ellis
November, 1979

---

[1] For a bibliography of J. J. Finkelstein's works, see that compiled by Peter Machinist and Norman Yoffee, in Maria deJ. Ellis (ed.), *Essays on the Ancient Near East in Memory of Jacob Joel Finkelstein*, Memoirs of the Connecticut Academy of Arts and Sciences, **19**, (Hamden, 1977): pp. 227–229. The bibliographical entry referred to on p. 229 as "Mesopotamia 2500–1000 B.C." has now been published as "Early Mesopotamia, 2500–1000 B.C.," in Harold D. Lasswell, Daniel Lerner, and Hans Speier (eds.), *Propaganda and Communication in World History*, **1**: *The Symbolic Instrument in Early Times* (Honolulu, University Press of Hawaii, for the East-West Center, 1979): pp. 50–110.

[2] **46** (1973): pp. 169–290.

---

[3] The discussions of the classical sources and the ethnographic material were combined into one chapter, VII.

THE OX THAT GORED

J. J. FINKELSTEIN

CONTENTS

INTRODUCTION

The present book undertakes to explore a few fundamental assumptions that underlie the Western view of the world. It does not attempt to get behind these assumptions, but focuses rather on certain of our laws and institutions in which they have taken on concrete form. My primary aim is to reveal them by analyzing the institutional and ideological phenomena in which they are embedded. The point of departure for this investigation consists of a handful of biblical verses found in the first five books of the Old Testament ("The Law" or the Pentateuch) which prescribe the legal disposition of various cases of homicide, including accidental death. The title of the book derives from the sequence of rules set down in the Book of Exodus chapter 21 verses 28–32, all of which concern cases in which a human being is butted or gored to death by an ox.

The theme of "the goring ox" was a popular one in the legal thought of the civilizations of the ancient Near East, particularly in that of ancient Mesopotamia. The "Code" of Hammurapi, the best known of the law collections left us by that civilization, has a series of three rules devoted to the theme, but "the goring ox" is treated also in other law documents. All of the Mesopotamian sources bearing on the subject antedate the laws in the Book of Exodus by many

centuries and, as I hope to demonstrate, the biblical rules derive their inspiration from these earlier prototypes or from as yet undiscovered sources that, in turn, derived from Mesopotamian prototypes.

The first part of this study is devoted to a thorough exposition of all the known ancient statements of the rules about goring oxen together with other statements of law, both in the Bible and in the cuneiform sources of ancient Mesopotamia, that shed light on our general theme.

In scrutinizing the institutions of any civilization we must first be sure that we know the conceptual postulates of the society under consideration, its system of values, its ways of classifying and categorizing the world of experience. In applying this rule to the laws of the goring ox it becomes evident that the conceptual context of the Mesopotamian statements of these laws is vastly different from that of their biblical counterpart, and that this difference is the most fundamental factor in determining both the inner structure of the laws themselves and the substantive differences in their juridical resolution. The biblical author appropriated a legal theme out of the common ancient Near Eastern heritage, but transposed these laws into a distinctly different framework and in effect transformed them in the most profound sense even while retaining much of their original form and language.

It is my opinion that the system of categorization reflected in the biblical statement of the laws of the goring ox is essentially the same as our own. In other words, the cosmic apprehension of the biblical authors, the way in which the Bible perceives and classifies the world of experience, is in every fundamental respect identical with ours, that is, with that of the civilization we usually describe as "Western."

Part Two of this study considers the trial of animals in primitive and non-Western societies, and traces the effect of the laws of the goring ox as stated in the Book of Exodus on the legal thought and practice of later phases of Western civilization, particularly in medieval Europe and in the United States. Under this aspect, it will be shown that the principle underlying the biblical laws of the goring ox has had direct literal and near-literal counterparts in the legal experience of later Western society, where we find the curious phenomenon of trials and punishment of domestic animals for attacks upon persons. In contrast, we shall see that such behavior is unknown to any society, past or present, which falls outside the Western cosmological tradition, and that this observation is valid also for "primitive" or "savage" societies, concerning which there remains much misapprehension in this connection.

Overshadowing this aspect of the thesis, however, is the development of the deeper rationale underlying the biblical law of the goring ox into a legal and politico-philosophical doctrine of extraordinary power. The essence of this doctrine is the transcending power of sovereignty and the prerogatives in law this transcendence bestows on those who exercise sovereignty in the realm of law, prerogatives which enable the sovereign entities to enforce legal standards that do not conform to elementary standards of justice or human reason. This extraordinary power, reserved to the sovereign alone, is the right to impose liability for a harm to its interest upon a person or subject who could bear no blame for that harm. The principle involved is that of "objective liability": a person can be compelled to suffer a penalty for a harm of which he was not the cause. The principle of the biblical law of the goring ox—which required the execution of the ox that had gored a human being to death—underwent its first transformation in the English law of the early Middle Ages. Under it, almost any accidental death of a human being and even the case of suicide became the occasion for the forfeiture of a sum of money to the Crown, that is, the sovereign. The instrument which served as the agent of an accidental death, whether it was an animal or an inanimate object, was declared *deodand* ("to be given to God"), and its value became forfeit to the king as a sum of money.

In the third and last part of the study the ultimate transformation of the biblical law of the goring ox is traced from the abolition of the deodands in England in the middle of the nineteenth century until the present. The sovereign retreated voluntarily from its interest in wrongful death and from the fiscal benefits that had accrued to it from the prosecution of crimes of violence in general. But the sovereign's special prerogative did not disappear; it was shifted into new fields, largely, but not exclusively, connected with state revenue and the public welfare. In the earlier phases of that shift the thread by which the new policy could be traced back to the biblical law of the goring ox was still visible to American jurists, and even until quite recently the biblical law of the goring ox was occasionally cited by judges in the course of decisions upholding government forfeitures. For the most part, however, the organic link to the biblical antecedent has been lost from sight, and the principle of objective liability to the detriment of individuals has been extended into new domains.

The final chapters of this section of the study review two leading contemporary legal issues, automobile accidents and compensation to victims of crime, both of which obviously incorporate legal factors of the older approach to the problem of wrongful death. I will show that government policy as regards these questions, as well as the discussions of their various aspects by professional jurisprudents, have ignored the crucial historical dimension which would have revealed the direct link between current attitudes toward these problems and the basic rationale underlying the biblical law of the goring ox and other scriptural legislation. This link is the transcendent quality of sovereignty, which is seen as conferring upon the sovereign the exclusive right of measuring liability by an objective standard while allowing it to claim immunity against liability for itself on an almost absolute standard.

The study closes with a return to the theme set in the Introduction to Part I. This is meant to suggest that the study as a whole is an essay in comparative cosmology rather than in comparative legal institutions. I have tried to demonstrate how closely linked social institutions are to a society's intuitive or axiomatic mode of classification. This classificatory mode, which remains unconscious and unexamined, possibly limits the options available to that society in confronting problems under new and pressing circumstances. The study may therefore be viewed as being essentially a historical investigation for illustrative purposes, an essay in "institutional and conceptual archaeology." By laying bare the background and demonstrating the existence of alternative modes for the perception and the classification of experience, one may hope that additional options, based on a critical assessment of even our most cherished assumptions about man and the universe, will increase our chances of success in contending with some of the problems confronting society at home and throughout the world.

PART ONE

And Lord Man created God from the very stuff of his own Being, and breathed into Him
the breath of Life; thus the Living God came to be.

(*see Genesis 2:7*)

I. APPERCEPTIONS AND CATEGORIZATIONS

It is a commonplace of modern anthropology that descriptions of exotic societies and analyses of their institutions cannot be undertaken properly if, at the outset, the observer does not have an adequate comprehension of the world view or the categorical framework of the society under investigation. This framework gives definition to the single institutions constituting the whole, while interaction between the intellectual and the categorical framework and constituent institutional elements reinforces the total structure and helps to maintain the integrity of the society at large. During the process of classifying observed data from other societies the investigator must constantly be aware of his *own* inherited categorical system, through which the data being observed must inevitably be filtered and assimilated.

By and large the scientific study of societies, whether ancient or contemporary, exotic or Western, is a preoccupation that developed within the intellectual life of a *particular* civilization, namely our own, the one we conventionally refer to as "Western." It is hardly necessary to observe that this civilization is defined by bounds that are far less territorial or even cultural than they are spiritual and intellectual. That is to say, they define a commonly held cosmology, a way of automatic and immediate apprehension of experience. This cosmology, this distinctively "Western" mode of cognition, is generally acknowledged to be the product of a fusion of what were originally two separate and distinct cosmologies and cultural traditions, namely those of the biblical and Hellenic civilizations. While in most respects the elements of these two traditions can no longer be isolated out of the amalgam of Western cosmology, it is nevertheless usually acknowledged that the more dominant effect on the *value* component—the moral quotient—in our classificational structure has been exerted by the biblical source. It is by virtue of this understanding that the designation of our civilization as "Christian" or "Judaeo-Christian" has come to be accepted as synonymous with the term "Western." The conditioning provided by this cosmology therefore makes it inevitable that the observer sees and studies the phenomena of alien societies and cultures with what may be succinctly characterized as "Western eyes."[1]

When we turn to the study of the civilizations of the ancient Near East, the observations just made are especially pertinent. We cannot enter here upon a detailed rehearsal of the long history of interaction between biblical scholarship and the study of the ancient Near East—more particularly of the civilization of ancient Mesopotamia—and must ignore altogether the inordinately large number of works from either field of study that display a blatantly tendentious cast. The fact remains that even the most disinterested or impartial investigations in this area have been adversely affected by a limitation of perspective common not just to biblical scholars and assyriologists, but to their audiences as well; all of them are, ultimately, Westerners addressing other Westerners.

A more specific, and probably the most fundamental, obstacle to our unobstructed vision in confronting the cosmological information of ancient Mesopotamia is that there is inherent in our own apperceptions a dichotomized view of the experiential universe: we perceive the phenomenon of "Man" on one side, and all the rest of the phenomenological universe, or "Nature," on the other. In the biblical stage of this conception, which is the primeval form of this cosmic apprehension, the division is of course threefold: God, Man, and Nature, in descending *hierarchical* order. The reality of the first constituent of this triad is not of the same order as that of the remaining two, however. The distinction is made manifest in the very first chapter of the Book of Genesis, verses 26ff., where the description of man as having been created in God's "image" and "likeness" begs the question, inasmuch as the incorporeality of this god is the fundamental tenet of biblical and ultimately, of all Western belief.[2] As has been observed often, however, the issue is easily

---

[1] The dilemma of the ethnographer was very succinctly stated by R. Needham in his Introduction to E. Durkheim and M. Mauss, *Primitive Classification* (Chicago, 1963), pp. vii–iv. He compares the crisis faced by the ethnographer confronted by a chaos of strange phenomena to the situation in which a congenitally blind person who has acquired full vision as a result of surgery finds himself.

[2] This sense is most vividly expressed in Yahweh's classic epiphany to Elijah, I Kings 19:11–12, and less colorfully but with the same intent in the epiphany to Moses, Exod. 33:20ff. In both instances the context is the aftermath of nationwide defection to the worship of more visible or palpable deities, Ba'al in the I Kings episode and the Golden Calf in Exodus. (These may well be synonymous; they involve other contextual parallels that it would take us too far afield to discuss here.) These two epiphanies were intended as a direct response to the issue of corporeality

resolved if the sense of the passage is reversed and the unitary deity of the Bible explained as the "creation" of man in his own image. The statement in the first chapter of Genesis is then to be seen as the expression of an awareness of the unique position of man in the universal scheme of things as it was apprehended by man himself. It is the biblical author's way of abstracting, isolating, and apotheosizing precisely those characteristics of man which he senses as the most significant, those which set him apart from the rest of the visible universe.[3] The essence thus abstracted of necessity stands outside this natural order, yet dominates it through the agency of man. Within the more strictly construed experiential universe, therefore, the effective categories remain only two: man, and the rest of natural creation.[4] This is brought home with particular force in the sequence of God's acts of creation as narrated in the first chapter of Genesis: the terrestrial and celestial phenomena, including all other living beings, are created and set in place by the deity so as to constitute a fully furnished environment for man, who appears last, as befits a regal figure whose domiciliary amenities must be seen to in advance.[5] Creation is completed with the making of man, who is enjoined by God to conquer and keep in subjection all the rest of the visible universe.[6]

The universe of the Bible is thus to be seen as unreservedly man-centered. Man is its focus and apex. God, to be sure, stands above man in this hierarchy, but he is the overlord who is not *physically* a part of this universe despite the belief that his force—and, on occasion, an even more palpable presence—is manifest within it. The visible universe is for man alone to conquer and dominate. Man is to rule wisely and justly; he is God's steward, to be sure, but he is to rule and dominate all the same.[7]

Turning now to consider briefly the elements in Mesopotamian cosmology that might correspond to the biblical scheme as just outlined, the initial difficulty confronting the investigator is that there exists no single "canonical" or systematic Mesopotamian exposition of its cosmic point of view. That we should look for, and expect to find, some such statement in cuneiform literature testifies to nothing more than the cosmic orientation of the observer, that is, of ourselves. But that the Mesopotamians provide no such statement is actually a logical concomitant of their own pluralistic and multi-dimensional response to such themes. In order to extract anything resembling a coherent cosmological "system" out of varied and often "contradictory" sources deriving from various localities within the "cuneiform world"[8] and spanning a period of more than two thousand years, the investigator must create his own synthesis. It is as inevitable for us to seek to fashion such a synthesis

---

and visibility of the deity. As such they differ from the epiphany at the Burning Bush (Exod. 3:2ff.): although it occurs in the same locale (Mt. Horeb or Sinai), it was spontaneous, and not in response to any question about the deity's form. Needless to say, the anthropomorphic descriptions of the biblical deity elsewhere in the biblical narratives do not really contradict this understanding.

[3] George Steiner put it tellingly recently when he defined monotheism as "that transcendental magnification of the image of the human self" ("The Language of Human Animals." *Encounter*, **33** [1969]: p. 9). This definition is set in the context of an exposition of the recognition and the experience of the individual self as opposed to other persons, with particular stress on the self-definition of God as "I am that I am" (Exod. 3:14). While this approach is not irrelevant to my present theme, the definition itself may well serve to express a more generalized and objectified sense of that component of man not shared by other sentient creatures.

[4] This has long been well understood: "The truth is that the image [of God] marks the distinction between man and the animals and qualifies him for dominion" (J. Skinner, "A Critical and Exegetical Commentary on Genesis," *The International Critical Commentary* [Edinburgh, 1910], p. 32).

[5] It is noteworthy in this perspective that even the sun, moon, and stars are stated to have as their purpose "to serve as markers for specific times, for days, and for years; they shall serve as lights in the expanse of the sky to illuminate the earth" (vss. 14f.). I fail to see how anyone can doubt that the Hebrew word *mo'adim* in verse 14 denotes anything other than the fixed seasonal celebrations which the Israelites were enjoined to observe, since the first chapter of Genesis is part of the P source (the Priestly document in the scheme of Higher Biblical Criticism), where this term always bears precisely this meaning. Nor is it proper to regard the use of the word in this context as anachronistic or even as anticipatory. From the writer's vantage point in place, time, and outlook, these "fixed times" are as patently part of the "natural" and universal order as are the demarcations of the "days and years." The great medieval commentator Rashi, with his rarely erring instinct, understood the term here in exactly this way. It is the only correct one.

[6] Gen. 1:28ff., and especially 9:1–7. The texts, of course, speak here only of the Earth, since the writers could hardly have imagined that the celestial bodies and their regions would one day come within the physical reach of man. Nevertheless, the fact remains that they are viewed as having been set in place to serve the Earth, that is, Man. Now that man has brought these celestial regions into his physical reach, the original biblical injunction to "fill the Earth and conquer it" (Gen. 1:28) approaches maximum fulfillment. The "conquest of space" has become as familiar a phrase and as valid a notion as the "conquest of Earth." Together they constitute the "conquest of Nature," a concept which expresses the quintessence of biblical cosmology. It is a concept which, as we shall soon see, is alien to Mesopotamian thought.

[7] Pursuing our own theme and the observations made in the previous note, I may point out here that the astronauts who first circled the moon read aloud the first chapter of Genesis. The inherent import of this act was made triumphantly explicit by the first words spoken by Neil Armstrong as he made the first human step on the lunar surface, when he declared it "a giant leap for mankind." The obvious piety that prompted these utterances does not alter the fact that they were not nearly as much a magnificat to God as to man.

[8] This designation is often used to indicate the broad territorial area reaching from Asia Minor and the Syrian coastal region in the West to the western portion of Iran in the East. For extended periods of time the inhabitants of those separate culture areas utilized the Babylonian cuneiform writing system and were in that respect influenced by the cultural traditions of the cuneiform homeland in Babylonia and Sumer in the lower half of the Tigris and Euphrates valley.

as it must of necessity do violence to the Mesopotamian testimony when we have finally created one. Apart from this dilemma, we face the difficulty that explicit statements bearing on Mesopotamian cosmology are, more often than not, allusive or laconic since they are not directed towards the issue that is engaging *our* attention, but are subordinate to some other expositive purposes, or are interpolated within some magical or ritual text having a particular and immediate cultic function. I shall here attempt no more than a series of generalizations about Mesopotamian cosmology in its largest dimensions which may be useful to our immediate purpose.

If we could distill the essence of Mesopotamian polytheism out of the varied and colorful mythological sources which have come down to us, we might define it as being a perception of the universe that sees it as being sustained and ruled by a large—and in principle probably infinite—number of independent forces. Some of these are apprehended as wielding authority over great domains of the visible universe and as affecting the fortunes of all people everywhere, while others exert only limited "supervision" within narrow bounds (that are not necessarily territorial) and are meaningful only to specific areas or groups of people. All, however, are basically conceived in anthropomorphic guise. The truly major deities are very few in number, and it is not surprising that the domains which they govern or with which they are identified comprise the three primary regions of the visible or tangible universe: the celestial, the atmospheric, and the chthonic. Mesopotamian theological speculation in different centers of learning and in various ages was preoccupied with systematization of the pantheon, with the grouping and regrouping of deities into families, courtly organizations, and even large manor-type organizations, in accordance with the political structure and ideological emphases of any particular time and place.[9] The single most significant constant through this entire theological history is that speculation never arrived at the notion of the absolute omnipotence of any single deity. In regard to matter from the opposite end, it was never the Meso-

potamian view that the authority exercised by any of the major gods was only "delegated" power that was ultimately the sole possession of a single divine overlord. The supremacy of Enlil—deriving from the theology of Nippur, which achieved dominance in Sumer early in the third millennium B.C.—did not entail the absorption of, or even any real encroachment upon, the jurisdictional province of other major gods. Enlil's supremacy—as that of Marduk of Babylon and Ashur of Assyria, which were little more than adaptations of this theology for other times and places—lay chiefly in his relationship to humanity. Enlil personified the vital forces inherent in that part of cosmic geography—from the surface of the earth up to the vault of the skies—which most immediately affected the well-being of mankind (and of all living things). These forces included the life-sustaining ones of fertility, vegetation, and all the phenomena associated with the maintenance of an abundant food supply. In relation to the other gods, however, Enlil's overlordship was more honorific than substantive. He was the overlord of such gods as An, Inanna, Utu, and Nanna;[10] but he neither delegated to them their respective jurisdictions, nor could he usurp them. Even more to the point, the Nippurian theology did not seek to eradicate the older and "rivalling" theology of Eridu, in which Enki was the supreme deity. Enki (Ea in the later Semitic literature) remained throughout totally independent of Enlil. He was the fountainhead of all the arts of civilization and of wisdom in general; the archetypal Promethean god; the patron of, and spokesman for, mankind. In this guise he even retained the power to thwart Enlil's decision to destroy mankind through the primeval Flood: he warned Atrahasis (later identified by the additional name of Utnapishtim, the Mesopotamian Noah) of the impending catastrophe and gave him explicit and detailed instructions for securing the means to escape the fate awaiting the rest of mankind.

The Mesopotamian gods were, in short, independent and limited in authority or power at one and the same time.[11] The fundamental fact to be grasped is

---

[9] The various divisions and groupings of the Mesopotamian gods may often be perceived as a kind of "code" for describing shifts in the political and military fortunes among the city-states and kingdoms that made up what we usually refer to as Sumer or Babylonia. (Periods of political unity were relatively rare, and mostly of short duration.) A more important point, and one to which I will return below, is that the notion of "deity" in Mesopotamian thought entails no uniform set of attributes or qualities. Similarly, the pantheon is "open-ended" as to number. Almost any phenomenon might at one time or another be apotheosized, so that the very idea of a pantheon as we understand it is somewhat misleading. Nevertheless, the elemental forces that are sensed as governing the universe are few in number. Mesopotamian theological speculation consists in large measure of arranging the great host of deities into extended families and groups of retainers of the major gods.

[10] An or Anu is "deity" and majesty personified. He is immanent in the vault of the heavens, and in his concerns is most remote from the affairs of man. Inanna (Ishtar), the most potent of the female deities, is the personification of nubile womanhood as characterized by sexual attraction rather than by birth and motherhood. Utu or Shamash is the personification of the Sun, and Nanna or Suen (later Sin) personifies the Moon.

[11] When, in the context of some particular cosmogony, a single god is elevated to supremacy and proceeds to parcel out the cosmic domains to the rest of the pantheon—as Marduk does in *Enuma Elish*, the so-called "Babylonian Epic of Creation"—the scheme is best understood as reflecting chiefly local, time-bound, political realities that have been transposed onto a cosmic plane. We are thus not offered an authentic insight into the more profound constants of Mesopotamian cosmology, such as its apperceptions of the nature of "deity," and the immutable interrelationships between the great gods.

that the essence, the individuality, of any given deity could not be thought of in isolation from the province which constituted that deity's domain, be it part of the natural universe or of some cultural institution created by man. Just as these provinces are autonomous though interrelated, so were the gods who personified them autonomous. A god's very being was in effect coterminous with the phenomena he "controlled." It is, of course, this quality above all that differentiates the "immanence" that characterizes Mesopotamian deity from the "transcendence" which characterizes the god of the Bible.

Although the major Mesopotamian gods are independent in their respective spheres, they nevertheless act in concert if not always in complete harmony. The interdependence, or interrelationship, of the gods has been aptly characterized as an "integration of wills";[12] this integration resulted in the conception of "the cosmos as a state." Just as the terrestrial environment and human society itself had been organized into a polity that (ideally, at least) assured stability against the threat of anarchy, so too were the gods, the otherwise autonomous powers of the universe, organized into a divine polity which held at bay the dark powers of chaos. Indeed, Cosmos denotes the very structure that came into being at the beginning of mythological time, when the domination of primeval Chaos was brought to an end.[13] The conception of a polity of the gods modeled on the structure of human society, however, entails a corollary analogy between the individual person and the individual deity: the gods are subject to all the human frailties and limitations. The sole human disability from which the gods were exempt was that of mortality.[14] The Mesopotamian deity was, in effect,

little more than a "superhuman" being in almost the precise literal sense of that term. The anthropomorphic conception of deity in Mesopotamia served to reinforce the limitations already implied in the identification of a particular god with a specific sphere of the objective universe. The autonomy of the god within his or her sphere meant that viewed as a polity the gods, whether acting individually or collectively, could never exert absolute universal sovereignty. The Western mind, with its biblical orientation, has tended to regard this Mesopotamian conception of deity as restricted, if not "flawed." But, apart from the fact that we have to do here with an immediate mode of cosmic apprehension and not a conscious choice among alternatives, the Mesopotamian conception of deity was not without its advantages. Being restricted, or unable to realize themselves fully as individual personalities, the gods could not give their undivided attention to the concerns of mankind, since the cosmic equilibrium required first and foremost that they keep an eye upon each other.[15]

The sympathetic attention of the gods might be implored by man as circumstances prompted, but above all the course of a person's fortunes might be advantageously advanced by resorting to magic. Magic rests on the belief that there is a latent potency in things, as well as in words and sounds, singly or in combination, beyond the more obvious effect such entities exert in their normal intrasocial use. Seen from the human perspective, this power is neutral as regards good or evil. Any adept, human as well as divine, may have recourse to it in his own interests. It can be invoked by personified forces of Chaos as well as by the gods of Cosmos.[16] For man the appeal

---

[12] T. Jacobsen, "Mesopotamia: The Cosmos as a State," in Henri Frankfort, H. A. Frankfort, John A. Wilson, and Thorkild Jacobsen, *Before Philosophy* (Harmondsworth, 1949), pp. 139ff.

[13] We must observe here that the Mesopotamian thinkers could not, any more than their biblical counterparts, really envisage a universe of absolute chaos. Thus the malevolent forces comprising that pre-creation era were conceived of as a body of monstrous personalities (or the like) acting concertedly and purposefully. In *Enuma Elish* Tiamat leads her host of demonic forces with at least a semblance of order against the benevolent gods of Cosmos, championed by Marduk. This entire scene is also a transposition onto a cosmic level of hostile encounters between superhuman beings that can, with greater or lesser certainty, be tied to historical human conflicts.

At bottom, we are confronted here with further evidence that the human mind, regardless of the culture which has trained its mode of apperception, remains a *rational* instrument; it automatically rejects the idea of randomness. Catastrophe and misfortune must be the result of a *conspiracy*: purpose *must* be imputed, and it must have an identifiable locus. The locus may be ascertained by what we would describe as reasonable means, such as tracking down a tangible identifiable source, or by "irrational" methods, such as blaming human or imagined sorcerers, or a host of demons. All were equally "real," however, to the Mesopotamians, and to many other peoples as well.

[14] In certain contexts, of course, specific gods—especially "evil" or malevolent deities—could be killed. Thus in *Enuma*

Elish Kingu, the "commander-in-chief" of Tiamat's demonic army, is executed by Marduk and the first human is created out of his blood. This, in turn, is an echo of the creation episode in the early Atrahasis epic in which the god slain for this purpose of creation was one of the rebellious gods (perhaps the instigator of the rebellion) who had refused to go on doing the heavy manual labor for the major gods and had threatened war against them. Another special case in respect to divine mortality is that of Dumuzi (Tammuz), whose annual "death and resurrection" is intimately linked with the seasons. Otherwise gods do not die; they are eternal. The Mesopotamians themselves stated this emphatically.

[15] It was due to the frequent engagements of the gods in affairs other than those which concerned mankind, as well as to the absence of the power of real omniscience, that the gods could be cajoled or even outwitted.

[16] Thus in the opening lines of *Enuma Elish* the opposing forces of Chaos, led by Tiamat, and those of Cosmos, led by Marduk, utilize magical formulas in the battle that led to the formation of the ordered universe. Marduk's victory was assured by the greater potency of his magical arsenal, as opposed to that available to Tiamat. The same energy source may be tapped by man to advance his own fortunes, through the engagement of professionals expertly trained in its use. The technique necessary to make magic effective is a craft not much different from other kinds of craftsmanship except that it depends on secret knowledge of a higher order. As such, the invention of magical techniques, incantations, and the like, is credited to Enki (Ea), the Mesopotamian "culture hero," the god to whom I referred above as the Mesopotamian Prometheus.

to magic is in some degree dependent on the notion that the gods' attention is often focused elsewhere than upon mankind, so that man must fall back upon the impersonal but more reliable power of magic for the support of his interests.[17] Man must for the most part shift for himself; at best he can hope to engage the gods' attention only at times.[18]

It is a different matter entirely when the question is that of punishment. Misconduct on the part of man was sure to trigger divine retribution. Indeed, it would not be too far off the mark to say that it is largely in the context of misbehavior that mankind comes to the gods' notice.[19] Wisdom lay in maintaining a "low profile," threading one's way cautiously and quietly through the morass of life with an occasional helping hand from the magician or the diviner, but otherwise attracting the gods' attention as little as possible.[20]

In contrast to the Mesopotamian gods, the God of the Bible while transcending the experiential universe is seen as omnipotent within it, mankind occupying the center, if not the exclusive focus, of his attention. Unlike the Mesopotamian gods the biblical god has no peers to be watched; he is thus free to give his undivided attention to the affairs of mankind, taking constant cognizance of its conduct and being ever solicitous of its welfare, individually and collectively. The biblical god is "wholly other" in a sense that is in sharpest contrast with the otherness of the Mesopotamian gods. Apart from his incorporeality, he is not identifiable with, nor is he immanent in, any single physical or visible force of nature. Yet, in further contrast to the Mesopotamian gods, his presence and immediate accessibility to mankind are intrinsic to man's conception of him. The conception is more readily comprehended if it is perceived that the biblical god is the human moral ideal personified and apotheosized. Man is barred from attaining the ideal —as distinct from identifying with it—not so much by virtue of the limitations inherent in his physicality as by the impediments presented by his equally immutable condition as a social creature.[21] The God of the Bible is therefore the extrapolation of the individual's aspiration, depersonalized and yet personal, achieving recognition through the merging of the individual self in the common socialized ideal. The incorporeality of the biblical god is an essential condition for the achievement of this kind of recognition. To be at once "wholly other" and so immediate and personal is no more of a paradox than the combination of humanlike attributes and remoteness that characterizes the gods of Mesopotamia.

We must probe further, however, if we are to reach the underlying sources of the contrast between the biblical and the Mesopotamian conceptions of deity. We have already touched upon the two primary elements in the respective configurations: consciousness and society. Both are integral to, and indeed define, the "nature" of man to the extent that *Homo sapiens* senses himself as in some fundamental quality "different" from the natural order, and, more particularly, from all other creatures that live and die. *Homo sapiens* everywhere and in all ages has grappled with the enigma "What is Man," and it is of relative insignificance whether this question is posed explicitly with responses provided just as directly, or whether it remains unarticulated with its resolutions taking the most apparently devious routes. It would, in this perspective, hardly be an overstatement to define "culture" (other than "material culture") as the intellectual stock of any discrete human society accumulated over time for the purpose of resolving precisely this enigma. In the process of formulating a distinctive response to this universal issue, the component of consciousness is by and large rendered subservient to, and is submerged in, the societal factor. The fusions and tensions of these two drives

---

[17] Through the use of magic a person may achieve a measure of control over his fortunes in a manner which, at least in principle, either did not involve the gods at all or at most assigned them a passive role.

[18] On Mesopotamian belief in intercessory gods and "guardian angels" see A. L. Oppenheim, *Ancient Mesopotamia* (Chicago, 1964), pp. 198ff. It must be stressed that this role was never taken by the major gods. Indeed, the need for such divine intermediaries—plainly modeled on the common predicament of the powerless individual seeking to gain access to and to enlist the aid of the high and mighty—is sufficient testimony to the "communication gap" between the major gods and mankind. Here, again, the contrast with the biblical God-man relationship stands out boldly.

[19] The most frequent mythological metaphor for this relationship is that of the noise or din made by mankind, which disturbs the gods' sleep.

[20] Oppenheim's characterization of the Mesopotamian religious climate as "tepid" (*Ancient Mesopotamia*, p. 176) is apt in this respect, and the gulf between it and the biblical climate is too obvious to require comment. There is, nevertheless, some possibility of misunderstanding. The religious unconcern of the populace relates to the formal cult only; those occasions involved the formal clergy and the king. There is ample evidence from all periods that it was thought meritorious for the individual lay citizens to present offerings to the temples on appropriate occasions, and it may be presumed that they did so in accordance with their rank and means.

[21] Moral awareness, consciousness of the individual's limitation, began with the creation of Eve. Her arrival on the scene—and it is to be remembered that her creation was prompted by God's concern and was not in response to any need sensed by Adam— provided man at once with conflict and with consolation; the dilemma is, of course, at the heart of the Garden of Eden episode. It was read back by the Jewish sages into the very words describing Eve's creation (Gen. 2:18). The ancient rabbis interpreted God's words stating as the purpose of Eve's creation that she should be a "help by his side" as meaning that Eve would be Adam's "helpmeet" if he was meritorious, but his antagonist if he were not, playing on the root sense of the word for "by his side" which denotes "opposition." Another rabbinic midrash shows greater perception by having Adam, after he ate the forbidden fruit and was confronted by God, lament his fate in having been provided with a companion and observe that he was without sin so long as he was all alone in the world (L. Ginzberg, *The Legends of the Jews* 1 [7 v.; Philadelphia, 1936–1937]: pp. 76f.).

within any cosmology are nevertheless of varied relative force. It is the total amalgam of these forces that provides each system with its unique character. The cosmology of any society may, indeed, be characterized succinctly as "the institutionalization of consciousness."

The biblical response to the question of the relationship between consciousness and society is forthright: the social organism is perceived as a magnified extension of the individual. Here it is consciousness which assumes the dominant role in creating the person's image of society and of the universe that is external to himself. The universe is experienced, and in large measure described, from the perspective of the first person. The biblical god speaks, commands, and expresses his moods in direct discourse and in explicit language. Revelation, ultimately, is self-revelation. The prophets, beginning with Moses, correctly perceived their function to be that of mediums. They served as the channel whereby the several individual "I"'s were put in communication with the universalized "I." Their particular gifts, which set them apart from their contemporaries, were those of insight and eloquence. They provided the articulation for the all but mute individual yearning for recognition and expression. At the cost of the suppression of the specific and the idiosyncratic the individual was afforded self-expression through the external generality of the society or nation, and self-recognition through God, the externalized projection of the self. From the perspective of the biblical "I" one may well describe the cosmic geography as consisting of a series of concentric spheres joined by a force radiating outward from ego and kept in equilibrium by the reflection of the same force. The biblical god represents the outermost and broadest of these spheres, encompassing all the others, and of infinite reach beyond. The biblical god is, in sum, the image of man magnified to infinite dimension.

Mesopotamian cosmology, on the other hand, was an attempt to resolve the tension between consciousness and society by effecting the submersion of the self in society and by assimilating the phenomenon of man—individually and in the aggregate—to the external and objective universe of nature. Far from seeing man as its nucleus or focus, normative Mesopotamian thought perceived the universe as an ordered entity, a cosmos, entirely apart from the presence of man. As varied as Mesopotamian speculation was about the precise methods and circumstances of man's creation, there was a unanimous assessment of his position within the cosmic scheme: man's place in the scheme was of secondary importance. Indeed, and as incongruous as it might appear, terrestrial creation, centering about the great cities of Sumer and Babylonia, was conceived of as complete *before* the appearance of man. It was the gods themselves who,

with their own manual labor—either as chafing serfs[22] or as fawning sycophants of their divine overlords[23] —built the cities and excavated the rivers and canals of southern Mesopotamia. It was only to relieve these oppressed gods of their intolerable burden that humankind was created: man's *raison d'être* was little else than "the care and feeding of the gods," and the performance of the more onerous tasks necessary to maintain the cosmic equilibrium. In the final formulation of the creation of man, as set down in the sixth tablet of *Enuma Elish*, the purpose of this crowning achievement by Marduk is plainly stated:

Upon it (i.e., mankind) shall be imposed the service of the gods that they (i.e., the gods) may be set at peace; thus adroitly transforming the routine of the gods.

Nowhere in Mesopotamian cosmological literature is it ever suggested or even implied that man is destined to dominate nature, the mandate which the first chapter of Genesis emphasizes and reiterates. It is not that the Mesopotamian thinkers held a truly low estimate of man's place in the cosmic scheme, or that they were oblivious of his uniqueness within the visible order of nature. They were, on the contrary, fully conscious of it, and in at least some of their speculations on this point set forth the proposition that man partook of the palpable substance of deity. Indeed, in its most explicit formulation, in the Old Babylonian epic of Atrahasis, the human prototype was formed by the great god Enki out of clay which was mixed with the flesh and blood of a god who was slaughtered expressly for this purpose.[24] This notion

---

[22] This is the conception in the Old Babylonian Epic of Atrahasis. The slave-gods are described as suffering forty years of heavy labor (W. G. Lambert and A. R. Millard, *Atrahasis: The Babylonian Story of the Flood* [Oxford, 1969], pp. 43ff.).

[23] This is the way the motif reappears in *Enuma Elish* Tablet VI. There the host of gods set about building Esagila, the main temple complex of Babylon, in a spontaneous expression of gratitude to their heroic leader Marduk, who had singlehandedly defeated the host of Tiamat. They complete their task in one year. The latest translation of *Enuma Elish*, incorporating portions of the epic discovered in the last decades, is that of R. Labat (in R. Labat [ed.], *Les religions du Proche-orient asiatique* [Paris, 1970], pp. 36ff.).

[24] The most detailed description of man's creation is that given in Atrahasis I 190–218. (Lambert and Millard, *Atrahasis,* pp. 57ff.). In that account the prototypal mother-goddess (Nintu:Mami) fashions man on the instructions of Enki. The narrative poses interpretive difficulties that cannot be elaborated upon here. They center upon the correct reading of the name of the god slaughtered, the special attributes he possessed or the particular reason which caused this deity to be marked for this purpose, and the special qualities which, by virtue of god and man having been "mingled together in the clay" (lines 212–213), were acquired uniquely by man and set him apart from all other living creatures. For the present see, in addition to the comments of Lambert and Millard, W. L. Moran, "The Creation of Man in Atrahasis I 192–248," *Bulletin of the American Schools of Oriental Research* 200 (1970): pp. 48–56.

The notion that the slaughter of a god was necessary for the creais echoed in the passage in *Enuma Elish* which deals with the creation of man. In that version, written down perhaps as much as a thousand years later than that of the epic of Atrahasis, the accomplishment is explicitly described as being extraordinary: it is the capstone of Marduk's transformation of chaos into cosmos. In the admiring words of the narrator: "That piece of handiwork was beyond comprehension."[25] It was only after the completion of this act that the assembly of gods acknowledged that their deliverance was an accomplished fact, and they were at last "free." The vital importance of man in the mundane sphere is also underscored by the fact that the creation of man is, in contrast with the first chapter of Genesis, all that the text included of terrestrial creation. For the rest, the creation episodes of *Enuma Elish* are concerned exclusively with cosmographic phenomena: the heavens and the abyss; celestial geography; the meteorological and atmospheric phenomena; and the creation of the Tigris and Euphrates rivers, which in Mesopotamian terms were quite understandably conceived of as being as fundamental to the universe as the heavens themselves.[26]

It is therefore clear that the Mesopotamian response to our question "What is Man?" was troubled and ambivalent. The Mesopotamians' apprehension of man's unique position and significance in the visible universe of nature emerged not only in the context of their specific views on creation, but came to the surface also in other literary manifestations of their thought, particularly in their religious literature. Yet the crucial characteristic of the Meso-

potamian intellectual drive was its assimilation of man to the external universe consisting of society and nature. Where biblical consciousness assimilated the not-self to the self, Mesopotamian consciousness was at pains to explain the self in terms of the not-self. We need to be reminded that the very framing of the question "What is Man?" is biblical, not Mesopotamian. And even then the question was not the verbal expression of a sensed difficulty, but a rhetorical introduction to a triumphant response which bears recalling here in full:[27]

When I regard your heavens—the handiwork of your fingers—the moon and the stars which you have established.
What is man, that you should be mindful of him; humanity, that you should take account of it?
Yet you made him lack but little of divinity,[28] and crowned him with honor and glory.
You gave him dominion over all your handiwork, placing everything under his feet;
All the flocks and herds, as well as the beasts of the steppe,
The birds of the skies, the fish of the sea (and) all that traverse the tracks of the oceans.

The first two verses of this conscious epitome of the first chapter of Genesis express sentiments to which a Mesopotamian thinker could easily have subscribed; indeed, they may be found in Mesopotamian hymnic literature in virtually identical diction. But the remainder of this panegyric to man's worth is in diametric opposition to a Mesopotamian's appraisal of man's stature in the universal scheme. Had these thoughts been uttered in his hearing, he would have regarded them as the acme of hubris and deemed them an invitation to divine chastisement.

Post-biblical Jewish thought gives even more eloquent expression to the biblical view by explicitly extending transcendent worth to the individual human life. The idea is, of course, implicit in the first chapter of Genesis and in the psalm just quoted. Thus we find in the tractate Sanhedrin of the Mishnah the following statement:

A single man was created in the world, to teach that if any man caused a single soul to perish, Scripture imputes it to

---

tion of man is so far not attested in Sumerian sources; T. Frymer has suggested—in an unpublished paper—that it may be an idea brought to Mesopotamia from western Semitic sources early in the second millennium B.C. The Mesopotamian texts from all periods, however, are unanimous about the subservient status of man in the cosmic scheme, by whatever means he was created. On such sources see A. Heidel, *The Babylonian Genesis* (2nd. ed.; Chicago, 1951), pp. 61ff.

[25] That is, it was a prodigy that could not be grasped by the human mind, and even by the other gods.

[26] The origins of plant and animal life and other terrestrial phenomena are totally ignored by Mesopotamian cosmologists; they are, however, taken up in the context of consciously aetiological stories or in similar kinds of compositions which would fall within the rubric of "wisdom" literature. Often these stories are not even independent in themselves, but serve rather as proëmiums to magical and ritual prescriptions designed for concrete use. In such cases, the cosmological background is wholly secondary, and is set forth for the purpose of providing explicit identification—the full pedigree, as it were—of the phenomena that constitute the focus of the text. For examples, see the introduction to an incantation related to the rededication of temples, in which the focus is upon bricks and brickmaking (that is, the basic element in building), and "The Worm and the Toothache," which sets forth the cosmological background according to which the specific toothache-causing worm had been primevally authorized to establish its "residence" in the teeth and jawbone of the man. Both of these compositions are translated by Heidel, *Babylonian Genesis*, pp. 72ff.

---

[27] Ps. 8:3–8.

[28] This is the line from Ps. 8:6 which has become familiar in the Authorized Version as "a little lower than the angels," a translation which violates the Hebrew in two ways. To take the "angels" first, this is an arbitrary rendering of *elohim*, "god, deity"; such a translation bespeaks only a late, pious sensibility which recoiled from the implication of comparing man with God. Second, the translation "lower" connotes the idea of status within a hierarchy, whereas the Hebrew verb here is *HSR*, which denotes "deficiency, lack (of some quantity or quality)." The plain sense of the line, bold as it is, is that God endowed man with a measure of qualities that just barely falls short of a level that might have placed him on a footing equal to that of God himself.

him as though he had caused an entire universe to perish. . . . Again, [but a single man was created] to proclaim the greatness of the Holy One, Blessed be He; for man stamps many coins with the one seal and they are all like one another; but the King of Kings, the Holy One Blessed be He, has stamped every man with the seal of the first man, yet not one of them is like his fellow. Therefore every one must say, "*For my sake was the Universe created.*"[29]

This statement is set forth as part of the adjuration of witnesses who were about to testify against a defendant in capital cases. Its burden was to impress upon a witness the extreme gravity of his undertaking, lest he expose himself to eternal blood-guilt for having helped bring about the death of a possibly innocent fellow human. It is a pithy summation of the first chapter of Genesis, and demonstrates how directly and effectively this foundation of biblical cosmology could be invoked in a judicial context— a hypothetical one, to be sure—when a life was at stake. It is to be doubted that a bolder or more eloquent profession of the anthropocentric world view will be found in Scripture or in post-biblical literature. This Mishnaic adjuration may be too guilelessly formulated for contemporary sensibilities, but it embodies the most fundamental principle underlying all of Western cosmology. Its burden, and the classificatory consequences that flow from it, stand at the opposite pole from the cognitive mode and categorical system which characterized Mesopotamian experience of the self and the external world.

In the ensuing pages of this part of the study I shall again take up the question of the need to take cognitive approaches into account, by considering a limited set of seemingly parallel statements found in the Bible and in the cuneiform sources of ancient Mesopotamia. The rules dealing with the legal (and implicitly moral) aspects of the contingency in which an ox belonging to one person gored another person to death are seemingly parallel; but we can demonstrate that despite their similar wording they are incommensurable when considered in the context of the societies and the cosmological frameworks within which they were formulated.

II. THE MESOPOTAMIAN AND BIBLICAL LAWS OF THE GORING OX: SOME CATEGORICAL CONSIDERATIONS

Ancient Near Eastern sources contain groups of rules relating to wrongs committed by goring oxen, and prescribing the ways in which these wrongs are to be adjudicated. These rules are embedded in several texts belonging to a distinctive genre which has con-

---

[29] H. Danby, *The Mishnah* (Oxford, 1933), p. 388, emphasis added.

ventionally been given the designation of "legal code." This designation applies not only to the separate compositions in the cuneiform sources which exhibit the formal features which the term "code" is intended to connote, but also to those biblical passages of shorter or greater length which bear the same or nearly the same characteristics. It is of importance to the discussion which follows that some preliminary considerations be devoted to the textual sources in which the goring-ox rules are found. Only then can we begin to analyze the rules themselves.

A. The Laws of Eshnunna

The text of these laws is known from two clay tablets, of which one is an incomplete duplicate of the other. The laws were probably drafted about 1850 B.C., but the extant copies appear to have been written some decades later. They were found between 1945 and 1947 at a site on the outskirts of Baghdad, which in early times was a small township named Shaduppum and was part of the independent kingdom of Eshnunna. The center of that kingdom was the city of Eshnunna, the ruins of which lie twelve miles to the northeast of Shaduppum. It is to be presumed that the rules or "laws" found in the Laws of Eshnunna were intended for the kingdom as a whole, and not merely for the locality in which the tablets were found.[1]

The range of topics touched upon in these laws is very limited, and a considerable part of the text cannot even be described as containing "laws" in any strict sense. The earlier portion of the text particularly would be more accurately characterized as a "tariff," that is, a list of prices for a series of staple commodities, and of fees and wages for certain kinds of services. The text itself provides no formal clues to the way it might have been divided in the conception of its original author(s). Basing himself on the precedent established for this purpose by the modern editors of similar texts found earlier (particularly the "Code" of Hammurapi, to be discussed immediately below), and using common sense, A. Goetze, who published the standard edition of these laws, divided the text into sixty "sections" or "laws." For the most part this division is satisfactory, at least for purposes of reference. There are instances, however, where it is still a matter of scholarly debate where one "law" concludes and the next "law" begins; con-

---

[1] These laws were first edited by Albrecht Goetze, in "The Laws of Eshnunna Discovered at Tell Harmal,"*Sumer* 4 (1948): pp. 63ff.; the standard edition is A. Goetze, *The Laws of Eshnunna*, Annual of the American Schools of Oriental Research 31 (New Haven, 1956). Other translations in English and other European languages which incorporate some important new readings and interpretations have since appeared, but they have not superseded Goetze's main edition. Except when otherwise indicated, reference to these laws will be understood as being to Goetze's edition of 1956.

sequently the interpretations of the legal import of the text at such junctures may vary considerably.[2]

B. The "Code" of Hammurapi

The difficulties just broached in connection with the Laws of Eshnunna stand out more prominently in the case of the "Code" of Hammurapi.[3] The full text of Hammurapi's laws first became known in 1902 when the large stone monument on which they were inscribed was discovered in the ruins of Susa (biblical Shushan) in southwestern Iran. It was the first editor of the text, V. Scheil,[4] who without pausing to consider the appropriateness of the term designated the text as a "code" of "laws," thereby suggesting structural and legal analogy with the codified statutes of ancient Rome, and with the codifications of law in modern sovereign entities. The designation of Hammurapi's inscription as a "code" has persisted in both assyriological and jurisprudential literature. The issue of whether or not the term "code" is appropriate as a denotation for Hammurapi's collection of rules (as well as for other cuneiform texts of the same genre) is far from a trivial one.[5] The mere use of the

term in referring to such compositions instantaneously creates a frame of reference which predisposes the reader—and the user—to ascribe a greater or lesser measure of legal reality to the material before him without asking himself whether any but the most neutral disposition about what this material represents is at all warranted. In following the lead initially given by Scheil, the modern reader subconsciously assimilates Hammurapi's text into the mental set consisting of the codes and statutes of modern political entities and jurisdictions.

The dictates of responsible scholarship, however, oblige us to reject at the outset any prior assumptions about Hammurapi's text—and about all other prescriptive documents of similar cast from the cuneiform sources—and to confront such materials in a totally neutral attitude with regard to their nature, category, purpose, or function in the social milieu within which they were composed. We cannot undertake to provide here the full reconsideration of the "law code" texts in light of the caveats just entered about the current status of their interpretation, but it is necessary to have called attention to the validity of such questions inasmuch as they bear directly on the theme of the present study. We shall henceforth speak of these texts as laws, but only for convenience of reference. By the use of the term "laws" to denote such documents I *do not* imply that they represent either in whole or in part "the law," that is, the rules that were actually enforced within the several communities or territories in which copies of these documents were written or studied. The term "laws" as used here denotes nothing more than a distinctive genre of epigraphic material consisting essentially of a larger or smaller collection of posed hypothetical situations or actions involving one or several persons, typically revolving about property, personal integrity, and status, which require consequential action in accord-

---

[2] For some examples of ambiguities of this kind see B. Landsberger, "Jungfräulichkeit: Ein Beitrag zum Thema 'Beilager und Eheschliessung' (mit einem Anhang: Neue Lesungen und Deutungen im Gesetzbuch von Ešnunna)," *Symbolae iuridicae et historicae Martino David dedicatae* 2 (Leiden, 1968): pp. 73ff., and H. Petschow, "Zur 'Systematik' in den Gesetzen von Eschnunna," in the same volume, pp. 132ff. (see his n. 4 for a bibliography on the question of the division of the laws in general). See also R. Yaron, *The Laws of Eshnunna* (Jerusalem, 1969), pp. 9ff., and my article "On Some Recent Studies in Cuneiform Law," *Journal of the American Oriental Society* 90 (1970): pp. 249f.

[3] Of the numerous editions and translations of the Laws of Hammurapi, the most exhaustive is the two-volume work by G. R. Driver and J. C. Miles, *The Babylonian Laws* (2 v., Oxford, 1953–1955). It remains a landmark even if it is not the most acute rendering and analysis of the text; I will use it as the reference basis for discussion here. The most up-to-date translation of the law is by A. Finet, *Le Code de Hammourabi* (Paris, 1973).

[4] "Textes Élamites-Sémitiques," *Mémoires de la Délégation en Perse* 4 (Paris, 1902). This amazing tour-de-force, which appeared within months of the recovery of the original monument and includes the best photographs of the original text that have been published to this day, remains indispensable.

[5] Not much forethought, and less consistency, have gone into the issue of what to call any of the cuneiform law corpora, and it is rash indeed for a jurisprudent to accord any weight whatsoever to the designation that has been chosen for any single one of them. The fragmentary remains of the Laws of Ur-Nammu (*ca.* 2100 B.C.), which appear to have amounted to a relatively short group of rules even when complete, were called a "code" by S. N. Kramer, their first editor (*University Museum Bulletin* 17 [Philadelphia, 1952]: pp. 23ff. and *Orientalia*, N.S. 23 [1954]: pp. 40ff.), presumably because they are introduced by a prologue. The Laws of Lipit-Ishtar (*ca.* 1925 B.C.), which have an epilogue as well as a prologue, were also called a "code" by their first editor, F. R. Steele (*American Journal of Archaeology* 52 [1948]: pp. 425ff.). The Laws of Eshnunna, on the other hand, are similar to these two earlier corpora in almost every respect (other than the fact that the text is written in Akkadian while the earlier texts were

drafted in Sumerian), but have never been referred to as a "code"— presumably because there is neither a prologue nor an epilogue. Yet the full year-name of the date of its promulgation, which precedes the text, may be taken as an indication of some formal and public status. F. Hrozný called the Hittite Laws a "code" in his primary edition (*Code Hittite provenant de l'Asie mineure* [Paris, 1922]), although the text lacks both a prologue and an epilogue and is in general similar in structure to the Middle Assyrian Laws (see G. R. Driver and J. C. Miles, *The Assyrian Laws* [Oxford, 1935]), which have never been referred to as a "code."

Clearly, then, the fact that a cuneiform law corpus has a prologue or an epilogue, or both, is not a useful criterion for trying to decide whether or not to call such a group of rules a "code." It should perhaps be pointed out that Driver and Miles's edition of the Laws of Hammurapi, which have both prologue and epilogue, uses the term Babylonian Laws in the title of the book not out of any desire to avoid the connotations of the term "code"—which the editors do in fact use in referring to Hammurapi's text—but because the work also includes a few other minor collections of "Babylonian laws" of various periods and provenience (see *The Babylonian Laws* 2: pp. 305ff.).

ance with an explicitly prescribed formula either by the parties directly involved or through the intervention of an impartial adjudicative authority. A "law" in the meaning used here is therefore nothing more than a statement of a hypothetical situation characteristically introduced by a word meaning "If, Given that," and the like, and concluded by the specification of the normative or corrective action consequent upon the posited facts. For the purposes of the present inquiry we will remain neutral as to the degree of "reality" represented by these laws. We will, in other words, ignore the question of whether any given case ever occurred, was likely to occur, or even *could* occur. We will similarly disregard the issue of enforcement, namely, the question of whether the norms represented by these cases were ever enforced, or were *ideally* intended to be enforced, or even of whether they were at all capable of being enforced. We will, in short, have little to say here with respect to the otherwise serious considerations regarding the actual purposes and function of these laws in their original social and historical contexts. Our concern centers rather upon the conceptual framework and moral standards implied in the normative prescriptions which these law collections explicitly set out. Their arrangement and internal structure will afford us valuable insight into the categorical system (that is, the "world view") of the societies which produced them.

There is yet another difficulty which must be disposed of before we can consider Hammurapi's law collection with the detachment necessary to our present purpose. This relates to the division of the legal part of the text into an exact number of individual "laws" or "paragraphs," and the perception of larger or smaller groups of these laws as constituting distinct "sections" or "chapters" devoted to specific topics. These divisions and categorizations, like the designation of the entire text as a "code," were first made by V. Scheil, who has been followed by others ever since. The problems faced by Scheil in this respect were of a practical nature. Even if one ignores the long prologue and epilogue which are not of a legal nature, the text of Hammurapi's laws as preserved on the stone monument is extremely long. It is in fact one of the longest inscriptions to have survived from ancient Mesopotamia. There are no divisions within the text to indicate where one "law" ends and the next one begins. Since citation of any part of the text by column and line number only would not have been efficient for easy reference, Scheil divided the text into separate paragraphs, or "laws." With a few exceptions he used the rule-of-thumb that a single law consists of a statement beginning with "if," setting forth the circumstances of a case and giving the ruling or decision appropriate to it. The text of Hammurapi's laws was in this manner divided into 282 "paragraphs" or "sections," each being conventionally treated in the literature as a separate

"law." It was obvious that these "laws" were grouped in sequences, each of which had its own theme or "title," even though these were not marked. Assyriological literature since Scheil's time has considered the larger divisions as self-evident; in the legal commentaries, especially, one finds Hammurapi's laws divided into groups either under explicit subject headings coined by the commentator or without explicit titles, but with such divisions implied in the typographical arrangement.

Fragments of numerous copies of Hammurapi's laws have come to light since Scheil's edition of the text. Some date to as much as a thousand years after Hammurapi's lifetime; others are of the same age as the original monument or of only slightly later date. The textual variants among all these different manuscripts are relatively minor. The most noteworthy difference is that in a significant number of instances the scribe provided clear indications of how he perceived the text to be divided, either by drawing ruled lines between the individual laws or by leaving a line blank for this purpose. In a few instances title headings were supplied for groups of laws.[6] The copies bearing these indications all date from the latter half of the Old Babylonian period (*ca.* 1800–1600 B.C.); at least one comes from the time of Hammurapi himself. All of the fragments of these other copies of Hammurapi's laws do not, even taken together, cover more than a portion of the known text, so that our knowledge of how the original scribes perceived the division of the text into sections and groups, and of the titles they might have applied to such groups, remains limited. The evidence is sufficient, however, to demonstrate that Scheil's idea of what constituted a discrete "law" often did not coincide with the understanding of the original scribes. Nor do the modern notions of what constitutes distinct groups of laws coincide with the ancient conceptions insofar as these can be gleaned from the few title headings that we now have. These considerations will materially affect our discussion of the laws relating to the goring ox. They furthermore provide confirmation of the wide discrepancies between the conceptual and classificatory patterns that guided ancient Mesopotamian thought and those of the modern investigator who has been inclined to impose his own system upon this alien world.

C. The Laws of the Book of Exodus: The Covenant Code

Chapters 21–23:19 of the Book of Exodus contain the only collection of Old Testament "laws" which

---

[6] A manuscript of Hammurapi's laws which dates to about a century after Hammurapi's reign includes topical headings preceding groups of laws, and illustrates at the same time by ruled lines between separate "laws" the inappropriateness of Scheil's divisions; see the fragment published by me as "A Late Old Babylonian Copy of the Laws of Hammurapi," *Journal of Cuneiform Studies* **21** (1967): pp. 39ff.

may to any significant extent be compared in either style or substance with the law collections in the cuneiform sources from Mesopotamia. Like the latter, they are (with a few exceptions) drafted in the "casuistic" formulation; that is, each law consists of a statement of the hypothetical facts of a case introduced by the circumstantial "If," followed by the judgment or ruling that is to be applied. By comparison with the legal material embedded elsewhere in the Pentateuch, the subject matter of the Covenant Code (as this section of Exodus has come to be called) is of a secular cast in that the wrongs treated in it are mainly those man might commit against his fellow man rather than against the religious or cultic norms. I shall attempt to demonstrate, however, that in biblical conceptualization there was no sharp dividing line between these two spheres of human conduct. The scope of the laws in the Covenant Code, that is, the range of topics treated in it, is extremely limited, especially in comparison with the relatively broad range of topics touched upon in the cuneiform legal collections.

A word must be said about the age in which the Covenant Code may have been set down, even though this issue will not materially affect our discussion. As is well known, the question of the age of the various constituent sources of the Pentateuch is the subject of a vast scholarly literature conventionally designated as "Higher Criticism," the canons of which were laid down more than a century ago. While there is a general consensus of opinion that the Pentateuch is the end product of numerous redactions of a handful of originally independent sources, there is little agreement about the date of these sources. There is also considerable disagreement with respect to the particular source to which passages, verses, or even phrases are to be ascribed. The Covenant Code, for example, is attributed to the source known as JE (itself a redaction of two still earlier sources designated as J and E) which, in the majority view, is the earliest of the major "documents" out of which the Pentateuch was constructed. In the view of many authorities, however, it did not retain its "pristine" state but underwent further redaction at the hands of those responsible for the other primary pentateuchal sources, each of whom interpolated additional textual material reflecting viewpoints characteristic of presumably later times.

The relative merits of conflicting opinions concerning the attribution of any of the laws in the Covenant Code to any particular source document are not significant in the context of this study. Regardless of the date when the Covenant Code assumed the form in which it is now preserved in the Book of Exodus—and some authorities would place it as late as the fifth century B.C.—much of its substance reflects the legal thought and expression of far earlier times, possibly even earlier than the "Mosaic" era itself (thirteenth-twelfth centuries B.C.). More cogent to our present purpose is the fact that, disparate as the viewpoints of the different documentary sources may appear to be among themselves, they present to us a cosmological perspective that is integral, especially when it is considered in relation to the cosmology reflected in the Mesopotamian sources with which the biblical material bears comparison.

D. Interrelationship of Sources

The preceding discussion inevitably leads to the further question of the possible interrelationship between the Covenant Code and analogous material in the cuneiform legal sources. I do not propose to enter into this issue in any depth since, as with the considerations just reviewed, it will not materially affect the kind of analysis I propose to undertake. Nevertheless, biblical and ancient Near Eastern scholars have been perennially absorbed by this question since the discovery of the "Code" of Hammurapi, and I therefore feel obliged to set down here, however briefly, my own observations on the question. I hope these will add to the perspectives from which the entire subject may ultimately be approached.

As regards the inner interdependence of the cuneiform sources there is little room for dispute. Since the discovery of the stela of Hammurapi in 1902 a variety of analogous collections of laws have come to light in the ruins of ancient Mesopotamia, including, of course, the Laws of Eshnunna. In this perspective Hammurapi's text, far from representing an early legal formulation—it was at one time thought to be the earliest—is now more accurately to be perceived as an expanded and relatively late exemplar of a genre in the literary-legal tradition of ancient Mesopotamia that began to take form hundreds of years before the reign of Hammurapi. Some of these earlier examples are also in the form of "codes" promulgated in the name of monarchs; we have, for example, the Laws of Ur-Nammu of the city of Ur (*ca.* 2100 B.C.) and the Laws of Lipit-Ishtar of the city of Isin (*ca.* 1925 B.C.).[7] These and virtually all other collections of cases drafted or copied in the scribal schools in Mesopotamia are written in Sumerian,[8] in contrast to the Laws of Eshnunna and the Laws of Hammurapi which are drawn up in Akkadian, the Semitic language of ancient Mesopotamia. It can nevertheless be demonstrated without difficulty that all of these sources

---

[7] The text of the Laws of Ur-Nammu has recently been reedited by me in *Journal of Cuneiform Studies* 22 (1969): pp. 66ff. As for the Lipit-Ishtar Laws, in recent years additional fragments of the Lipit-Ishtar Laws have been discovered, as have other pieces that can be ascribed to that corpus with a high degree of probability, although not with certainty. A new edition of the corpus incorporating the new material is now needed. Much that is now extant also indicates a need for re-interpretation. This, in my view, would tend to demonstrate the dependence of Hammurapi's text on such earlier corpora to an even greater extent than is currently appreciated.

[8] For a translation of an "anonymous" group of laws drafted in Sumerian, see *Ancient Near Eastern Texts Relating to the Old Testament* (ed. J. B. Pritchard, 3rd. ed.; Princeton, 1969), pp. 525f. That volume also includes translations of all extant cuneiform law corpora of significant extent; see pp. 159–198 and 523–528.

represent a single tradition, for in many instances the Akkadian of the Eshnunna laws and of Hammurapi's text proves to be little more than a word-for-word equivalent of the Sumerian of earlier sources. The various texts are not, to be sure, mere duplicates of each other. There is a considerable degree of variation both in terms of substantive legal prescription and in expansiveness or economy of expression with respect to any given legal topic. But the range of topics remains relatively uniform throughout the tradition, and the phraseology employed, whether in Sumerian or Akkadian, is completely homogeneous. It is therefore unnecessary to raise the question of whether the scribes who drafted Hammurapi's text did or did not have direct access to the Laws of Eshnunna. The frequent use of identical expressions and of legal prescriptions in identical cases such as occur, for example, in the series of rules concerning the goring ox are due mainly to the fact that the authors of both these texts drew on essentially the same corpus of prototypal material.[9] The differences in detail between the statement of the goring-ox laws in the Eshnunna laws and in the Hammurapi text are a secondary issue that will be taken up below.

The heart of the question of interdependence of sources, the issue which has provoked the most heated discussions, is that centering on the influence of the cuneiform legal sources upon biblical law, particularly upon the material in the Covenant Code. To some degree, at least, an emotional factor rooted in religious conviction is at once responsible for making the issue crucial and for hindering a disinterested consideration of the facts. We cannot, of course, take issue with those for whom the acknowledgment of Mesopotamian influence on biblical law would amount to placing in jeopardy the millennia-old dogma that the Pentateuch is the revealed word of God, hence innately unique and incapable of being "influenced" by non-Israelite sources. But for others—the preponderant majority of the scholars who have come to grips with the question—the factor of religious conviction is not the dominant one; they are prepared to acknowledge Mesopotamian influence on the Covenant Code (as well as on other parts of the pentateuchal tradition) directly or indirectly. Yet the power of the biblical tradition over Western thinkers is such that, however attenuated their conscious belief in the qualities as-

cribed to it by dogma may be, they are led to focus on the issue of interdependence to a degree which is out of all proportion to the increase in knowledge and understanding this special attention could conceivably produce.[10]

---

[9] This subject requires a full exposition which I cannot undertake in the present context. It must be observed here, however, that the prototypal material is of the paradigmatic school-exercise type, and is only another "subject" of the scribal school curriculum. Since it is almost self-generating in the sense that grammatical paradigms are in a more obvious way, it is a futile exercise in most instances to attempt to determine which examples were drawn from "real cases" and which were invention. The tendency of juristically trained students of cuneiform law to assume that all of this material, and the "codes" themselves, had more or less legal validity is wholly an *a priori* judgment which in the circumstances is inadmissible.

[10] M. David is probably the foremost of recent investigators of the subject to declare against such cross-influence; see *Een Nieuw-ontdekte Babylonische Wet uit de Tijd vóór Hammurabi* (Leiden, 1949), a response to the publication of the newly discovered Laws of Eshnunna, and "The Codex Hammurabi and its Relation to the Provisions of the Law in Exodus," *Oudtestamentische Studien* 7 (1950): pp. 149ff., which addresses the issue more broadly. Strangely, the plainly contrary indications of the evidence are ignored rather than confronted and refuted. Other recent opinions of the same case depend in large measure on David's arguments. R. Yaron provided a summary of these views in "The Goring Ox in Near Eastern Laws," *Israel Law Review* 1 (1966): pp. 50ff., and restated them in his *Laws of Eshnunna*, pp. 192ff. While Yaron rejects David's position and assumes an interrelationship between biblical and cuneiform sources, he does so on the ground of the presupposed existence of "customary laws and practices common to the ancient Near East" which according to him existed side by side with the "local positive law" of the various states which constituted "rules of political entities not dependent on each other." Both these primary assertions rest on the kind of *a priori* bases that I consider unacceptable (see previous note). The idea of a customary law common to the entire ancient Near East is an unwarranted extension of the concept of "cuneiform law" beyond its limits as a convenient label for subsuming those ancient Near Eastern societies that utilized syllabic cuneiform writing (mainly but not exclusively in Sumerian and Akkadian) in their daily life. The common use of the writing system also resulted in a common repertoire of documentary forms and formulas for civil purposes; this is evident *prima facie* and in fact continued into post-cuneiform times. See, for example, Y. Muffs, Studies in the Aramaic Legal Papyri from Elephantine, Studia et documenta ad iura orientis antiqui pertinentia 8 (Leiden, 1969): p. 9: "In all probability the Aramaic formulary is based, on the whole, on actual cuneiform models." Then, again, to speak of a "positive" law in the context of ancient Near Eastern "political entities" is a gratuitous intrusion of a notion peculiar to Western jurisprudence into an alien milieu. One must first demonstrate that certain conditions obtain in which something that can be identified as "positive law" can conceivably operate. I might adopt a recent observation as being pertinent to this issue: "Legislators and judges, and other officials of the system, must believe that the laws can be obeyed; and they are to assume that any orders given can be carried out. Moreover, not only must the authorities act in good faith, but their good faith must be recognized by those subject to their enactments. Laws and commands are accepted as laws and commands only if it is generally believed that they can be obeyed and executed. If this is in question, the actions of authorities presumably have some other purpose than to organize conduct." (J. Rawls, *A Theory of Justice* [Cambridge, Mass., 1972], p. 237). The mere existence of a monument inscribed with a body of rules or "examples" for conduct, ostensibly "legislated" by Hammurapi, is not even the beginning of a proof that these rules constitute "positive law" in any way. And this holds for all similar corpora of so-called cuneiform "laws." The authority of such documents can be ascertained *only*, if at all, from evidence *external* to the document itself. We must have information about the administration, the organs of enforcement, the possibilities for the dissemination of such documents on a local level, knowledge of them by judicial officials and laity alike, and, ultimately, some indication that the rules—not necessarily all—were in fact enforced, with the unmistakable evidence that this enforcement is in direct response to the "legislated" law in question. To bandy about such terms as "positive law" before any of these factors are considered is nothing but

When one pauses to consider the almost infinite number of areas of human behavior from which a scribe or "lawgiver" might draw his illustrative cases, the appearance in the Covenant Code of much of the subject matter found in the Mesopotamian law corpora cannot plausibly be explained as coincidental. Nor could it be claimed that the basic wrongs which one person might commit against another are essentially identical in all societies; some of those chosen for illustrative purposes are most unusual, and sometimes even bizarre, kinds of occurrences.[11] The series of cases concerning the goring ox are among those that stand out in this respect. Finally, the specific wording of the biblical rules of the goring ox is so close to that of the cuneiform antecedents that any explanation of the resemblances other than one based on some kind of organic linkage is precluded.

The real difficulty is that however compelling the assumption of interdependence may be, it cannot be definitively demonstrated on the basis of the evidence now available. Through most of the second millennium B.C. the Syro-Palestinian coastland lay at the outer orbit of the cultural world of which Babylonia was the nucleus; cuneiform writing with its varied learned traditions defined the bond of whatever degree of cultural unity may be imputed to that world. In many respects, but especially in the political sphere, the Syro-Palestinian region was at the same time within the orbit of Egyptian culture to whose heartland it lay in even closer geographical proximity. The cuneiform system of writing was utilized in Palestine until about the thirteenth century B.C., though it would appear not to have been widespread and seems— as far as the preserved evidence indicates—to have been limited in application. The alphabetic system of writing (ultimately derived from Egyptian hieroglyphic sign forms) developed in Palestine during the second half of the millennium B.C. and, by virtue of its simplicity, soon overtook the cuneiform system as the common recording medium. The earliest elements of what we now know as the Pentateuch—and we may for the present purpose at least include the Covenant Code in this category—might have been committed to writing about the tenth century B.C. By that time the cuneiform writing system was long extinct in Palestine, and the traditions which it carried, including the legal corpora which concern us here, would no longer have been directly accessible to the early Israelite scribes. It does not help to fall back upon the assumption of an oral tradition, for we would still have to account for a gap of hundreds of years. Moreover, the form which the goring-ox laws take in the Covenant Code is so close to its cuneiform analogues

---

question-begging; consequently much of contemporary expositive literature on the biblical as well as on the Mesopotamian "law" corpora is little more than irrelevant ingenuity.

On the other hand, there can be no objection against the convenience of referring to the ancient corpora as "laws" provided that we do not lose sight of the special sense in which the term "law" is used: it designates an injunction to follow a particular course of conduct in a particular set of hypothetical circumstances. Whether such an injunction actually had the status of a "law" in the more commonly understood usages of that term is an entirely separate matter and is *a priori* not determinable. It follows then that the nature of these epigraphic artifacts (and I include here the biblical law corpora) is such that their elucidation confers no priority of authority on investigations conducted according to the canons of jurisprudence or the history of law. Indeed, the creative application of the resources of those disciplines especially equipped to fathom the written and material artifacts of remote and alien societies, such as anthropology, linguistics, philology, and archaeology, provides a more reliable approach to what such "law corpora" represented in a literary, historical, and moral way within the structural framework of a total culture. Nothing, of course, prevents a jurisprudent or historian of law with a deep interest in these cultures from participating in the same enterprise on the same terms.

[11] Probably the most convincing evidence that the explanation of the phenomenon confronting us is to be sought in the literary rather than the legal sphere is provided by the case of the pregnant woman who, either as a consequence of a deliberate assault, or through being caught in a mélée, is caused to abort her fetus. While one can be persuaded that in a typical agricultural setting (modern as well as ancient) the goring of a person by a bull, ox, or the like, was not so rare an occurrence, the same cannot be said of the case of the pregnant woman. There is, of course, no record of such a case actually having occurred in the ancient Near East. I have not made a thorough search in legal records elsewhere, but a cursory survey turned up no case of this kind, though I would suppose that a more diligent pursuit might yield a few instances. At any rate, I have been advised that from a medical point of view the occurrence is statistically highly improbable. Why then should we find this topos in almost every law collection from the ancient Near East, expressed in virtually identical terms? The earliest extant Sumerian formulation was set down *ca.* 1800 B.C. (see *ANET* [3rd. ed., 1969], p. 525b). It is not found in the extant portions of the laws of Ur-Nammu and Lipit-Ishtar, but that is most probably due to the fragmentary state in which those collections are thus far known. The topos appears to have been omitted in Eshnunna, but it is treated at length in Hammurapi's laws, (§§209–214); the Middle Assyrian laws (§21); the Hittite laws (§§17–18); and also in Exod. 21:22. The explanation which appears to me inevitable is that we have to do here with a *literary* phenomenon rather than with a legal one. The case of the pregnant woman had entered into the scholastic tradition in Nippur or Ur some time between the Ur III and the early Old Babylonian periods (*ca.* 2100–1800 B.C.). It may well have begun with an actual case, very plausibly one involving a woman who because of some physiological abnormality was not likely to carry a pregnancy to full term. This is a common defect which, though subject to some effective counteraction today, cannot have been well understood or counteracted in ancient times. A sudden jostling of a pregnant woman having this defect could easily have precipitated a miscarriage that very likely would have occurred anyway at some later time. But at the time the jostling could in all honesty have been blamed for the miscarriage, and liability would have been laid accordingly. Once this case entered the tradition, however, it soon assumed the *canonicity* which characterized the various topoi that came to comprise such "law" corpora, a canonicity that bore little relationship to local legal usage. The variations that are found among the various corpora in the actual formulation of the cases illustrating a particular topos may reflect certain local conceptions and standards in some measure. But they are largely a function of the variation technique that is an intrinsic feature of the paradigmatic structure of the law corpora from their very inception, and that paradigmatic structure is *the* most characteristic feature of the cuneiform scholastic tradition.

that it bespeaks the presence in Palestine of an almost canonical knowledge of the precise phraseology of the earlier Akkadian formulations. There is, in short, no certain way at present of explaining the verbal identity between sources that are perhaps as much as five hundred years and as many miles apart. But the fact of this identity is incontrovertible and compels us to postulate an organic linkage between them even if this linkage cannot be reconstructed. With this I consider the subject of the interdependence of sources to have been paid its sufficient due for our present purposes. We may now turn to examining the goring-ox laws in some detail.

III. THE LAWS OF THE GORING OX

A. The Laws of Eshnunna

§53. If an ox has gored another ox and caused its death, the owners of the oxen shall divide between them the sale value of the living ox and the carcass of the dead ox.

§54. If an ox was a habitual gorer, the local authorities having so duly notified its owner, yet he did not keep his ox in check[1] and it then gored a man and caused his death, the owner of the ox shall pay two-thirds of a mina of silver (to the survivors of the victim).

§55. If it gored a slave and caused his death, he shall pay fifteen shekels of silver.

B. The Laws of Hammurapi

§250. If an ox, while walking along the street, gored a person and caused his death, no claims will be allowed in that case.

§251. But if someone's ox was a habitual gorer, the local authority having notified him that it was a habitual gorer, yet he did not have its horns screened nor kept his ox under control,[2] and that ox then gored a free-born man to death, he must pay one-half mina of silver.

§252. If (the victim was) someone's slave, he shall pay one-third mina of silver (to the slave's owner).

C. The Biblical Laws (Exod. 21:28ff.)

i. If an ox gores a man or woman to death, the ox shall be stoned to death, its flesh may not be eaten, but the owner of the ox is innocent.

ii. But if the ox was previously reputed to have had the propensity to gore, its owner having been so warned, yet he did not keep it under control,[3] so that it then killed a man or a woman, the ox shall be stoned to death, and its owner shall be put to death as well. Should a ransom be imposed upon him, however, he shall pay as the redemption for his life as much as is assessed upon him. Whether it (i.e., the ox) shall have gored a minor (lit.: a son or a daughter) this same rule shall apply to him.

iii. If the ox gore a slave or slavewoman, he must pay thirty shekels of silver to his owner, but the ox shall be stoned to death.

At this point in the biblical text the series of rules concerning the goring ox is interrupted and the succeeding verses take up the subject of restitution to be paid to the owners of oxen and asses that had been killed as a result of falling into an open pit dug by some other person. After this interruption[4] the text returns to the subject of the goring ox in verses 35–36:

iv. If an ox belonging to one man gores to death the ox of his fellow, they shall sell the live ox and divide the proceeds, and they shall divide the dead one as well.

v. But if the ox was previously reputed to have had the propensity to gore, and its owner had not kept it under control, he shall make good ox for ox, but will keep the dead one for himself.

This, then, is the complete statement of the rules of the goring ox as they are found. The similarities in diction stand out as sharply in the original languages as they do for us, due to the affinities of Hebrew

---

[1] It is now generally accepted that there was a scribal error here. The verb in question cannot mean, as Goetze at first hesitantly conjectured, that the owner failed to "dehorn" the animal. The verb is to be restored as *ú-⟨še-⟩ši-ir*, possibly written **ú-ši-ši-ir* in the prototype text from which the extant manuscript was copied, so that the error is merely one of inadvertent omission of a single ŠI sign. This is as good a point as any to note that Goetze's original reasoning that MS. A is only a copy of an earlier manuscript now lost (*Laws of Eshnunna*, pp. 14ff.), is confirmed by the text of MS. A itself. The dubious sign after *šum-ma* in §28 which was read by Goetze as UL, and which has caused much desultory debate in the literature, is proved by collation of the original by Maria deJ. Ellis to be the signs *hi-pí*, "broken," the conventional scribal notation signaling that at that point the original tablet which was being copied was damaged. In §28, however, it would appear from the context that very little, if anything, was actually missing in the original, despite the break. The paragraph merely notes that the owner of the beast failed to exercise due care while leading or driving it through an area of public access, and thus expresses in characteristic Mesopotamian fashion the "due/proper care" doctrine essential to negligence law.

[2] Hammurapi here uses the verb *sunnuqu*, which means "to act promptly, to do something with exactitude and efficiency." It is, to all intents and purposes, here used exactly as the verb discussed in the previous note is used in the Eshnunna rule. In neither case can it denote the idea of keeping the animal penned and guarded, as that would raise further questions of trespass and contributory negligence. The due care principle is best illustrated on the neutral ground, in this respect, of a public thoroughfare.

[3] The Hebrew verb here is *ŠMR*, in the general sense "to guard, keep, observe (commandments, covenants, etc.)." I take it here to denote the same notion as do the parallel verbs in the cuneiform laws; see the two previous notes.

[4] The significance will be discussed below, p. 37.

and Akkadian as members of the Semitic family of languages. The similarities in the formulations are also immediately apparent, strikingly so in the case in which the ox had gored another ox, represented by §53 of the Laws of Eshnunna and Exodus rule iv. In that case the resemblance extends to the form of the "sanction" to be applied or, more exactly, to the judicial disposition of the case. In those cases in which the victim of the ox was a human being, however, there is a striking divergence between the biblical and Mesopotamian rules in respect to sanction.

One further point must be stressed by way of emphasizing my belief that we are confronted here not with independent developments, but with a single, organically interrelated, literary tradition. This has to do with the fact that in all of the tens of thousands of cuneiform documents relating to legal matters which have thus far come down to us, there is hardly a single allusion to a real instance in which an ox killed or injured a person or another animal.[5] I do not mean

to imply that such occurrences never happened or that they could not happen, but merely intend to suggest that such occurrences would have been rare at best. It is possibly the very rarity of such an accidental occurrence that was the cause of its first incorporation into the body of law cases that were part of the curriculum in the scribal schools. Once it was so incorporated, a series of related hypothetical cases was constructed by permutation of the circumstances as they might have occurred in the— hypothetical—prototypal instance. It is also the very unlikelihood of such an accidental occurrence that makes us concede that the biblical goring-ox laws must have been dependent upon their *literary* Mesopotamian prototypes; it would be too unreasonable to posit that such an unusual incident occurred also in early Israelite experience, and then became quite independently the source of the goring-ox laws of the Book of Exodus.

IV. THE MESOPOTAMIAN LAWS AND THEIR CONTEXTS

A. Grouping and Arrangement

1. **The Eshnunna rules.** To provide some perspective on the textual context of the goring-ox laws which are contained in §§53–55 of the Laws of Eshnunna, we may note here that the group of rules which immediately precedes them concerns the subject of kidnapped and runaway slaves, a theme essentially unrelated to the goring ox. §§56–57, which follow the goring-ox rules, take up the subject of attacks on persons by vicious dogs. §58 considers the subject of the killing of a person by the collapse of a dangerously decrepit wall upon him. It is not difficult to perceive that the goring-ox rules serve to introduce the central principle of culpable negligence and its consequences.

---

[5] The goring of a person by an ox is mentioned in Old Babylonian omens: "If a perforation is located in the left side of the threshold of the 'palace-gate': Goring by an ox." (The 'palace-gate' is a term denoting a natural feature of the liver.) "If a perforation in the left side of the threshold of the 'palace-gate' has pierced it all the way through: Goring by an ox; the 'man' will die." ('Man' in this context is thought to mean the king or ruler.) Cited from A. Goetze, *Old Babylonian Omen Texts* Yale Oriental Series, Babylonian Texts **10** (New Haven, 1947): no. 23 rev. 5f. (see the *Chicago Assyrian Dictionary*, A/1, 365b sub *alpu* 1a). In this context we must also note the following statement from the Standard Babylonian omen series *šumma alu* (*CT* **38** 33: 18): *šumma ina nikip alpim šumma ina ziqit zuqaqīpim imât*, "Be it by the goring of an ox or by the sting of a scorpion, he will die." The collocation here suggests that the goring to death by an ox was not more frequent than being stung to death by a scorpion. Both were occurrences of such relative infrequency or rarity as to render them suitable for the omen literature. Presumably non-lethal gorings by oxen and scorpion stings were somewhat more common, though hardly an everyday occurrence.

The goring of one ox by another is attested in one court record of about the late fifteenth century B.C. The defendant in the case claims that it was not he, but another ox belonging to the plaintiff that had caused the destruction of the ox. The text is JEN 4 341 (E. Chiera, *Proceedings in Court*, Publications of the Baghdad School of the American Schools of Oriental Research Joint Expedition with the Iraq Museum at Nuzi 4 [New Haven, 1934]).

ᵐTe-ḫi-ip-til-la DUMU *Pu-ḫi-še-en-ni* (2) *it-ti₄* ᵐTa-a-a DUMU ARAD.ŠEŠ (3) *a-na di-ni i-na pa-ni* DI.KU₅MEŠ (4) *i-te-lu-ú* ᵐTa-a-a SIPA.GU₄.MEŠ *ša Te-ḫi-ip-til-la* (5) *ù* 1 GU₄ *ú-še*(!)*-bi-ir* (6) *um-ma* ᵐTa-a-a-ma GU₄*ina*(AŠ) EDIN.MA (7) *tap-pu-šu ú-še-bi-ir* (8) *ù* DI.KU₅ *a-na* ᵐTa-a-a (9) *iq-ta-a-bu* LÚ.MEŠ IGI.MEŠ.KA₄ (10) *bi-i-la ki-i-me-e ina* EDIN.MA (11) *tap-pu-šu ú-se-bi-rù* (12) *um-ma* ᵐTa-a-a-ma LÚ.MEŠ IGI.MEŠ-*ya* (13) *ya-nu um-ma* DI.KU₅.MEŠ (14) *ša tù-še-bi-rù ki-i* GU₄ *i-din* (15) *i-na di-ni* ᵐTe-ḫi-ip-til-la (16) *il-te-e ù Ta-a-a* (17) *a-na* 1 GU₄ *ša sú-gu₅-ul-li* (18) *a-na* ᵐTe-ḫi-ip-til-la (19) *i-ta-du-uš* (20) NA₄.KIŠIB ᵐSa-qa-ra-ak-ki(!) DUMU *Ar-ti-ni/ir-we* (21) NA₄.KIŠIB ᵐNi-nu-a-ri DUMU *A-ri-pa-nu* (22) NA₄.KIŠIB ᵐTa-an-ni-mu-ša DUMU *Im-bi-*AN (23) NA₄.KIŠIB ᵐNa-i-še-ri DUMU *Qa-pu-ta* (24) ŠU ᵐIt-ḫa-bi-ḫe DUB.SAR

(1–6) Tehiptilla son of Puhišenni appeared together with Taya son of Warad-ahi before the judges (on the complaint that) Taya,

the oxherd of Tehiptilla, had brought about the destruction of one ox. (6–7) Thus Taya: "Another ox had brought about the destruction of that ox out in the field." (8–11) The judges declared: "Produce your witnesses to the effect that another (ox) had destroyed it in the field." (12–13) Thus Taya: "I have no witnesses." (13–14) Thus the judges: "You shall pay one ox like the one you caused to be destroyed." (15–19) Thus Tehiptilla prevailed in the lawsuit and Taya was remanded to Tehiptilla for (the payment of) one ox from the herd.

Seals of five witnesses and the "hand" of the scribe.

The case is an interesting one since the suspicion is strong that Taya was telling the truth. If the attack took place out in the field ("plain") it would hardly be likely that there woud be any witnesses. The judges' demand that they be produced was in effect an empty gesture. Tehiptilla being the most powerful figure in the town, and Taya being a mere oxherd, the decision of the judges in favor of Tehiptilla is in keeping with all that we know about Tehiptilla's financial and legal affairs from many other records in the same archives. Regardless of fault, however, we do have in this text at least a documented assertion that one ox had so injured another in an attack that it died or had to be destroyed. The liability of herdsmen for cattle put in their care is dealt with in Hammurapi's laws, §§264–267.

This is the larger theme of all the cases from §53 through §58. The scribe did not label the group, but the arrangement itself serves as evidence that he was conscious of the principle he undertook to illustrate. By the progression from goring oxen to vicious dogs to decrepit walls the scribe also appears to have attempted to illustrate negligent wrongs in a series of situations of increasing gravity: the tortfeasor is progressively more liable prima facie in that he has less and less ground for pleading extenuating circumstances. An ox, after all, is a valuable and crucial component in the economy; moreover, an ox—even one with a reputation for having a tendency to gore—will not *predictably* attack persons at any opportunity. A vicious dog, on the other hand, is nothing but a menace with little redeeming economic utility, and once turned vicious will predictably attack people given the slightest opportunity. There remains only the somewhat mitigating factor that a dog, however vicious, nevertheless "acts on its own" in some sense; it is a living being capable of movement and escape from its owner's control despite the latter's most diligent efforts. A decrepit wall in danger of imminent collapse, on the other hand, affords its owner no margin for extenuation after he had been made aware of its condition and he had failed to make any repairs. The wall is sure to collapse, and is in a condition amenable to correction, as goring oxen and vicious dogs are not. Should the wall collapse and kill a passerby, the proprietor is not only liable for damages; his negligence in this case renders him subject to the death penalty at the king's discretion. The punishment indicates that the negligence in this instance borders on the criminal, as it does not in the case of a goring ox or a vicious dog.[1]

2. **Hammurapi's rules.** As noted earlier, the text of the Laws of Hammurapi remains by far the longest surviving document of its genre; it achieved the status of a "canonical" literary work, and was still being copied in the libraries of Assyrian kings as late as the seventh century B.C. It exhibits throughout a rational structure such as cannot be discerned in any other text of the genre, certainly not in the Laws of Eshnunna.[2] It is composed as a sequence of broad themes

within which subsidiary themes and individual topics are arranged in meaningful order. The classificatory notions which govern the arrangement do not, of course, conform to those followed in modern drafts of legal codes, but it would not be difficult to perceive its structure in terms of "title, chapter, paragraph, section," and so on, similar to the structure of modern legal codes. The textual "environment" of the goring-ox rules in Hammurapi's laws will therefore disclose to us something of the classificatory canons we are seeking.

The "title" or "chapter" within which Hammurapi's goring-ox rules are situated may be said to begin with §228, a rule which lays down the rate to be paid to a builder for construction of a house. This "law" inaugurates a short series of rules, §§229–233, which concern various sanctions against the builder for wrongful death and damage attributable to faulty (that is, negligent) construction work. §234 sets the rate to be paid for boat construction, and is followed by a group of rules concerned with faulty boat construction, faulty navigation, and establishing compensation for consequent loss of the boat and/or its cargo. §239 establishes the wage-rate for a hired boatman. The series concludes with a law establishing compensation for loss of a boat and its cargo in a collision resulting from the violation of the right-of-way rules of river traffic. With §241 the subject of oxen is introduced. §§241–249 deal with the wrongful taking of an ox from its legal owner (§241), the rate of hire of plough oxen (§§242–243), and liability or non-liability of the lessee of the ox for its death or injury in various circumstances while it is in his possession (§§244–249). Then come the goring-ox laws, §§250–252.

The method of organization is thus clearly discernible. With §228 the drafter enters upon the area of major economic activity, construction, boat building and navigation (that is, the primary mode of long-distance transport in Mesopotamia), and the use of oxen—the major "vehicle" for local transport, but primarily the basic unit of energy in field husbandry. Indeed, the goring-ox laws themselves serve to introduce a long series of laws, which continues to §272,

---

[1] In general, Goetze perceived the underlying thread of this entire sequence of laws as well as the reasons for the progression from lesser to greater culpability; see his remarks in *Laws of Eshnunna*, p. 140. It must be observed, however, that the use of the term *napištum* or *dīn napištim*, "life," "a case where life (is in the balance)," does not have the full sense of "capital case" in our terminology, and is ambiguous from that point of view. There exists at least one instance from the Old Babylonian period in which the phrase is followed by an explicit amplification that the penalty is a specified sum of money; see G. Boyer, *Textes Juridiques*, Archives Royales de Mari, 8 (Paris, 1958), no. 1.

[2] For a general introduction to the structural features of Hammurapi's text see H. Petschow, "Zur 'Systematik' im Kodex Hammurapi," *Zeitschrift für Assyriologie* 57 (1965): pp. 146ff. The same scholar provided an analysis of the same aspects of the

Eshnunna Laws in *Symbolae. . . David*, pp. 131ff. It says something about the traditional orientation of scholars who confront these documents—especially Hammurapi's text—that Petschow's is the first attempt to find the rational bases for the internal suborder of these compositions and for their structure as a whole. Earlier scholars, finding that these structures did not conform to *their* ideas of what a rationally ordered "judicial code" should look like, had by-and-large dismissed this aspect of the documents with such characterizations as "unscientific" or "chaotic." Petschow proved the facts to be quite the contrary. As the present study is designed to illustrate, a disinterested examination of the structure of texts of this kind (or any other, for that matter), is a *sine qua non* for the understanding of their substance, since the structure is the embodiment of the basic classificatory system of which the single groups or items are but the manifestations.

dealing with various aspects of agricultural labor, animal husbandry, and local transport; most of these revolve around the use of large and small cattle. Each of the three subgroups of this sequence consists of normative rules setting out the rates deemed proper (that is, "just") to a particular activity, followed by a series of rules illustrating some instances of wrongful conduct in the pursuit of that activity, and the liability attaching to it. The goring-ox rules as a group occupy the same position within the third sequence that the law about boat collision (§240) occupies in the second sequence. Both deal with "traffic accidents" that are thought to illustrate wrongful conduct characteristically arising from the use of boats and oxen, respectively. The group of goring-ox rules in Hammurapi's text thus serves to illustrate culpable negligence within the framework of a theme of larger scope, namely the area of agricultural-economic activity in which the employment of oxen is central. In this respect the setting of Hammurapi's statement of the goring-ox rules represents a more thought-out organizational plan than does the statement of these rules in the Laws of Eshnunna, where the focus is on negligence as an almost abstract principle, as is indicated by the succeeding rules about mad dogs and decrepit walls.

B. Internal Structure

1. **The Eshnunna rules.** For purposes of analysis the three Eshnunna rules may realistically be reduced to two. Of these, the first, §53, offers the instance in which (1) there is no indication of whether the goring ox already had a reputation for such tendencies, or whether such a circumstance would have affected the rule, and (2) the victim was another ox. §§54–55 must be construed as a single rule or "case," since the only distinction between them concerns the status of the victim, a detail which affects only the amount of compensation to be assessed. Otherwise §§54–55 contrasts with §53 in that (1) the ox is now said to have had a reputation for a dangerous disposition, (2) that its owner had been warned of it by public authority but had nevertheless taken no precautionary measures, and (3) the victim of the animal was a human being. In other words, from §53 to §§54–55 the drafter presents us with a number of crucial variables. Our own notion of a logical progression would have suggested the introduction of one variable at a time.[3]

Thus, if we were dependent for our information on the Laws of Eshnunna alone, we would remain in the dark as to what the Mesopotamian feeling would have been if (a) the animal that gored a person to death had not previously given any indication of vicious tendencies so that its owner could not have been forewarned, or (b) whether, as regards the case of §53, the owner of the ox that had gored another ox to death would have come off as lightly had his animal already been known for vicious tendencies and had he been warned of them.

The Eshnunna rules provide some basic juridical elements that are vital for comparison with the biblical laws in Exodus: (1) When an ox has gored another ox to death, there having been no prior indication that the goring ox was of vicious disposition, there can be no *presumption* of fault in the owner of either animal. In resolving such a case, however, the society does not follow the rule which in our own times is stated as "letting the losses fall where they may";[4] in the view of the ancients that would be tantamount to a "penalty" against the owner of the gored ox. The principle of "loss distribution" is invoked instead: An unforeseen accident ought not to be an occasion on which one party is made to bear the entire loss; the loss must be borne by both parties equally. We may legitimately view this resolution of the case as a perception—however simplistic or crude—of the social need for a form of loss equalization or distribution which in modern times has been supplied by the more complex institution of accident insurance.[5] (2) The immediate progression from the case in which the victim of the goring ox was another animal (§53) to the case in which the victim was a person (§§54–55) bespeaks the absence of any sense that this factor alone changes the nature of the case; the controlling variable is plainly the factor of negligence and the presumption of fault consequent upon that. The owner of the ox becomes liable for compensation to the surviving kin in the amount of two-thirds of a mina (that is, forty shekels) of silver if the victim was a free citizen, and fifteen shekels (that is, one-quarter of a mina) if he was a slave. The money was in the latter instance presumably to be paid to the slave's master. (3) It is to be noted that in §§54–55 the author has nothing to say about the disposition of the animal itself.

2. **The Hammurapi rules.** Hammurapi's treatment of the goring ox theme, like that of the Eshnunna series, consists of three illustrative cases. Unlike the Eshnunna sequence, however, all three are in-

---

[3] I have demonstrated elsewhere ("Sex Offenses in Sumerian Laws," *Journal of the American Oriental Society* **86** [1966]: p. 368), that in selecting a sequence of cases to exemplify some specific theme the Mesopotamian writers were not guided by a casuistic purpose. It was not their intention to progress from case to case by the alteration of one circumstance at a time in order to demonstrate how variation affects the appropriate judicial disposition, although on occasion this was done. Their aim, rather, was to exemplify the *just* and "true" disposition as unambiguously as possible; to this end it was often necessary to "stack the deck" in

such a way as to point unmistakably to the one disposition or "verdict" in each separate case that illustrates the fulfillment of those criteria.

[4] This is a generally prevailing principle of the common law in the realm of torts.

[5] See *Temple Law Quarterly* **46**(1973): pp. 256ff.

stances in which the victim was a human being. The case illustrated in §250 is adjudged to be one of non-liability, and corresponds only in that limited sense to §53 of the Eshnunna series, where the victim was another ox rather than a person. It may be recalled at this point that there is a contextual distinction between the Eshnunna and the Hammurapi statements of the goring-ox rules. The former group is set in the limited framework of illustrations of negligent omissions, for that purpose treating also vicious dogs and decrepit walls. Hammurapi's series, on the other hand, is set within a much broader framework which encompasses a wide variety of activities involving the use of oxen, including normative rules as well as instances in which the animal is the victim of accident or negligence, or the agent or instrument of misfortune. The case represented by §250 would therefore have been wholly out of place in the Eshnunna series. It is by the same token relevant to the more comprehensive context in Hammurapi's laws: Prior to setting down the two rules §§251–252, the circumstances of which exactly parallel Eshnunna's §§54–55 in providing the ground for liability, it was particularly pertinent to delineate an instance in which the victim of the ox was a human being, but in which the owner of the animal could not be held culpable. The decisive circumstance in §250 is that the accident occurred while the ox was "walking along the street." This is careful and deliberate language. It implies that the ox was "walking along" under proper control by its owner (or whoever was in charge of it), so that the ensuing accident was not the result of negligence on the owner's part. The further implication is unavoidable that the death was due to the victim's own carelessness; he apparently wandered—perhaps absentmindedly—into the animal's path. The case is intended as an illustration of contributory negligence, for which the owner of the ox cannot be held liable. It exemplifies the prime objective of Hammurapi's "Code": the dispensing of even-handed justice. Before giving the owner of an ox notice of his responsibility towards pedestrians, the law seeks to reassure him that his liability is not absolute: there are circumstances in which he would not be held liable should his beast be the agent of a fatal accident. Having established this principle in §250, the author feels free to move on to the major concern, namely, the prescription of appropriate indemnities for loss of life when the owner of the ox is liable by reason of a culpable omission. §§251–252 follow the same principle as §§54–55 of the Eshnunna laws, except for discrepancies in both rules in relation to the amount of the indemnity for the free man and the slave, respectively. The scholarly literature has been at some pains to attempt to account for this relatively minor difference between the Eshnunna and Hammurapi rules; the issue need

not detain us here.[6] The principle of both statements is the same. §§250–252 of Hammurapi's laws, in which a person is the victim of a goring ox, follow directly upon a sequence of cases in which the ox was itself the victim of wrongful human action or of an unforeseeable accident. In both sets of rules the compensation or indemnity, when it is warranted at all, is strictly pecuniary. As in the Eshnunna rules, nothing is said in Hammurapi's laws about the possible fate of the ox, however dangerous it might have proved to be.

To sum up the salient features of the goring-ox laws in the cuneiform sources of Mesopotamia, it is first of all obvious that all of these rules—the laws in which the ox is the victim of a wrongful act or omission as well as those in which the ox is the immediate agent of a wrongful injury—are conceived of as operating wholly in the legal realm which in modern terms would be denoted as *torts* or, in the earlier common law, as *trespass*. They constitute, in other words, palpable harms to private interests which are amenable to remedy in equivalent, that is, pecuniary, terms if they are committed under circumstances in which the wrongdoer may be held culpable for negligence. The killing of a person by an ox constitutes an economic trespass against the dependent kin of the victim, and is to be made good as such once liability is properly established. The loss is conceived of in quantitative and objective terms: the killing of a free adult is a more severe injury than the killing of a minor or a slave, and justifies a proportionately greater indemnity, and the killing of any human being by an ox is, in general, more grave than the killing of an ox by a person who was not its owner. The setting of the goring-ox laws in Hammurapi's text, following immediately upon the laws dealing with boats, suggests

---

[6] I do not want to get side-tracked into an analysis of the implication of the different assessments which the Hammurapi rules and the Laws of Eshnunna make against the tortfeasor in identical circumstances. In the present instance the indemnity in the Eshnunna laws is fifteen shekels for the loss of a slave, while Hammurapi (§252) assesses ⅓ mina, that is, twenty shekels of silver. This is, however, the kind of difference that poses a conflict only if one comes to the text with the mind of a literalist. Indeed, even greater contradictions can be found within the *same* text as regards awards for loss or injury based on status and age of the parties involved. Without pursuing the matter here more deeply, it may be asserted that from the standpoint of effective law these "posted tariffs" are among the least reliable elements in such documents. They are merely meant to illustrate—usually only within the particular context of a sequence of rules of greater or lesser length—the differentials among groups of different status (or age, when this is a relevant criterion) as regards awards for damages to which each group may be entitled with reference to the other groups. The sums prescribed should not therefore be examined and compared in isolation from the *textual* contexts in which they occur. This observation applies throughout the legal corpora where graded awards are laid down for members of the major status or age groups.

that, just as the boat rules may be viewed as constituting a simple "maritime traffic code," the goring-ox rules may be seen as a rudimentary "vehicular traffic code." In either sphere the injuries are private and their remedies pecuniary. Throughout there is not the least suggestion that the wrong in any sense entailed a public offense that might require some form of expiation. The public interest is presumably satisfied completely by having made the remedy of compensation available to the victim or to his survivors.

V. THE BIBLICAL RULES

A. Grouping and Arrangement

Following the analytical procedure employed for the cuneiform sources, we will first consider the goring-ox rules of the Covenant Code in relation to their context. To do this we must survey the total structure of the Covenant Code, beginning with its first laws, set down in Exodus chapter 21. The following is the sequence of themes taken up in the Code:

1. **Slavery:** Exod. 21:2–11. The subject here is not slavery in the conventional sense—human beings owned outright by their masters and subject to the same laws, more or less, as non-human chattels— but "term" enslavement of "Hebrew" persons. A more precise terminology would define the status of such persons as "indentured servants" rather than as "slaves." In biblical usage the status of real slaves is reserved for persons of foreign (that is, non-Israelite) origin; they do not come within the purview of this group of laws, which seek to protect the right of Hebrew slaves to regain their freedom. The Covenant Code obviously does not even visualize the possibility of Israelites being outright slaves of fellow Israelites except upon their own explicit demand.

2. **Capital crimes:** Exod. 21:12–17. The major capital crimes are homicide, kidnapping, assault against one's parents, and cursing one's parents.

3. **Assault and battery:** Exod. 21:18–27. The major thrust of this group of laws is towards establishing the talionic principle of punishment, "an eye for an eye," which begins in verse 23.[1] It includes, how-

ever, two cases that are emendable by pecuniary means: injuries which cause only temporary disability, in which case the injurer is obliged to pay only for the injured's loss of earnings and for his medical costs (vss. 18–19), and the curious case of a miscarriage which is precipitated by someone's striking a pregnant woman in a brawl (vs. 22). In that instance the husband of the woman may demand an indemnity for the loss of a potential child. This section of the Code also includes the unusual rule (vss. 20–21) which makes the master of a (presumably non-Israelite) slave liable to blood-vengeance (?) for whipping him to death, although he is immune if the slave should survive for one day or more and then die, on the ground that the slave is "his asset."

4. **The goring ox that has killed persons:** Exod. 21:28–32. Except for the first instance given, in which the ox had no previous record of viciousness, the sequence is aimed at illustrating negligent homicide and its juridical consequences.

It will be noted that the themes in 1–4 above revolve about "persons," either in connection with status (Hebrew slavery) or in relation to physical invasions, including homicide, kidnapping, maiming, and simple assault. We should not be far off the mark if we were to refer to this entire portion of the Covenant Code as the "Law of Persons." Beginning with verse 33 the biblical author proceeds along a different course:

5. **Negligent omissions causing death of cattle:** Exod. 21:33–37. Two types of cases serve as illustrations. The first is that of someone who dug a cistern and failed to cover the top, so that large cattle (that is, an ox or an ass) fell into it and died; restitution is prescribed. The second case is that of the ox that had gored another ox to death.

---

[1] The *ius talionis*, or "eye for an eye" formula, and its full context in the relevant section of the Covenant Code and in the framework of the parallel laws in the cuneiform corpora, has yet to receive a satisfying exposition, as do the relevant ethnographic data. The topic was last discussed by B. S. Jackson, in "The Problem of Exodus XXI 22–5 (Ius talionis)," *Vetus Testamentum* **23** (1973): pp. 273ff. For our present purpose it is relevant to stress that the *aim* of the section in the Covenant Code is to mute the widely practiced custom of paying for injuries and wounds, whether they were inflicted deliberately or accidentally. These "laws" notwithstanding, that practice must—apart from some exceptional and isolated instances, which we may imagine occurred from time to time—surely have continued in Israelite society. The fact

that the full formula, following that of "a life for a life," is commonly regarded as a late interpolation strengthens rather than weakens this view. It bespeaks the sense that however impractical and even inappropriate physical talionic punishments might be for the crimes of assault and injury, the principle nevertheless deserves statement as a *moral* doctrine: if "a life for a life" is an eminently feasible method for "making the punishment fit the crime," *eo ipso* "an eye for an eye, a tooth for a tooth," and so on, despite the unfeasibility of the latter. A punishment is moral *only* if it fits the crime. The talionic formula is merely a dramatic and effective way of stating this principle, which is more explicitly formulated in Lev. 23:19–20: "When a man inflicts a permanent injury upon his neighbor the same shall be done to him." The absurdity lies not in the statement of the principle but in the solemnity with which it has been debated as "law" in the modern scholarly (and not so scholarly) literature. That over the ages the principle has come to serve as the epitome of the stern and uncompromising justice of the Old Testament, as contrasted with the forgiving cast of the New Testament, is a historical fact whose consequences will hardly be reversed even by the most sober and dispassionate treatment the subject may be accorded. It is clear, then, that this theme deserves scrutiny from the perspectives of Western intellectual and moral history rather than from that of jurisprudence.

6. Larceny: Exod. 21:37–22:3. The illustrations involve theft of small cattle, conversion, and the special case of burglary (that is, breaking and entering).

7. Negligent damage to agricultural land: Exod. 22:4–5.

8. Damage or loss of chattels while they were held in bailment or on loan: Exod. 22:6–14.

9. Seduction of an unbetrothed virgin: Exod. 22:15–16.

With the single exception of certain acts arising in the context of burglary—which I will consider below—it will be seen that the object of the tortious acts or omissions of the cases illustrated under themes 5–9 (Exod. 21:33–22:16) consists of chattels, real property, or a recognized economic interest, the last represented by the potential bride-price realizable for one's virgin daughter. The sanction in all these cases is uniformly pecuniary; restitution or compensation is prescribed for negligent acts or omissions, and multiple damages for theft or conversion. The exception just alluded to concerns a most remarkable interruption by the biblical writer in his exposition of the laws of larceny. Having set forth in Exod. 21:37 the principle that theft and subsequent conversion of large and small cattle entail quintuple and quadruple damages respectively, he shifts his focus in the next verse, Exod. 22:1, to the question of the life of the burglar: under what circumstances would the slaying of the intruder be privileged, and when is killing not justifiable, warranting instead blood-vengeance against the killer, presumably even if he had been the would-be victim of the burglary? Only in the middle of Exod. 22:2, having disposed of this separate issue, does the writer return to his main theme, that of larceny, to emphasize that the culprit is obliged to pay the full multiple damages set down in Exod. 21:37; should he be incapable of satisfying this penalty he is to be sold into slavery. The writer then concludes his rules relating to larceny in verse 3, with the prescription of double damages for simple larceny without conversion. The verses that deal with the killing of the would-be burglar have been seen by many modern authorities as intrusive in their textual location; some have been bold enough to suggest that this is a real displacement arising from some early redactional fault.[2] Whether such a conclusion is warranted or not, the discordant effect of these verses on the modern reader cannot be disputed. I shall return to consider this problem in due course.

B. Internal Structure and Analysis

The arrangement of the goring-ox laws of the Covenant Code presents no problem apart from the textual gap between those cases in which the victim was a person and those in which the victim was another ox. This issue is part of our juristic analysis

---

[2] See below, p. 39 n. 34.

of these laws as a whole, which revolves about four salient points:

1. The stoning of the ox to death.

2. The prescription of the penalty of death, or "ransom" for the owner of the ox in circumstances presuming negligence.

3. Specifications regarding the age and status of the victim.

4. The textual gap between the cases in which the victim of the goring ox was human and those in which the victim was another ox.

1. **The stoning of the ox to death.** In contrast to the parallel cuneiform laws where, as we have seen, there is no mention at all of the fate of the animal, the biblical statement accords this question particular prominence. The ox is to be stoned to death not only if it had already established a record for viciousness, but even if it had no such record at all, and presumably even in circumstances in which the death of the victim might have been attributable to his own carelessness. Nor is the stoning of the ox contingent upon the status of the victim; it must be stoned even when the victim was a (presumably foreign) slave. Finally, the biblical law underscores its special concern with this facet of the case by the specific prohibition against the consumption of the flesh of the ox as food. All of this presents a sharp contrast not only with the Mesopotamian rules, but also internally in the biblical distinction between the fate of the ox and that of its owner when the latter is held to be guilty of "criminal" negligence: while the ox is condemned to be "stoned" to death, the owner is simply to be "put to death" without specification of the mode of his execution. This distinction in wording—in the very same sentence—cannot be dismissed as fortuitous; it suggests rather that the guilt or "crime" of the ox is of a different order than the crime of its owner.

Was the ox to be "executed" for having "committed murder"? The answer is clearly negative: The sanction in biblical law for intentional homicide, as set forth in Exod. 21:12–14 and elsewhere, is simply death. The sentence is identified merely by the phrase "He shall die" or "be put to death," as it is in the case of the owner of the goring ox; the mode of execution has traditionally been understood to be death by the sword.[3] Never is stoning prescribed for someone condemned to death for intentional homicide. Death by stoning, in biblical tradition and elsewhere in the ancient Near East, is reserved for crimes of a special character. In those cases there is no designated

---

[3] This is to be understood from Num. 35:19, which ordains that the execution of a criminal homicide must be accomplished by the blood-avenger of the victim; the execution is indicated by the Hebrew verb *pāgāᶜ*, "to strike (with a weapon)." The same verb is elsewhere used explicitly in association with the sword, as, for example, when Joab was slain on the orders of Solomon, in the fulfillment of the mandate set by David and as the expiation for his murder, years earlier, of rival army officers. See I Kings 2:28–34.

"executioner," for the community assembled is the common executioner of the sentence. Offenses which entail this mode of execution must therefore be of a character that, either in theory or in fact, "offend" the corporate community or are believed to compromise its most cherished values to the degree that the commission of the offense places the community itself in jeopardy.[4] The ox that gored a human being to death obviously committed an offense of this magnitude. To identify the particular quality of this offense requires us to place it in the context of other offenses in biblical law or tradition which similarly entailed the penalty of death by stoning. These must now be reviewed:

The worship of "foreign gods," as set forth in Deut. 13:7ff. It is there laid down that even should the person attempting to lure others into idolatry be a member of one's immediate family, he must be publicly denounced and executed by stoning: "Your hand (that is, that of the witness) being the first in his execution, and the hand of the entire people afterward." Should the entire population of a town be seduced into idolatry, stoning is no longer feasible; the population must then be exterminated by the sword. But—and this bears emphasis—nothing of its goods or wealth is to be taken as booty; all of it must be collected, piled up in the main square, and be incinerated. The town must then be totally burned down, to remain an everlasting ruin (as a permanent example) never to be rebuilt. "Nothing may cling to your hand of the proscribed material in order that the divine wrath relent etc." (vs. 18). The same mode of execution is ordained for those engaging in worship of astral bodies (Deut. 17:2–7).

The disobedient and profligate son: Deut. 21:18–21. Should a son persist in such unfilial behavior after repeated admonition, his parents are to deliver him up to the authorities of their town and denounce him, whereupon "all the townspeople are to stone him to death. Thus will evil be purged from your midst and all Israel will hear of it and be fearful."

A newly-wed bride found by her husband not to have been a virgin. Deut. 22:20f. prescribes that she is to be stoned to death by the townspeople "because she had committed a depraved act in Israel by having fornicated whilst still in her father's house, so will you purge the evil from your midst." Similarly, a fornicating couple must be stoned to death when the woman involved was already betrothed to another man, "the woman for not having cried out for help within the town, and the man for having violated his neighbor's wife" (Deut. 22:23f.).

We may briefly list other offenses which entailed

the penalty of death by stoning: child sacrifice (Lev. 20:2ff.); sorcery and necromancy (Lev. 20:27); blasphemy (Lev. 24:10ff.); and violation of the Sabbath (Num. 15:32–36). In addition, I Kings 21 tells the story of the false accusation and execution by stoning of Naboth, for blasphemy and sedition against the king. This surely indicates that stoning was the formal procedure for execution in authentic instances of sedition.

But stoning a person to death was not just a formal mode of execution. It could also serve as the manifestation of spontaneous popular outrage beyond the bounds of judicial sanction. Thus when Rehoboam, the son and successor of Solomon on the Israelite throne, increased the tax burden on the Northern tribes instead of granting relief as he had been petitioned to do, the Israelites in their fury stoned to death the king's chief tax official, who had been sent out to enforce the royal policy (I Kings 12:18). Again, it is told in the seventh chapter of Joshua that when Achan violated the explicit proscription of all of Jericho's wealth by secretly taking some booty, the divine wrath was promptly manifested—as the people interpreted it—by a military defeat in the first attack upon the city of Ai. Having learned the cause of this setback by a divine message and having further been instructed how to identify the guilty party, Joshua was commanded to burn him and all his possessions in fire. After Achan had confessed his crime, he was taken, with his illicit booty and also "his sons, his daughters, his ox, his ass, his sheep, his tent, and all of his possessions," to the vale of Achor. There "all of Israel threw stones upon him, burned them with fire" and heaped a rock tumulus over the remains (Josh. 7:25f.); after that Yahweh's wrath abated and the Israelites were victorious. Incidents such as these strongly suggest that stoning to death was, par excellence, the form of killing used in a lynching. It was particularly suited to the purpose: rocks were abundant; death was relatively slow, and dependent upon mass participation; and the physical remains were, literally, spectacular. Against this background we may perceive in the formal sentence of death by stoning the modulation of an otherwise uncontrolled and spontaneous lynching process into a solemn, ritualized execution carried out under formal judicial authority, to be invoked for a limited number of capital offenses. In the same way ordinary execution by the sword (as, for example, for the crime of murder) is but an attenuated and judicially controlled form of the blood-vengeance which allows the kin of the murdered victim to wreak his private vengeance upon the condemned by serving as executioner, as it were, on behalf of the community.[5]

The common denominator of all the offenses

---

[4] A still valuable study of the subject is that of R. Hirzel, "Die Strafe der Steinigung," *Abhandlungen der königlichen sächsischen Gesellschaft der Wissenschaft*, phil.-hist. Klasse **27** (1909): pp. 223–266. While based mainly on classical Greek sources, it covers other evidence of the practice, including the biblical.

[5] On this point see M. Greenberg, "The Biblical Concept of Asylum," *Journal of Biblical Literature* **78** (1959): pp. 128f.

entailing the punishment of death by stoning is that they are thought to strike at the moral and religious fibers which the community as a whole sees as defining its essence and integrity. Such crimes, in other words, amount to insurrections against the cosmic order itself. Viewed in their mundane or strictly physical effects, most if not all of such offenses would, in modern juristic terms, be categorized as "victimless crimes." They are, at the same time, crimes of the most serious kind for they are "revolts" against God, or the world order which is ordained by the divine word. That most of the crimes to be expiated by stoning which were enumerated above answer to this description needs no further comment. Mundane "insurrections" against legitimate authority such as citizens against the king, sons against parents, and the fornicating daughter against her father, as well as religious crimes like idolatry and blasphemy fall into this category of offense. The violation of the Sabbath is of equal gravity, even if less obviously so, for the Sabbath is part of Creation itself and was indeed its capstone (Gen. 2:1–3). Yahweh himself designated its observance by the Israelites for all eternity as *the* perpetual symbol of Creation and of the special covenant between him and the people of Israel (Exod. 31:12–18). The desecration of the Sabbath was therefore tantamount to a challenge to God's order of Creation, and was as grave an offense as idolatry.

Despite God's statement to Noah that he will hold animals as well as man responsible for the shedding of human blood (Gen. 9:5), the "crime" of the ox that gored a person to death is not just to be found in the fact that it had "committed homicide." As we have seen, the intentional shedding of blood by human murderers does not call for execution of the criminal by stoning. Furthermore, as we have also noted, the ox is to be stoned even on a first occurrence, and presumably even when it was not "at fault." The real crime of the ox is that by killing a human being—whether out of viciousness or by an involuntary motion—it has objectively committed a *de facto* insurrection against the hierarchic order established by Creation: Man was designated by God "to rule over the fish of the sea, the fowl of the skies, the cattle, the earth, and all creatures that roam over the earth" (Gen. 1:26, 28). Simply by its behavior— and it is vital here to stress that intention is immaterial; the guilt is objective—the ox has, albeit involuntarily, performed an act whose effect amounts to "treason." It has acted against man, its superior in the hierarchy of Creation, as man acts against God when violating the Sabbath or when practicing idolatry. It is precisely for this reason that the flesh of the ox may not be consumed.[6] That prohibition corresponds exactly to

the total proscription of a town condemned to extirpation for idolatry, that is, treason against God, the Lord of Creation and the summit of the cosmic hierarchy: the wealth of the town must be destroyed and the taking of booty is forbidden. "Guilt" or "innocence" of the offending object or animal is immaterial; it offends solely because it has become a source of contamination and hence poses a danger to the well-being of the larger community. It must therefore be totally destroyed. The episode of Achan provides us with the starkest example of the principle. While it was only Achan himself who was *morally* responsible for his offense in violating the proscription of the wealth of Jericho, his punishment entailed the simultaneous destruction of his entire family and wealth. The principle is analogous to the treatment of a physical malignancy, the drastic excision of which entails the removal of some surrounding and apparently non-infected tissue, the better to insure the survival of the total organism. Achan's family and property had to be destroyed for the same reason: the survival of the organism of the entire Israelite community required the eradication of everything and everyone that had been in contact with Achan, the seat of the malignancy.

As a last example we must consider here the unique episode involving Qorah and his associates narrated in Num. 16:1ff. Although the spectacular punishment meted out in that case was not that of execution by stoning, it is nevertheless extremely pertinent to the present discussion. Qorah was a leading member of the prestigious Levitical clan of the Qehathites. Together with a large number of high-ranking Israelite chieftains he accosted Moses and Aaron with the charge that they had arrogated to themselves the exclusive prerogatives of priesthood, in alleged contradiction of the understanding that Yahweh was directly present amidst all of Israel. At the foot of Mount Sinai, on the eve of the receipt of the Ten Commandments and the Law, Yahweh had explicitly ordained that the whole of Israel be "a kingdom of priests and a holy nation"; as such, every Israelite— and especially every Levite, without distinction— enjoyed the privilege of serving the cult without the mediation of a professional priesthood. One senses that Moses's failure to respond promptly to the challenge—upon hearing Qorah's accusation Moses "fell upon his face" (vs. 4)—was due to his percep-

---

[6] *Ibid.,* and also the same writer's observations in "Some Postulates of Biblical Criminal Law," *Yehezkel Kaufmann Jubilee Volume* (Jerusalem, 1960), p. 15: "The establishment of a value hierarchy of man over beast means that man may kill them—for

food and sacrifice only . . . —but they may not kill him. . . . The religious evaluation inherent in this law is further evidenced by the prohibition of eating the flesh of the stoned ox. The beast is laden with guilt and is therefore an object of horror." This is all correct as far as it goes, and clearly expresses sensitivity to the hierarchic implications of the law. But it does not, to my mind, adequately stress the difference between mere "execution" of the ox for homicide in accordance with the law of Gen. 9:5f. and the stoning of the beast and the prohibition against its consumption as food, a mode of execution which, as I demonstrate here, is tied to a set of coordinates that do not embrace the crime of homicide.

tion that the complaint was not without merit. Nevertheless, the accusation amounted to a direct confrontation with God's election of Moses and Aaron to the exclusive rights of the priesthood, and thus constituted an insurrection against the divine order. Since the circumstances of the case were such as to preclude punishment by a human tribunal, punishment appropriate to the offense could be effected only by divine intervention. Thus "the ground underneath them split apart; the earth opened its mouth, swallowing them up together with their dwellings including all of Qorah's family and all the property; they and all they possessed descended to Sheol alive, the Earth covering them over, and they disappeared from amidst the assembled population" (vss. 32–33).

Apart from the fact that this extraordinary occurrence was seen as a deliberate and prompt punishment of the offenders by God, it bears in all other respects the indicia of the standard form of execution of those guilty of treason or insurrection: the contaminating quality of the offense required not only the execution of the criminals but also the simultaneous extirpation of their households—that is, of all animate and inanimate things that were directly in contact with them—to prevent spreading the "infection" into the wider community. Further, and for the same reason, the punishment took place in the full sight of the community, so that the appropriate lesson would be driven home with maximum effect. The net result of the punishment was precisely the same as the consequences of the Achan episode, and parallels the prescription for the destruction of cities whose population had fallen into idolatry. Finally, the punishment of Qorah and his associates strikingly echoes the prescriptions found in the Hittite Laws, §173, for executing those guilty of insurrection and treason:[7]

If someone challenges a royal decision, his house
　shall be turned into a rubble heap.[8]
If anyone challenges the decision of a dignitary,
　his head shall be cut off.
If a slave rises up against his master, he shall
　go down into a pithos.[9]

It will be seen that the fate of Qorah and his group combines the main element of the first sub-rule—their dwellings (that is, tents), possessions, families, and livestock were destroyed with them—with the main characteristic of the third sub-rule, which prescribes being buried alive. Taken altogether, then, the Qorah story, for all its fabulous elements, is perhaps the most vivid witness to the biblical view of the kind of death proper for those guilty of insurrection.

To sum up, in the context of other biblical laws where execution by stoning is ordained, the biblical prescription requiring that the ox that had gored a person to death be stoned emerges as the salient feature of the judicial procedure. In this it stands in sharpest contrast with the treatment of the theme in the cuneiform sources, where the fate of the ox merits no judicial attention whatever.[10] Conversely, the culpability of the owner of the ox enters into consideration only when circumstances create a presumption of negligence, and even then the biblical law almost deliberately leaves the sanction ambiguous. The cuneiform laws consistently view the situation as demanding pecuniary emendation from the owner of the ox, except when circumstances indicated that the victim died as a consequence of his own negligence.

2. **The death penalty or ransom against the owner of the ox.** When the previous record of the ox creates a presumption of negligence on the part of its owner, biblical law promptly alters its view of the wrong. It obviously considers the misfortune as a variety of criminal homicide, and ordains the death penalty for the owner of the ox. Having done so, however, it offers the alternative of commuting that sentence to a pecuniary ransom. The wording "If a ransom be imposed upon him" suggests that this plainly more lenient sanction is discretionary only, to be invoked only at the pleasure of the victim's kin, or of the judicial authority, or both. The diction chosen by the biblical author in broaching this alternative hints also that this is a mode of resolution that does not altogether meet with his approval, and is offered by him only as an accommodation to the practical realities of cases of this kind. It is the only case in all of biblical law in which the wrongful

---

[7] See also the translation by A. Goetze in *ANET*³, p. 195b.

[8] As pointed out to me by my colleague H. Hoffner, the Hittite word used here, *pulpuli*, is equated with the Akkadian *tillu*, "a hillock of ruins"; the same word, *tel-*, is used in modern Arabic in the names of the mounds representing the ruins of the ancient cities. Note also Deut. 13:13ff., which ordains the total destruction of a city that reverted to idolatry; it is stipulated there that such a city "shall remain a ruin (*tēl*) forever; it must never again be rebuilt."

[9] That is, he is to be buried alive in a large storage vessel that is sunk into the ground.

[10] It is perhaps not entirely redundant to remark that this lack of attention is not to be thought of as an oversight or as implying that the ox was to be destroyed as a matter of course. It is rather that the disposition of the ox was not thought to be a matter for legislation, just as in contemporary laws with regard to domestic animals or pets that have turned vicious the sole interest of the statutes relates to the liability of the owner. It may be presumed that in ancient Babylonia, just as today, the question of whether to destroy the animal or not was left to the common sense and prudence of local administrative authorities. This understanding of the situation is not refuted by the fact that in some jurisdictions in the United States where there are special economic interests, say, in sheep-herding or poultry-farming, the statutes retain laws *permitting* any police officer or even a private citizen to shoot on sight a dog caught in the act of killing a lamb or a chicken. These are all laws relating to nuisance, and have nothing to do with a judicial sanction ordaining the execution of the animal. With regard to the occasional occurrence of the latter phenomenon in certain contemporary contexts, see chapter XI, pp. 83f. below.

extinction of a human life is formally emendable by a pecuniary settlement. Elsewhere in biblical law it is expressly forbidden to compound for a killing, even when that killing was unintentional: The homicide by inadvertence is obligated to flee for his own safety to the city of refuge (Exod. 21:13, Num. 35:11ff., Deut. 19:1ff.). The prohibition against compounding is stated fully in Num. 35:31–32: "You may not accept a ransom for the life of a slayer guilty of a capital crime; he must be put to death. Nor may you accept a ransom in lieu of flight to the city of refuge, (or) for return to dwell (at liberty) in the land before the death of the high priest." It is of course the case *a fortiori* that homicide that is criminal in any degree is not amenable to pecuniary resolution (Num. 35:31f.). Against this background the case of the negligent owner of the goring ox stands out as peculiarly aberrant.

There is, however, still another variety of homicide treated in biblical law that requires our attention. This is the case in which the victim of a murder is found in the open, the killer remaining unknown. The "legal" procedure governing this case is given in Deut. 21:1–9. It provides that the "responsibility" for the slaying rests upon the entire citizenry of that town which, by precise measurement, is determined to lie closest to the spot where the corpse was found. This extraordinary procedure is prescribed also in precisely parallel cases treated in the Hittite Laws, and in the laws relating to robbery in Hammurapi's laws, §§22–24. As in the laws of the goring ox, the conclusion is unavoidable that these cuneiform antecedents provided the inspiration for the biblical considerations of this theme. But whereas the procedure as delineated in the cuneiform rules is explicitly directed towards establishing a basis for providing appropriate restitution to the kin of the victim—the liability being borne by the community within whose territorial perimeter the body was found—the biblical rule invokes the measuring procedure towards another end altogether. The biblical author makes no mention whatever of restitution to the victim's kin; it obviously never even entered his mind as a possible mode of resolution. Instead, the community situated nearest to the point of discovery of the body is to undergo a purificatory rite designed to absolve it of responsibility for the blood that was shed. The killing is requited vicariously: a heifer is "executed" by breaking its neck in a fast-flowing stream while the authorities of the town, under the supervision of priests, wash their hands and pronounce a solemn declaration that none of them was guilty of, or witnessed, the criminal murder. The concluding verses of the prescript demonstrate explicitly that it was inspired by the fear of communal taint for blood-guilt rather than the desire to right a private wrong. In this it is completely consistent with other biblical laws of homicide.

That a "ransom" is allowed for the life of the owner

of the goring ox thus stands out very boldly as an anomaly. It was already suggested earlier that the biblical author broached the topic in a grudging manner. This is indicated by two features of his statement on the subject: the word chosen to designate the "ransom" or "commutation," and his failure to designate any precise sum by which such commutation is to be effected. The "ransom" is indicated by the Hebrew term *kôfer*. That term connotes unambiguously that the payment serves to redeem the life of the one who pays it, which otherwise would be forfeit;[11] it is devoid of any implication of indemnification for the life of the victim of the ox. By paying a *kôfer* the owner of the ox secures his *own* "redemption" (Hebrew *pidyôn*, Exod. 21:30). This approach admirably suits the biblical writer's deeper predilections, since it absolves him from the necessity of naming an appropriate sum that would resolve the case. For it is a well-established phenomenon—as true today as in ancient times—that while there may be objective criteria by which to assess the "value" of a person already dead in terms of the financial loss his death has caused his survivors, no such criteria exist for assessing the value of a living person in order to rescue him from death. Thus the "value" of a person held for ransom depends entirely on the demands of those holding him for ransom, the victim's ability to pay, and/or the ability or the inclination of the victim's family to meet the demands. This is, of course, well understood and much appreciated by modern kidnappers. In the case of the owner of the goring ox the situation is similarly potentially extortionate and could easily result in the perversion rather than the implementation of justice. The plight of the owner of the goring ox is tempered only by the reasonable assumption that the

---

[11] To remove any possibility of implication that the *kôfer* is a kind of *wergild* (the "price" of a man, as used in Germanic and early English law) it is important to bear in mind the root sense of the Hebrew term. *KPR* describes an action, originally performed by a priest, which is meant to ward off or neutralize a potentially dangerous force that had been set loose, either by an individual sinful act or by a communal transgression. The act of *KPR* usually involves the transfer, or re-direction, of the evil force to a *vicarius*, an animal or other offering that is to be sacrificed for the purpose. Hence the idea of "atonement" associated with the root *KPR*—as in *Yôm Kippûr*, "The Day of 'Atonement'"—is only a secondary meaning, deriving from the *moral* implications of sinful conduct by either an individual person or by the community. That the basic idea is rooted in the belief in the existence of morally neutral evils is proved by the fact that the same action, *KPR*, is required of the priest in the ritual "cleansing" of morbid manifestations on a patient's skin or in the walls of a building after the apparent disappearance of the symptom, that is, the "healing" of the patient. See Lev. chaps. 4–5 and 14, especially 14:53. In connection with the goring-ox law the biblical author consciously tied the use of the term *kôfer* to the life of the owner of the ox; it represents the propitiation he would be required to make, in pecuniary terms, in absolution of *his* guilt. In the view of the biblical author this payment is *not* to be viewed as an award for damages to the victim's kin based on the victim's "worth" (that is, it is not a "wergild").

impartial judicial authority would have had the final word in fixing the appropriate "ransom." But even these impartial authorities are put under constraint by the biblical prescriptions, for the law states that "whether (the ox) has gored a son or a daughter (that is, a minor) the same rule will apply (to the owner of the ox)" (Exod. 21:31). In other words, the biblical writer pointedly rejects the principle guiding the assessment of damages which prevailed elsewhere in the ancient Near East[12]—the death of a minor would obviously not represent an economic loss to the survivors as great as that of an adult—and emphatically identifies the owner of the ox as the one whose life is to be assessed.

The implementation of the sanction against the owner of the ox, were the biblical rule to be followed literally, posed difficulties both of a juridical and of a practical nature. By any standard of justice the imposition of the death penalty upon the owner of even a vicious ox that had gored a person to death seems excessive, unless the circumstances of some particular instance clearly pointed to a deliberate homicide where the animal was used as an instrument of murder much as an automobile might be used in the same manner today. But this is not the situation envisaged in the hypothetical case delineated in the biblical text; the phraseology indicates nothing worse than negligent homicide committed by an animal that might have escaped even the most conscientious supervision. On the other hand, the alternative resolution of imposing a "ransom" upon the owner of the ox presented, as I have just indicated, the difficulty of arriving at an objective assessment.

In attempting to fit the biblical rule with their own sense of justice and reality, the rabbis of the talmudical period readily perceived the impossibility of following the biblical prescription. What they decided amounted, *de facto*, to total disregard of the biblical rule even though they believed and professed that they were merely interpreting that rule.[13] Thus they completely ruled out the possibility of the death penalty for such cases, treating the biblical prescrip-

tion in this instance as merely hyperbolic: for them it expressed only a moral condemnation of the owner of the ox for his negligence. The alternative of a "ransom" was thereby transformed from an option into an obligation. The focus of discussion could then be turned upon how this form of emendation was to be implemented, and on this point two views were expressed.

One school of thought declared forthrightly that the "ransom" was to be calculated on the value of the person killed by the ox, thereby ignoring once again the plain meaning of the biblical words but providing the only practical basis for settling the case. The opposing school insisted upon the literal interpretation of the biblical directive: the life to be calculated was that of the owner of the ox. But the difference between the two schools was more apparent than real, for the talmudical authorities were not much more constrained by considerations of practical jurisprudence than were their biblical forebears. The "law" as expounded in the talmudical academies of Palestine and Babylonia remained largely in the realm of theory and ideals; the jurisdiction of the rabbinical courts did not extend appreciably into the area of capital crimes, which might otherwise have compelled them to discuss such issues in more realistic terms. Thus the school which insisted that the "ransom" was to be calculated on the life of the owner of the ox did not proceed from that position to any explanation as to just how this assessment was to be determined. Since the entire discussion was speculative, the rabbis apparently felt that to discard the death penalty was a sufficient concession to justice; they were not prepared to set aside their prejudice against the idea that a human life could be converted into a pecuniary sum. That concept would of course be called into play if the estimate were to be based on the "value" of the victim. The more "lenient" school obviously arrived at its position by placing greater weight on the question of how a real court of law would, in the final analysis, arrive at an appropriate assessment against the owner of the ox. This is not to suggest that the proponents of this approach were less earnest than the opposing school in upholding the principle that a human life cannot be evaluated in pecuniary terms. Their position implies rather that they distinguished between a deeply held conviction affecting transcendent values and the mundane necessity of providing a practical remedy for those seeking just recovery of damages occasioned by the death. But in doing so they perforce transformed the strict sense of the biblical *kôfer*, the "ransom" for the life of the owner of the ox, into the straightforward meaning of "damages" for the wrongful death. The rabbis of the closing age of the Talmud saw that the two views moved on two different planes and were not essentially in conflict. They therefore reconciled them in characteristic talmudical fashion: the sum to be paid

---

[12] It was already suggested by D. H. Müller, *Die Gesetze Hammurabis und ihre Verhältnis zur mosäischen Gesetzgebung sowie zu den XII. Tafeln* (Vienna, 1903; repr. Amsterdam, 1965), p. 166, that this biblical specification would appear to be a deliberate repudiation of the *wergild*, or assessment of loss principle, as it is exemplified in the Laws of Hammurapi. See further below, pp. 34f.

[13] The *kôfer* in the goring-ox laws was discussed in the Babylonian Talmud, Tractate *Baba Qamma* 40b. The moral dilemma posed by the term *kôfer* is nicely illustrated in the next section (40c). The question is there put whether, if the goring ox was owned by two partners, each of them would be obliged to pay a full *kôfer* for himself, or only half. For it is obvious that if the *kôfer* is in the nature of a solemn propitiation it would only be logical to exact a full sum from each owner. Only if it is conceded that the *kôfer* is civil liability for the value of the dead person—a distasteful position—would a half-liability for each make sense. Rabbi Acha, to whom the question was put, confessed his inability to resolve this conflict.

to the kin of the victim was indeed to be understood as a "propitiation" (in the strict meaning of *kôfer*) offered by the owner of the ox that his own life might be spared, but the sum offered was to be calculated on the loss sustained by those kin as a result of the victim's death. Thus the biblical intent was not violated, while the practical emendation of the wrong was facilitated. For all essential purposes, however, the final talmudical position on the question is indistinguishable from that laid down in the Mesopotamian sources two thousand years earlier; it is indeed the same principle that governs remedies for wrongful death in almost every jurisdiction today.

In order to illustrate further the ideal and scholastic, rather than the practical, orientation of the talmudic sages we may here return briefly to the question of the fate of the ox and observe how the rabbis deal with the biblical prescription for its stoning. In contrast to their eagerness to modify the biblical penalty against the owner of the ox, the rabbis consistently treated the case of the ox itself in the context of capital crimes. From the tractate Sanhedrin I §4[14] we learn that the ox that gored a person to death was to be tried before the "Little Sanhedrin," a collegiate court consisting of twenty-three judges, which was the normal complement of the bench when capital cases were to be heard. In addition to the goring ox, cases of this kind involving animals included prosecutions of (domestic) animals that had been used by persons in acts of bestiality as well as prosecutions of wild animals—the wolf, lion, bear, and leopard are listed explicitly—that had killed persons. The last example, which obviously represents fancy rather than experience, might lead us to consider the entire discussion of the trial of animals as scholastic musing and as having no place in a serious legal inquiry. Yet we should fall into a number of methodological and other errors were we to dismiss the talmudic discussion of this theme as not deserving serious analysis, for the discussion of the trial and execution of animals is part of the halakhic component of the Talmud. That part of the Talmud treats legal topics seriously (if often ideally), in contrast to the haggadic component, which consists of tales, metaphysical speculation, proverbial wisdom, and similar matter, and in which the rabbis permit themselves free play of the imagination and hyperbolic expression to drive home some particular moral or ethical point in a homiletical manner. There exists, furthermore, another passage in the Mishnah, this time in Eduyoth ("Testimony") 6:1, which alludes to the stoning of a cock to death for having killed a man. This occurrence is alleged to have taken place in Jerusalem in an earlier age, and there is no way of determining its authenticity.[15] It is nevertheless a good indication of the seriousness with which later talmudical authorities treated the theme.

Other passages in the Talmud, such as in the tractate Baba Qamma, in which the biblical goring-ox laws in all their aspects receive their most detailed exposition, document that the fate of the goring ox in a court of law engaged the rabbis' attention in a serious way. Among other considerations regarding the fate of the ox the rabbis held, contrary to the clear intention of the biblical rule, that the ox was to be exonerated if the evidence showed that it had killed a person, not by a deliberate or vicious charge, but by inadvertence.[16] In addition to bespeaking the humane concerns of the talmudical authorities, this view attests, perhaps even more eloquently than do those instances in which the ox was to be condemned to stoning, the anthropocentric perspective upon all manner of experience. It is also the earliest unambiguous indication that the actions of an animal may be judged by human criteria to determine guilt or innocence, a view which is not only not implicit in the biblical prescription for the stoning of the ox but is, in my view, even alien to it. Nevertheless, it was the way in which the rabbis of the talmudical age understood the biblical rule. Evidence for the literal application of the prescription that the ox be stoned thus is lacking for the talmudical as it is for earlier periods; but the case is far otherwise in later times in Western society. There the understanding of the biblical goring-ox laws paralleled that of the talmudical authorities to a remarkable degree, but it was applied in the most literal fashion by authentic juridical tribunals.

3. **The age or status of the victim.** It will be recalled that the biblical text states that if the victim of the ox was an Israelite no distinction based on the victim's age was to be allowed in resolving the case. Assuming that in the biblical author's conception the wrong involved was more of a criminal offense than a civil injury, this specification appears to be especially redundant. In order to account for this otherwise gratuitous stipulation, we must assume that the biblical writer was aware that in the formulations of the goring-ox laws in non-Israelite contexts—and in other legal contexts in which the issue might arise

---

[14] English translation in Danby, *The Mishnah*, p. 383.
[15] *Ibid.*, p. 432.

[16] As I suggested above, p.24, §250 of the Laws of Hammurapi also illustrates the "innocence" of the animal. But consistent with the Mesopotamian approach which in no respect "anthropomorphizes" the ox, the rule simply states that if an ox that is walking along the street (that is, it is not engaged in a wild charge) gores a person who, we must presume, strayed into the animal's path, there can be no cause for action. The rabbis, on the other hand, taking their cue from the biblical rule, simply extended its "anthropomorphization" (as they interpreted it) by according the ox real justice. But apart from this aspect, the net effect of the talmudic view in such a case is exactly the same as that of Hammurapi's §250: there can be no liability if there was no fault, and the owner of the beast must not suffer its loss as a result of an accident for which the animal could not be blamed.

as well—the age or status of the victim had a substantive bearing on the nature and dimension of the penalty to be applied. It is indeed probable that in early Israelite times practice—as opposed to the ideal—took account of the status or age of the victim in determining the outcome of cases in a way which seemed offensive to the author of the biblical goring-ox rules. He therefore feels constrained to reject explicitly the practice by which the indemnity was fixed on the basis of the victim's status or age, and prescribes a uniform penalty instead.

Although the Mesopotamian laws of the goring ox as they are represented in the laws of Eshnunna and Hammurapi do not provide evidence that the damages were assessed on the basis of the victim's "worth,"[17] it cannot be excluded that such a procedure did occur in the (unknown) sources which inspired the biblical statement of the goring-ox laws. The principle was in any case commonly used in non-Israelite legal sources to establish indemnities. In assessing damages or pecuniary penalties for various wrongs the Laws of Hammurapi regularly distinguish between free man and slave, and sometimes take cognizance as well of members of an intermediate social class, the *mushkēnum*'s, who were personally "free" but were economically dependent on the Crown either wholly or in large part. Perhaps the most extreme example of penalty/damages gradation in the Hammurapi laws is the series of rules governing liability for damages arising from faulty house construction (§§229–232), to which I alluded earlier. §229 ordains that if the proprietor himself died as the result of the collapse of a newly-built house the builder must himself be put to death. §230 provides that if the son (that is, the minor child) of the proprietor is killed in the collapse, then a son of the builder is to be put to death. §231 provides that if the victim was a slave, the builder must supply another slave as a replacement. Finally, §232 ordains that the builder must replace all (movable) property destroyed in the collapse.

This sequence of rules has traditionally been seized upon by modern commentators as evidence that in Babylonia it was legally possible to put someone to death for another person's crime, in contrast to the often-quoted biblical injunction of Deut. 24:16 that "Fathers are not to be put to death for (the sins of) sons, nor sons for (the sins of) their fathers; each must die for his own sin." §230 of Hammurapi's laws is, of course, the particular rule singled out for obloquy in that it appears to order the killing of an innocent child as a "vicarious punishment" that was

really directed against his father.[18] We must note at the outset—and thereafter disregard the point—that there is no evidence whatsoever that even suggests that it was ever part of the legal practice of ancient Mesopotamia to inflict a "vicarious" punishment on a person for a crime or wrong committed by someone else. Reconsidering in this light the biblical author's specification of "redemption" based on the life of the owner of the goring ox (Exod. 21:31), it is evident that he almost certainly could not have been prompted to that prescription by any knowledge that there was an actual legal practice in Mesopotamia that might be characterized as being "vicarious punishment." Nor do we have any evidence, one way or another, as to whether the non-Israelite peoples of the Syro-Palestinian area resorted to such a practice within the framework of their secular legal institutions.[19] In contrast we have seen that the practice of punishing one person for a crime committed by someone else was followed in ancient Israel in cases in which the offense touched seriously upon the sacred, as in the case of Achan and his family, cited above.[20] The very approach used by the biblical author might therefore itself constitute yet another indication that the relationship of the Covenant Code as a whole to its Mesopotamian analogues is to be found in the diffusion of a literary, rather than a legal, tradition.

In the present context the really crucial point for us is that in the sequence of Hammurapi's laws about

---

[17] Except, of course, for the distinction between free persons and slaves. The biblical law makes the same distinction, Exod. 21:32, thereby signaling emphatically that a slave is a chattel, and that the case is civil rather than criminal. The ox, however, is to be stoned to death even if the victim was a slave, since by killing a human being, even a slave, it had overstepped its place in the earthly hierarchy.

[18] See, for example, Greenberg, "Postulates," *Kaufmann Volume*, pp. 20f. Greenberg, of course, is fully aware of the Mesopotamian rationale: "The members of the family have no separate individuality vis-à-vis the head of the family. . . . The person of the dependent has no independent footing." It is therefore inappropriate to speak of the Mesopotamian penalty in these circumstances as "vicarious punishment."

[19] We must observe here that "vicarious punishment" in the literal sense, and involving a human victim, was far from unknown in the ancient Near East. But it has nothing to do with mundane secular law. The "Sacrifice of Isaac" by Abraham was averted by divine intervention at the last minute (Gen. chap. 22), and may justifiably be interpreted as a rejection of such deeds as a matter of principle. Jepthah's sacrifice of his daughter in fulfillment of his vow that he would offer up to Yahweh the first person to emerge from his house to greet him if he should return victorious from the war against the Ammonites is narrated starkly and movingly, if with an undertone of disapproval (Judg. 11:30–40). In a later age, when Mesha the king of the Moabites sacrificed his crown prince atop the city wall in full view of the Israelite army that was besieging him, the act achieved the effect he desired: the Israelites recoiled at the sight in horror and terror and abandoned the siege (II Kings 3:27). Given the background of such experiences (and presumably many others that have not been reported), we can appreciate the particular vehemence with which the Priestly School denounced and outlawed child sacrifice (Lev. 20:1–5). Even as a propitiatory measure, however, the sacrifice of children seems to have been restricted to the Semitic populations of the Syro-Palestinian coastal regions, and does not appear to have been practiced in ancient Mesopotamia. There, instead, on very rare occasions a mock king was enthroned and subsequently slain. The death pit at Ur of the Early Dynastic period is probably the starkest example of this practice.

[20] P. 28.

the liabilities of a negligent builder the provision by which the builder's son would seem to pay the supreme penalty for an accidental death makes *logical* sense within the Mesopotamian categorical universe and, indeed, in the progression of the sequence of cases within the group of rules itself. One must first remember that Mesopotamian society is structured by status, each status being translatable into a corresponding "value" with reference to the other statuses on the scale. This is made very clear in the rules under discussion: adult free man for adult free man; minor free person for minor free person; slave for slave; chattels for chattels. Everything can be, and is, objectified. It is precisely the same viewpoint which required Utnapishtim, the Babylonian Noah, to bring into the Ark a representative practitioner of every known craft as well as of the animal species if human civilization was to be effectively resumed after the Flood.[21] Status is a form of "species," albeit a relatively fluid one. Status implies a certain standard of quality for persons, just as there exist different grades of quality in chattels, as, for example, in animals and slaves. When, in a tort case, it is ordered that the damage is to be made good in terms of the loss, it is commonly specified that the replacement must be of comparable quality to that of the chattel destroyed by the tortious act. Hence to require that a negligent builder should be put to death for the *loss* of a minor person would, in Mesopotamian terms, amount to gross imbalance of justice: a relatively minor economic loss to the houseowner (and one that might be presumed to be replaceable without cost by procreation) would be "remedied" by the killing of a head of household, an economic loss of major proportions, and a catastrophic one for his family.

Within the sequence of cuneiform laws concerned with the negligent builder §230 stands out as absurd in that while the other three cases in the group are capable of being enforced in any conceivable situation this does not hold true for §230. For what, one may ask, would the "law" do in the event that the builder had no minor son, or even a son of any age? Would his daughter do instead? And supposing he had no daughter either? And so on. Such considerations have been taken as further evidence—and I believe justifiably so—that this paragraph states a kind of ideal principle rather than a literal rule. That principle is stated in terms which reach the absurd, as is often also the case with modern illustrations that are used to explain a theorem in logic, for absurdity in terms of real possibility is no bar to the validity of the principle being illustrated. Indeed, the absurdity of the example often promotes a clearer focus upon the principle by disencumbering it of the clutter of the specific and the real. In Mesopotamian exposition

the paradigm serves in place of the abstract principle or the theorem (which is an innovation in thought and exposition that is Greek in origin); it is not necessary that all the constituents of the paradigm (or, in some contexts, any of them) be "real." Similarly the consideration that the talionic formula as stated in Exod. 21:23–24 is "absurd" from the standpoint of application in real life in no way vitiates its validity as an "ideal" or as a principle.[22]

In confronting a written statement of "law" such as that represented by §§229–232 of the Laws of Hammurapi, however, the biblical author of the Covenant Code would have been able to see only the bare statement; he could not have comprehended the classificational system that determined the shape and the form of expression of the principle underlying such a statement. To these basic elements he, as a representative of a culture with an entirely different mode of apprehension, was as one congenitally deaf and blind.[23] The response of the biblical author in this situation is precisely analogous to the well-known biblical misrepresentations of "idolatry." The polemical factor aside, the biblical writers, including the classical prophets, were fundamentally incapable of seeing deeply into the rationale of polytheism; to them the religion of the "nations" seemed patently to consist of little more than the worship of "wood and stone" or of "the sun, the moon, and the stars."[24]

It is quite clear therefore that the biblical writer was familiar with the type of graded sequence of cases represented by the "builder's code" in Hammurapi's laws. It may also be possible that the (to us unknown) source by which knowledge of the principle of gradation reached the biblical writers illustrated it precisely in the statement of the goring-ox laws. It is one thing, however, to understand why and how the biblical writer reacted as he did in Exod. 21:31. It is quite something else again for modern observers to give expression to a certain moral partisanship, be it ever so restrained, which is clearly implicit in the very description of the Mesopotamian statement of the rule as an example of "vicarious punishment." In pointing out this phenomenon here I do not wish to be understood as standing for the suspension of moral judgment in all contexts. But, as I have suggested earlier, moral considerations often serve only to obstruct accurate vision in dealing with the social phenomena of ancient Mesopotamia (and with

---

[21] Gilgamesh Tablet XI line 85; see *ANET*[3], p. 94.

[22] The absurdity of the talionic principle (except for the idea of "a life for a life") has been illustrated by posing the question of how it could equitably be implemented in the case of a one-eyed man who had deliberately assaulted and destroyed one eye of a two-eyed man, or vice versa. This conundrum was posed not only in relation to the biblical talionic rule but also in discussions of early Greek laws, and presumably is to be found elsewhere as well.

[23] See the discussion at the outset of this essay.

[24] This observation has in recent times been made most forcefully by Y. Kaufmann; see *The Religion of Israel* (trans. and abridged by M. Greenberg; Chicago, 1960), pp. 7–20, especially p. 18.

records of comparably ancient and alien civilizations in general). §230 of Hammurapi's laws offends our sense of justice or even of plain reason. We are perhaps even more strongly repelled by the analogous rule in §210 which ordains the death of the daughter of a man who had struck a pregnant woman of the free class, precipitating a miscarriage and the lady's death. There too the rule is part of a graded paradigm (§§209–214), which must be read and translated in terms of the principle which it is attempting to illustrate and the postulates of Mesopotamian social structure.[25] It is not by any means self-evident, however, that the biblical view which apparently finds abhorrent the notion that one human life can be assessed at a lower "value" than any other human life—indeed, that human life is assessable by any humanly measurable standard whatever—is in all conceivable situations *the* moral position. Circumstances involving a human death could at times be such that the biblical view leads to a legal position which could hardly be considered as representing either morality or justice. But that is a subject which I will take up elsewhere in the exploration of our theme.[26]

One last consideration must be pointed out with respect to the offending Mesopotamian penalty prescriptions: they certainly were not *meant* to be complied with literally even when they were first drawn up, any more than were the equally offending biblical rules, be it the goring-ox laws, the *ius talionis,* or others. Apart from our obligation to analyze these rules from the perspectives we have just discussed, we must recognize that both the biblical and the Mesopotamian statements serve an admonitory function. If one would be bold enough to restate Hammurapi's §230 as a direct admonition it might run to this effect: "Woe to the contractor who undertakes construction and in his greed cuts corners, or is otherwise careless in his work to the point of endangering life and limb." A possibly more convincing illustration is Hammurapi's §218, which ordains that a surgeon whose patient dies under the knife or is blinded as a result of an eye operation is to have his hand amputated. Were this to have been meant literally as "law" it is inconceivable that any sane

person in ancient Mesopotamia would have been willing to enter the surgeon's profession. The message conveyed by the prescription is, clearly, that a physician or surgeon has a particularly grave responsibility in the performance of his duties, which typically put in the balance the lives and limbs of the patients under his care. Hammurapi merely cast the warning into the casuistic form to maintain a stylistic uniformity throughout his "code." Similarly the various price and wage "tariffs," which elsewhere in the Mesopotamian sources are "posted" in simple apodictic form, are presented by Hammurapi in the casuistic "case" formulation;[27] since they are patently unsuited to that kind of statement, their presentation in that form can be due only to the desire to maintain a uniform style throughout the text.

In summary, then, the provisions in the Mesopotamian law corpora, and those in the "code" of Hammurapi in particular, while cast in a uniform style are not all to be read on a uniform level, nor were they meant to be. Different *kinds* of messages were encoded in a single form; if we are to understand them properly, they must be decoded accordingly. It is similarly necessary that the same general procedure be applied to the material in the Old Testament commonly denominated as "biblical law," the rubric that subsumes much else besides the Covenant Code of Exodus. There remains, however, one essential difference that is central to the purpose of the present study: Whatever might have been the proportions of realism, idealism, hyperbole, and scholasticism in the amalgams that took the shape of the "law corpora" of ancient Mesopotamia, they left no palpable traces in the substantive law (as distinct from the forms in which the law could be made manifest) of subsequent civilizations. The place of the biblical law corpora in their original context is uncertain, though I have tried to demonstrate that they could hardly have had any impact on reality greater than that of their cuneiform counterparts. But they were part of Holy Writ, and as such they were ultimately invested with a moral, and at times even legal, authority that their authors could hardly have dared to hope for and, quite possibly, might not even have welcomed. Consideration of the absurd and the offensive in Mesopotamian legal expression and of the equally absurd—if not quite so offensive—in biblical legal expression thus results in a sharp difference in historical balance. Mesopotamian legal experience was never translated into action, but the biblical formulations have had

---

[25] The sequence of Hammurapi's laws §§209–214 also raises questions of a kind that do not apply to the rules in the builder's sequence, such as who is properly the victim of the loss, the father or the (presumably known) husband of the dead woman. These are, however, questions which would lead us too far afield and would not materially affect the present argument. The principle is exemplified once more in the Laws of Hammurapi in connection with forcible distraint for debt, §§113–116; §§116 prescribes that the son of the distrainor-creditor is to be put to death if the son of the debtor had been physically maltreated by the creditor while being held under distraint.

[26] I refer here to the biblical treatment of the subject of wrongful death in circumstances other than that of an intentional killing. See above, pp. 29f. and 31, and below, p. 37.

---

[27] Compare, for example, the straightforward "posting" of prices of commodities and of wages for certain kinds of labor in §§1–4 of the Eshnunna laws with Hammurapi's laws §L (interest rates), §228 (builder's fee), §239 (sailor's wage), §§242–243 (rates of hire of oxen), §§257–258, 261 (farm labor, herding), §§271–277 (transport work, handicrafts, maritime labor).

a subsequent history that has shown them to be anything but innocuous.

4. The textual gap between the cases in which the victim of the ox was human and those in which the victim was another ox. In the goring-ox rules which are concerned with the case in which the victim of the ox was another ox, the identity between the biblical and Mesopotamian formulation extends to substantive legal terms as well as to phraseology, as can readily be seen by comparing Exod. 21:35f. with §53 of the Laws of Eshnunna. The aim of the rule, both in Exodus and in the Eshnunna laws, is to achieve an equitable distribution of loss when the circumstances of the case suggest that there was no clear justification for shifting the burden of the loss from one party to the other. Towards this end both the biblical and the cuneiform rules ordain that the surviving ox be sold and the proceeds divided equally between the two parties; the carcass of the dead ox is to be divided as well. For this procedure to meet the writer's aim the precondition is implied that the two animals were of nearly equal quality. It is also to be assumed that the procedure is to be imposed by an impartial authority in the event that the two parties could not settle the matter amicably between themselves.

One other premise must be considered here, a premise which though it is basic to the rule is not made explicit: The court, or the public authority felt that it had the right and the duty to intervene in what in all respects was recognized as a private, that is, civil, matter, in order to allocate loss. In other words, the notion that "losses will lie where they fall" unless there is compelling ground for effecting a shift of loss[28]—a principle which prevails almost universally in contemporary tort law—is totally unknown to both the biblical and the Mesopotamian legal thinkers. A member of the community has sustained a loss through the agency of another member's property. In the absence of grounds for imputing fault to either party—at least none are offered in the first hypothetical case—the society feels that it would be contrary to its sense of justice to allow the full burden of the loss to be borne by the owner of the dead ox while leaving the owner of the goring ox without any liability at all. To have adopted such a position would surely have engendered resentment and ill will that might very well have led to some overt act on the part of the owner of the dead ox against the other party and might thus have touched off a chain of *socially* harmful consequences. In this instance therefore, the goal of the adjudication, which cannot be divorced from what the society perceived as the ends of justice, is the restoration of communal equilibrium.[29] This aim is not incompatible with the perception of fault as a factor to which the judicial process must give weight in allocating responsibility for restitution. That coordinate aim is not illustrated by the Mesopotamian rule, but appears clearly in the second case of the biblical sequence, set out in Exod. 21:36. In contrast with the case posed in verse 35, the second example adds the circumstance that the ox that had gored the other ox to death had already had a reputation for such a tendency, that this was known to its owner, and that the latter had failed to take adequate precautions. Under these circumstances the community feels that justice is best served by making the owner of the goring ox bear the entire burden of the loss, but expressly provides also that he keeps the carcass of the dead animal for himself. We can hardly mistake the intent in specifying this last, otherwise relatively trivial, detail. The primary focus of the adjudication is the compensation of the injured party for the full value of his ox. This is a substantial departure from the intent shown in the first case, which was to equalize the total loss between the two parties. In the case of the negligent owner, the jurist invokes the principle that the owner of the dead ox must be awarded full restitution for the exact damage he had suffered, but he is not to be granted a bonus by being allowed to keep the carcass of his own dead ox. That would not only have been tantamount to the imposition of a *penalty* against the owner of the surviving ox, but would have allowed the other party to reap something of a profit from the mishap. In the jurist's view, the net effect of such a procedure would have been the same as it would have been if in the first case posed he had let the owner of the dead ox bear the full burden of the loss (as a consequence of the absence of fault): a climate of resentment might well have been precipitated. In the second case, of course, it would have been the owner of the surviving ox who might have felt that he had been wronged. The equitable solution, therefore, was to *transfer* to him the carcass of the dead ox. In this way society indicates to him that his interests have not been overlooked: his obligation to make good the value of the dead animal to the other party is an appropriate mode of compensation for loss in circumstances that involved his own negligence, but the resolution of the case is not to be understood as punishment. In sum, then, the biblical jurist has at once served the end of justice by ordering full compensation for an injury entailing a negligent omission, and avoided social disequilibrium by allocating the residual good—namely the carcass of the dead animal—to the party charged with making good the loss.

---

[28] For the classic expression of the doctrine, see *Temple Law Quarterly* **46** (1973): pp. 256ff.

[29] This goal underlies much of the adjudicative procedures observed in traditional societies, especially in Africa.

The biblical writer's approach to cases of the goring ox in which the victim was another ox stands in sharpest contrast to his attitude to those cases set out in verses 28–32, in which the victim was a human. In the earlier cases the focus is almost exclusively upon punishment of the perpetrator of a social harm (the killing of a person). The agent of that harm must be punished appropriately: the ox must in all instances be killed by stoning; its owner, if guilty of a negligent omission, can escape the capital penalty only by paying a ransom of unspecified size. The predominant element here is one of moral disapprobation; this, with one exception, precludes restitution as a mode of adjudication. In instances in which there was no human victim the moral element is conspicuously absent; instead, the writer is at pains to signal his intent that no one is to be condemned even when the owner of the goring ox is presumed liable for a negligent omission.

In light of the preceding discussion the discontinuity in the biblical sequence of goring-ox rules takes on special significance. Verse 32 concludes the sequence of those goring-ox cases in which the victim was human; but the biblical author does not proceed directly to the second sequence. Instead he first sets out the case in which an ox or an ass is killed by a fall into an unprotected cistern. Under those circumstances there is *prima facie* evidence of a negligent omission; full restitution is prescribed, but the owner of the cistern keeps the carcass of the dead beast. Only then does the writer return to the goring-ox theme, taking up the cases of the ox that had gored another ox. This break in the sequence is very telling. The biblical author is, in effect, warning us that those cases in which the victim of the goring ox was another ox are of an entirely different legal order from those cases in which the victim was human. The sharpest way in which the biblical writer could make that distinction, other than by stating his juristic principles explicitly, was by breaking up the sequence as he did. We may perhaps even be driven to posit that the biblical writer was conscious of a sequence of goring-ox laws in a non-Hebraic prototype, such as that illustrated in the Laws of Eshnunna, in which no apparent distinction was made between cases in which the victim was human and those in which the victim was another ox. We might then be entitled to perceive in the biblical author's rearrangement of the material an implicit rejection of the Mesopotamian classificatory principle: by breaking up the series he reasserts the biblical outlook.

We have already noted earlier that Exod. 21:33, which closes the goring-ox cases in which the victim was human, also marks a larger caesura: it is the concluding law of the larger sequence which we have designated as the "Law of Persons," with which the entire chapter had been concerned up to that point.

Verse 34 introduces the category of the "Law of Things" and the sequence of cases that are concerned with property rather than with the person. We might have expected that the writer would have effected the transition by progressing from the last of the goring-ox cases, in which the victim was a slave and thus represented *both* person and property (the ox is to be stoned to death for killing a person and the slave's master is to be compensated by the owner of the ox for property loss) to the case in which the victim of the goring was an ox and represented property exclusively.[30] But the writer chose to avoid this otherwise logical progression; instead he begins his illustrations of the Law of Things with the case of the unguarded cistern into which an ox or an ass had fallen. Only after that does he return to the theme of the goring ox.

We may perceive in this disjunctive transition from the Law of Persons to the Law of Things not only the biblical author's sense of the juristic distinction between these two realms of wrongful conduct but also his sense of a disparity between them in terms of gravity. It is not merely that wrongs against the person are of greater gravity than wrongs against property. It is rather that the two realms belong to utterly different mental sets. Different scales are used to weigh the wrongs, and the corrective measures prescribed are of two distinct qualitative orders. Apart from the "ransom" which is available as an option in the case of the goring ox, and the compensation which is ordered for loss of earnings and for physician's fees for injuries inflicted in a scuffle (Exod. 21:18f.) and for a miscarriage caused in similar circumstances (Exod. 21:22), the biblical jurist does not countenance pecuniary remedies for crimes or wrongs against persons. They are expressly prohibited in all cases where death results, even when it was caused by accident and without negligence. Indeed, apart from the special instances just cited, in which non-intentional and non-permanent injuries were inflicted, the biblical jurist avoids altogether discussing the kind of case in which permanent maiming was caused by an unintentional or merely negligent act (or omission), for this would almost certainly have compelled him to deal further with pecuniary remedies, which he clearly found distasteful when the victim was a person. He therefore limited his consideration of permanent maiming to the context of intentional felonious attack, for which he could uncompromisingly prescribe a talionic physical penalty.

---

[30] The Laws of Hammurapi, for example, show such a transition in the sequences discussed above in connection with "vicarious punishment." Slaves are placed at the lowest level as persons but immediately precede other chattels, animate and inanimate, since they partake of the qualities of both categories.

It is to be noted that we never find in biblical law any physical sanction, whether it be death, mutilation, or scourging, for a felony involving wrongful taking or destruction of property if *no* physical harm had been inflicted upon the victim by the perpetrator. In such cases the sanction is uniformly pecuniary, and may take the form of simple or multiple restitution. The biblical attitude towards wrongful taking in instances which do not involve additional felonious elements such as sacrilege, or physical harm to the victim, may be described as almost complacent. This stands out especially in comparison with the severity with which biblical law treats wrongs against persons, and even more when we consider the stern treatment of wrongful taking in Hammurapi's laws, which often invoke the capital penalty.[31]

Perhaps the most eloquent evidence of the disparity between the biblical author's treatment of wrongs against the person and wrongs against property occurs in the Covenant Code of Exodus, in the middle of the exposition of the subject of wrongful taking. The subject of theft and conversion is launched in Exod. 21:37: "If anyone steals an ox or a sheep and has then slaughtered or sold it, he shall make restitution of five head of cattle for an ox and four sheep for each sheep." The next verses, Exod. 22:1–2, continue: "If the thief is caught while tunneling and is struck dead, there can be no blood-vengeance for him. But if the sun shone upon him, blood-vengeance may be exacted for him." Then in the midst of verse 2 the focus changes: "He must make full restitution; if he has not the means he is to be sold (into slavery) because of his theft. Should, however, the stolen property still be found in his possession, he makes (only) two-fold restitution."

This statement of the law shows a strange phenomenon. Having begun the exposition of the case of wrongful taking with a verb denoting the act of "theft," the author, suddenly and without transition, shifts his focus away from the subject of the perpetrator's liability and takes up the issue of his life. The context is no longer that of simple theft but that of burglary, that is, theft in the context of breaking and entering.[32] The problem of how such circum-

stances might affect the penalty for the felony, however, is set aside in order to consider the slaying of the burglar caught *in flagrante*. At issue is the question of when the slaying of the burglar is exculpable and when blood-vengeance, presumably by the slain burglar's kin, is justified. The criterion by which the question is resolved is that of the presence or absence of circumstantial indications that the life of the intended victim of the burglary (or of members of his family) might have been in jeopardy. The rationale followed by the biblical jurist is plain: nobody's life, even that of a would-be burglar, may be taken with impunity solely in defense of property; the issue of life or death, or homicide, overrides any question of guilt related to the wrongful taking of mere "things." Only when there is reason to believe that the intended victim of the burglary (or his kin) was in physical danger—that is, only if there is a presumption of self-defense in the most literal sense—is the killing of the intruder to be deemed justifiable.[33]

This section of the Covenant Code vividly demonstrates the biblical author's moral priorities and their legal consequences. Despite the fact that he had already concluded his exposition of the Law of

---

[31] For example in §6, death is prescribed not only for the person who steals objects belonging to the temple or the palace, but also for the "receiver" of the stolen goods (that is, the "fence"). This case contains elements of sacrilege or lèse majesté; even when these are absent, however, the death penalty is ordained for theft in certain circumstances (see §§7–13).

[32] It is commonly assumed in the scholarly literature on the subject that the breaking and entering is to be understood as being within the framework of the initial statement of theft, in other words, that the building being entered is the barn or sheepfold, and that the object still is to steal animals. This is most unlikely on a number of grounds. In the first place, when the biblical author shifts his focus away from the object of the theft to the issue of the life of the would-be burglar, a complete disjunction takes place; the specific example with which he had begun to illustrate the law of theft falls so far into the background of the writer's mind as to be irrelevant to the new point which engages him. It is this

new theme which requires an illustrative setting that better sets off the legal distinctions that the author intends to make. The dwelling of the intended victim of the burglary is far better suited to illustrate his purpose than a sheepfold or a barn. Second, we must consider the cuneiform formulations of this law. In the Laws of Hammurapi, §21, which is a close analogue to Exod. 22:1–2a, burglary is effected by "breaking through (a wall or the like)"— the verb is *palāšum*, "to pierce, to bore through"—and the building is, typically, a "house" (Akk. *bītum*). A similar formulation is found in §§36–37 of the Eshnunna laws; there, however, the focus is not on the burglary but upon the issue of liability for stolen goods that had been in bailment. In connection with the biblical rule it must be pointed out that it is not likely that corrals or sheepfolds in which domestic animals and flocks were kept at night would have been of such construction as to have required "tunneling into it" in order to effect a burglary. (See also the next note.)

[33] The two contrasting situations set out by the biblical author in Exod. 22:1–2a have generally been taken to denote surreptitious or nighttime entry on the one hand, and attempted daytime burglary on the other. In the first instance the killing of the intruder is justified by the presumption of self-defense: it is assumed that the burglar would know or could have known that the occupant of the premises would have been at home and that that knowledge implied that he would have been prepared to carry out his theft even at the cost of killing or incapacitating the occupant. Hence the slaying of the intruder is justifiable homicide. If, on the other hand, the entry was made in broad daylight, the presumption is that the intruder did not expect to encounter any occupant, and that he was not prepared to attack the occupant of the premises in the pursuit of his theft. The assumption is even made that the intruder would have retreated had he known the premises to be occupied. The slaying of the intruder is therefore not justified in this instance. This line of reasoning, as necessary as it seems to be, does not emerge unambiguously from the wording of the biblical text; one can, after all, "tunnel" into a building at any time of day or night, and the "sun shining upon him" does not necessarily mean that the burglary itself was attempted in daylight. But these are considerations which we cannot pursue here; see B. S. Jackson, *Theft in Early Jewish Law* (Oxford, 1972), pp. 204ff.

Persons with Exod. 21:32 and was already well into his discussion of the Law of Things, the subject of burglary prompted him to shift his concern from the issue of the theft itself to that of the burglar's life. As in the case of the goring ox, one might surmise that here, too, the biblical writer was aware of the comparable rules in extra-Israelite sources. §21 of Hammurapi's laws, for example, justifies the summary execution by hanging of anyone caught in the act of breaking and entering; no account is taken of whether or not persons on the premises were threatened. It is clear that in Hammurapi's view the act of breaking and entering with the intent to steal may itself be a capital crime. It is therefore not impossible to see in the biblical statement on this point a conscious rejection of the Mesopotamian approach. In other words, we may interpret the biblical statement, which is so patently out of place in its context, as underscoring the biblical writer's view that the issue of the death or life of the burglar is not to be decided by the rationale governing the Law of Things but by the principles that determine the Law of Persons. The author's digression to make that point may well have been deliberate. Only after making it does he return, in Exod. 22:2a–3, to the question of the burglar's liability for multiple restitution.[34] From that point onward the biblical author's theme remains the Law of Things. There are no further digressions, and in the case of every one of the wrongs discussed the remedies to be applied are solely pecuniary.[35]

In summary, then, the study of the cuneiform and the biblical versions of the laws of the goring ox in the context of their respective literary units discloses a disparity in outlook between them that far outweighs their admittedly close formal resemblances. More important, it is in this divergence in outlook, in the way the two different civilizations apprehend and classify experience, that we can detect the underlying rationales that are responsible for the divergence in the substantive rulings applicable to identical sets of circumstances. In Mesopotamia no qualitative discontinuity was perceived between the phenomenon of man and any other phenomena of the natural universe. An accidental untoward occurrence in which a person is the victim therefore did not, by virtue of that element alone, transpose the event or the procedure by which it was to be emended into some exclusive categorical sphere which would not have obtained had the victim been other than a human being. Thus Hammurapi deals seriatim with a whole sequence of cases involving the use of oxen, moving directly from illustrations of cases in which oxen are the victims in the course of their service to man to cases in which, in the course of service, men become the victims of the animals. The Laws of Eshnunna illustrate the same principle by placing in a single unbroken sequence cases in which the victim of the goring ox was either another ox or a human being. In the biblical scheme those goring-ox cases in which the victim was human belong to an entirely different sphere of experience—and hence, of law—than do cases in which the victim was another animal. They were accordingly separated, and dealt with in strikingly different fashion. In the biblical view whatever concerns man belongs to a realm of experience that is *qualitatively* removed from, and superior to, anything involving the rest of the experiential universe. The biblical laws of the goring ox offer an eloquent statement of this distinctive world view.

VI. REFLECTIONS

I reserve this section not so much for a summary of all that has preceded as for the purpose of discussing a phenomenon relating to comparisons of biblical and Mesopotamian law which cannot be directly integrated into the discussion of the laws of the goring ox and of the categorical considerations which we found to be at the root of the divergences between the biblical and the Mesopotamian statements.

We may begin by posing the issue as follows: The Mesopotamian laws of the goring ox arise out of, and reflect, a cosmological outlook which perceives the tangible environment, including man, as a phenomenological continuum. Within this continuum the individual phenomena can be located at different levels, but the same value scale is applied to all. This standard is not, however, exclusively pecuniary. We saw, for example, that if a death was brought about through negligence during house construction, the death penalty could at least in principle be invoked if the victim of the wrong was of a social rank which precluded the possibility of satisfaction in pecuniary terms. For our present purpose the crucial point is that a case which stipulates the imposition of a physical penalty upon the wrongdoer such as the negligent builder is almost invariably embedded in a longer sequence of similar cases which, if they prescribe a penalty at all, make it a restitutive and pecuniary one.

---

[34] The translators of the New English Bible (Oxford and Cambridge, 1970) obviously concurred with the widely held view that some verse displacement occurred in this section in an early stage of the redaction, and went so far as to rearrange the material by placing 22:2b–3 immediately after 21:37, concluding the passage with 22:1–2a. This, of course, accords with our own sense of order. But it does not follow that the biblical writer must needs have perceived the material in the same way. The more cautious approach is to accept the order of the verses as they now stand and to attempt to understand the *author's* or the *redactor's* sense of order or his scale of values. What I have offered here is one attempt to do just that.

[35] Among the cases included in this section is the seduction (without physical violence) of an unbetrothed virgin (Exod. 22:15–16). The wrong consists of the diminution of the girl's "value" for her father in prospective marriage. The father may compel the seducer to marry the girl or to pay him the equivalent of the bride price for a virgin.

I cannot undertake here to document fully the distinctive Mesopotamian rationale of punishment, but must be content with one or two illustrations. In the legal corpora the invocation of physical penalties is most striking. These penalties include bodily mutilations as well as the death sentence, and are prescribed in cases which we today should regard as civil actions (in fact these corpora themselves do also so regard them in certain circumstances). Thus §§218–220 of Hammurapi's laws stipulate that if a surgeon commits malpractice which results in the death or permanent blinding of his patient the penalty will be the amputation of one of the surgeon's hands if the patient was a free citizen, but only restitution of a slave if the patient was a slave. The point is made more sharply in cases involving assault and battery, §§196–205: An assaulter is liable to talionic physical penalty ("an eye for an eye") if the victim was of the free citizen class, while only pecuniary compensation is to be exacted if the victim was of a lower (yet still free) class, or was a slave. This is a far cry from the biblical approach to the same theme which, as we have already observed, does not countenance pecuniary satisfaction for attacks upon the person, apart from the specific cases of battery which cause only temporary incapacity or which cause a woman to miscarry.

Another, and in our context perhaps even more interesting, aspect of Mesopotamian law is the invocation of physical punishments in the context of civil suits, particularly those involving litigation over property. From the Old Babylonian period (*ca.* 1900–1600 B.C.) we have a number of trial records which prescribe that a plaintiff whose suit had been rejected—usually but not invariably on the ground that he had already lost a prior litigation over the same property and had been enjoined by the court from reopening the issue—be subjected to the penalty of having half his hair and beard shaved, a procedure that usually included the further pain and indignity of having his nose pierced and being marched around the main street of the city.[1] This penalty, to be sure, should be viewed as a sanction for the public offense of "contempt of court" rather than as a satisfaction for the successful defendant in the original suit. Yet there are other cases of the same type in which this penalty is not imposed, and the wrongful litigant is merely dismissed with the instruction to render to the successful defendant a final quit-claim document.[2] In contracts from elsewhere in Mesopotamia or nearby regions, and from different periods, the penalty clause for wrongful suit usually stipulates a pecuniary award. This award, to be paid to the other party, could be made in silver or other metal, or in movable property such as cattle, slaves, and the like. In Assyria the penalty could also take the form of a fine destined for the local temple. In other regions we find in texts roughly contemporary with the Old Babylonian records stipulations invoking severe mutilation,[3] and the pouring of molten lead into the mouth; the latter might well be interpreted as being tantamount to a sentence of death.[4] No record survives of the actual execution of such sentences for the offense of bringing suit wrongfully, and it is not likely that such penalties were ever really invoked. The extravagance of such stipulations is best understood as being formulaic—as oath-taking is today—in the sense that the terror of the words to which the parties subscribe vouches for the earnestness of their undertaking and their commitment to abide by it.

It is clear that in cases arising from situations of tort or contract (that is, cases in which the wrongs involved were not patently "public offenses") a Mesopotamian court was at liberty to invoke any *kind* of penalty it thought appropriate to the individual case before it. This latitude applied to different types of wrongs as well as to different instances of what was apparently the same wrong. It was the judge's assessment of the grossness of the behavior of the one to be punished that was the operative factor in

---

[1] The pain was of course incidental to the main purpose of the procedure, which was that of public degradation. Having the nose bored likened one to a beast of burden whose nose was usually pierced for the purpose of attaching a lead-rope. Important prisoners of war were often humiliated in the same way. It is possible that in the instances cited here a lead-rope was also attached, but the rope (or string, if the action was only symbolic) is never mentioned. For an example of a case in which the sentence of boring was actually executed see *ANET*[3], p. 544 Text B. The standing pillory and the stocks used in some parts of Europe and America well into the eighteenth century, largely for relatively minor public offenses, may be seen as somewhat subtler "variations" on this ancient Mesopotamian form of punishment.

[2] See *VAS* 13 7:8ff. "as the penalty to be imposed for (wrongfully) instituting claim against the field he shall render a 'no claim' document," and also *TCL* 1 157:50ff. "the judges imposed the penalty, compelling her to render this 'no claim' document." See *CAD* A/2 294ff. sub *arnu*. There are grounds for supposing that in some of these instances the penalty (*arnu*) was pecuniary and presumably was awarded to the successful defendant. See, in general, M. San Nicolò, *Die Schlussklauseln der altbabylonischen Kauf- und Tauschverträge* (Munich, 1922), pp. 187ff.

[3] Documents from Susa, in southwestern Iran, prescribe the cutting off of hands and tongues; see, for example, Scheil, *MDP* 24 p. 1 no. 328 (and *passim* in other texts in the series). In *MDP* 24 328 the penalty stipulation concludes a division of an estate among four brothers, and is in addition to a penalty of ten minas of silver, presumably to be divided among the three brothers who would have been the successful defendants in a suit by the fourth, the one to suffer the penalty. [The "touching" of the tongue is also known from the penalty clauses of two Old Babylonian documents from the kingdom of Eshnunna, *JCS* 14 (1960): pp. 30–31 no. 64, and *TIM* 5 4. The last text in addition prescribes that the fine of 2 minas of silver is to be paid to the king. See M. deJ. Ellis, "An Adoption Tablet from Tell Harmal," *Journal of Cuneiform Studies* 27 (1975): p. 147. *Ed.*]

[4] This stipulation occurs in documents from Alalakh, and involves very highly placed persons; in at least one instance it is in addition to the payment of the enormous fine of one thousand shekels of gold to the temple of the Storm God, and one thousand shekels of gold to the palace. For references see *CAD* A/1 36, sub *abāru* ("lead").

assigning the penalty, which could range from a nominal fine or the requirement to render a document solemnly renouncing all future claims, to severe physical punishment. The dire threat of severe mutilation or possibly even of death, even if mentioned only as a matter of form, should not be dismissed altogether. Taken as a whole, the evidence strongly indicates that Mesopotamian legal thinking was not conscious of any *categorical* gulf between various classes of wrongs. Had such a distinction been made, it would have restricted the form of the sanctions appropriate to particular classes of wrongs.

We have already observed that biblical law, in contrast, admits only of pecuniary remedies for civil wrongs, reserving physical penalties exclusively for wrongs against the person; indeed, biblical law appears in general to be far less concerned with civil wrongs, or wrongs to property, than with wrongs directly affecting the person. In this connection it is useful to compare the biblical treatment of larceny and misappropriation (Exod. 21:37ff., discussed at length above) with §8 of the Laws of Hammurapi.[5] The biblical rule specifies restitution by the thief; if he is unable to make it, he may be sold. Hammurapi's rule obliges the offender to indemnify the victim of a robbery ten fold; he may be put to death if he is unable to comply.[6]

___

[5] We will consider here only the second part of this law, in which the victim of the theft is denoted as a *muškēnum*. In the context of this rule that term must be understood as "commoner, ordinary person" or the like. In contrast, it is the "god" and "palace" that are the stated victims of the crime in the first part of the rule; these terms denote, respectively, the temple and crown property. I will not consider the latter two categories here since the wrongful taking of property belonging to the crown and temple involves the higher crime of lèse majesté or sacrilege. Theft from the temple or palace is described also in LH §6; in that rule it is presumed that the objects stolen were part of the direct equipment or property of the temple or palace. The death penalty is mandatory for that offense. In contrast to §6, §8 is presumed to speak of property legally owned by the crown or temple but not actually in use for royal or sacerdotal purposes.

[6] Once again, I must emphasize that we are dealing with ideal or prescriptive statements, not with facts. No extant texts record persons being put to death for theft. The execution of a convicted thief because he is unable to satisfy the victim of the theft would still offer the latter neither satisfaction, nor even simple restitution of the stolen goods. There is more reason for believing that convicted thieves were reduced to slavery, not necessarily because they were unable to meet some sum that might have been previously assessed. Enslavement of the thief assured some measure of compensation to the victim of the theft, who could either retain the thief as his own slave or could have him sold to another buyer and receive the proceeds of the sale. This latter procedure would have been more likely and, in fact, is what the biblical law prescribes in Exod. 22:2b in the event that the thief is unable to meet the requirement of multiple restitution. In either case, the penalty is only ultimately linked to the theft; it is more immediately and more properly to be understood as the typical fate of anyone defaulting on a debt or otherwise unable to meet some obligation that has fallen due. I. Mendelsohn (*Slavery in the Ancient Near East* [New York, 1949], pp. 23, 26ff.) discusses both the Mesopotamian practices and the "code" prescriptions; he also mentions allusions to the practice in the historical books of the Old Testament.

In the context of this discussion we must consider also the punishment of scourging. The penalty of scourging is nowhere in biblical law prescribed as a sanction for any specified delict, be it public or private. However, a Deuteronomic injunction (Deut. 25:1–3) limits the maximum number of blows to forty, indicating that scourging was a form of punishment frequently resorted to—often, presumably, without restraint.[7] The Deuteronomic passage might be taken to suggest that physical penalties could be imposed for wrongs that might be classified as "civil," since the language giving the circumstances which led to this sanction is ambiguous, and could indeed seem to suggest that the litigation was strictly over a private difference: "Should a quarrel arise between (two) parties, whereupon they have recourse to the court, which hears them and decides which of them is in the right and which in the wrong. . . .'' We are not told what the source of the disagreement might have been. The very word "quarrel" is ambiguous in this respect. It could indicate merely a verbal dispute over a real or alleged insult or over a matter of substance such as some presumed obligation between the disputants. The disagreement could also have led to blows. The biblical background, taken by itself, is thus unclear. However, the cuneiform law corpora, especially the collection of Middle Assyrian Laws, frequently invoke punishment by scourging; the contexts in which the penalty occurs enable us to identify the general range of wrongs which might in the biblical setting have been expiated by the same penalty.

The Laws of Hammurapi call for scourging in two instances. §127 prescribes it as punishment for the malicious slander of well-born ladies—either married women or (unmarried) women serving as "priestesses" of high rank.[8] In §202 the same penalty is imposed upon a person who slaps the face of another who is superior to him in social rank. In the Middle Assyrian Laws, §18 prescribes scourging for someone who defames his neighbor's wife, either by

___

In the treatment of default, then, as in the case of the goring-ox laws, we observe a convergence in practice between the law in biblical society and the prescription as well as the practice in Mesopotamia: the practice in biblical times with respect to property was not nearly so lenient as the biblical prescriptions might lead us to believe, nor was the punishment of Mesopotamian offenders for wrongs against property nearly as severe as the law corpora suggest.

[7] That this penalty was frequently invoked is suggested also by the fact that an entire tractate of the Talmud is devoted to the theme, under the title *Makkoth*, "Stripes." It follows directly upon the tractate *Sanhedrin*, which is devoted to the most serious crimes and their punishments.

[8] The latter is denoted by the title NIN.DINGIR in Sumerian and *ugbabtum* in Akkadian. Women with this or some of the related titles were not, strictly speaking, "priestesses," but there is no other English equivalent for these titles. Essentially they were to lead sequestered lives, and to serve the patron deity in some way. With certain exceptions they were not to marry or to raise children of their own. They invariably came from socially well-placed families.

spreading slander secretly or by insulting him to his face in the heat of a quarrel. §19 provides for the same treatment of someone who defames his neighbor indirectly with the slander of homosexuality, or insults him in the same terms to his face, in public, and in the heat of a quarrel.[9] One may well suspect, therefore, that the context of Deut. 25:1–3 was similar to that of the Mesopotamian cases, rather than being a dispute over some contractual obligation.[10]

The purpose of scourging is less to inflict pain on the convict than to degrade him. This is clearly emphasized in both §127 of the Laws of Hammurapi and §§18–19 of the Middle Assyrian Laws, which further prescribe the shaving of half of the wrong-doer's head and beard.[11] The object is to make him a butt of public derision, and the scourging is intended to suggest that he is—for the moment at least—no better than a beast of burden or a slave. In this light the Deuteronomic statement is especially significant since it sets limits upon the use of this punishment even when it is judicially sanctioned: "He shall administer upon him not more than forty stripes lest—should he go beyond this number to excess— your brother become degraded in your eyes." In sum, therefore, it remains the case that biblical law restricts the imposition of physical punishments to wrongs involving the life, limb (and, possibly, the good name) of persons, and to clearly public wrongs, such as transgressions against the sacral order.

The contrast between the biblical and the Meso-potamian legal corpora is underscored even further by the almost total absence in the former of normative rules, that is, formulations of the proper procedures governing commerce and economic life in general. The legal sections of the Pentateuch betray what amounts to complete indifference to the formalities without which the most elementary social institutions could hardly be said to function. This silence applies not only to contracts and obligations, but also to the normative forms by which family life is ordered, such as marriage, family property rights, and in-heritance. The Mesopotamian legal corpora dwell on these themes at great length; biblical law touches upon them only in the most cursory way, and then often within the framework of a narrative where it typically is a question of the unusual rather than the normative procedure. This is clearly illustrated by the petition of the daughters of Zelophehad for in-heritance rights in the absence of male heirs.[12]

The conventional view is that this state of affairs is to be ascribed to the comparatively primitive stage of development presumed for Israelite society and economy in early biblical times, in contrast to the complexity and sophistication which characterized Mesopotamian civilization. Whatever the degree of incommensurability of early Israelite and Meso-potamian society, however, it hardly accounts for the nearly complete silence of the Pentateuch—and, to only a slightly lesser degree, the rest of the Old Testament—about what must have been the main preoccupations of the overwhelming majority of the Israelite population over real time and space. In the fascination over isolated phenomena in the biblical record which all but beg for comparative investigation with Mesopotamian parallels one tends to forget how extraordinarily skewed the biblical evidence really is. It is not simply that the Old Testament is only the merest fragment of the history of a particular civilization over the course of perhaps one thousand years, for even what we do possess is not "history" in any modern sense. It is, indeed, a "testament," a cumulative but at the same time selective "legacy" out of a people's experience over that millennium. It is the final product of a process which involved continuous culling and pruning, refraction and redac-tion, by what was at any given time a highly special-ized minority of the learned sector of the population. Whatever the age, these writers represent, as they themselves candidly report, a particular point of view which was not representative of the population at large.

This viewpoint amounted to a distinct thesis: The Israelite nation was bound by an ancient and sacred pact with its deity to organize and conduct its life, both personally and institutionally, in accordance with the divinely ordained prescriptions. Directly or indirectly, whatever is included in the Old Testament by way of "historical" information is meant to rein-force that central thesis; the vicissitudes of the people through the millennium embraced by the bib-lical time span serve as hardly more than a barometer of the nation's fidelity to, or perfidy against, its pact with Yahweh. Everything is subordinated to this over-riding purpose, and whatever did not contribute to this "transcendent" end was not considered for inclusion, no matter how fundamental it was to the pursuit of daily life. As a consequence norms and regulations governing trade, property, the crafts, family law, and the like—the institutions that constitute the very fabric of daily life—were of little concern to the bib-lical authors and redactors. What little we can glean about such mundane matters from the biblical text is typically fortuitous; such items are included not for their own sake, but were utilized by the particular writer towards some other, or "higher," end. Thus our best and virtually only source of knowledge about ancient Israelite real estate conveyancing is in the form of an oracle by which Yahweh directed Jeremiah

---

[9] The slander here is pointed precisely: it accuses the other person of acting as the passive partner in the homosexual activity. The verb, which is the same as that used in §20, is the more vulgar Akkadian verb for sexual intercourse.

[10] This is also suggested by the noun used to characterize the one to be penalized: rāšāᶜ, "wicked, evil person," is the strongest Hebrew term of moral disapprobation, and would hardly have been appropriate if the issue had been purely a civil matter.

[11] The verb gadāmu in the Assyrian is to be understood thus; see CAD G 8, s.v.

[12] See Num. 27:1–11 and chapter 36.

to purchase a field from his cousin (Jer. 32:7ff.). The prophet carried out the command; in the course of the transaction we learn about the document of title and other attendant formalities. These formalities prove to have been not very different from those in use in Mesopotamia in similar contexts. But the only reason that this instance is reported in the Old Testament is that it provides the theme for the ensuing prophecy of ultimate return from the exile: the soon-to-be devastated land will be repossessed and will once again be the object of normal sale requiring the same normal formalities that the prophet had just completed (vss. 43f.). Abraham's purchase of the Machpelah cave from Ephron the Hittite (Gen. 23) was similarly executed with formalities that were obviously indispensable for the validation of such transactions, even if no mention was made of a written deed of sale. Yet it can hardly be doubted that we should not have learned in such detail about the circumstances of the site's acquisition were it not for its future significance as the sepulcher of the patriarchs.[13]

Other examples may be cited. Sheepherding was one of the most characteristic economic activities in ancient Israel, but all that biblical law has to say in that connection is to ordain repeatedly that the first-born of any ewe (or of cattle) is to be offered to God.[14] For our knowledge of the rules and customs relating to the business side of herding—which, as we know from the Mesopotamian documents as well as the cuneiform law corpora, entailed complex formalities and procedures—we must fall back on the patriarchal narrative of Jacob's dealings with his father-in-law Laban in Gen. 29–31. That narrative is most revealing about the law and lore pertaining to sheepherding in early biblical times.[15] Yet in the last analysis we come by this valuable information only because the biblical writer wanted to expand on the character and tribulations of Jacob, the circumstances of his marriages, and the origins of the twelve tribal ancestors.

The little that we do learn about everyday social and economic life from the legal sections of the Pentateuch most frequently does not derive from direct information. Instead, it comes by implication from what is mentioned about various activities in those biblical rules that aim at alleviating the inequities and imbalances arising out of the normal course of economic life. For example, the provisions in the Covenant Code regarding slavery (Exod. 21) were meant to set limits on an institution that was obviously widely practiced and that must have involved a host of usages and fixed procedures such as we find throughout the Mesopotamian law corpora. The Priestly Code amplifies the mitigating thrust of the biblical prescriptions (Lev. 25:39ff.), while the Deuteronomic rules on the same subject (Deut. 15:12ff.) add the terse apodictic and humanitarian injunction—characteristic of the source both as to substance and style—that a fugitive slave should *not* be returned to his master (Deut. 23:16f.).[16]

The same meliorative concerns are manifested by the Priestly rules in Lev. 25, affecting debt, the support of the poor and landless through limitations on cropping, redemption of sold land, and the prescription of moratoria and jubilee years, when all real property sold—it is assumed that such sales could be due only to financial hardship—is to revert to its original owner.[17] The Deuteronomic laws exhibit

---

[13] The Book of Ruth, a superb pseudo-historical romance, similarly provides unique glimpses into the customs and formalities relating to marriage and the inheritance of patrimonial land. But it is impossible to determine whether those practices were current in the (uncertain) time of its composition or in the time in which the story is set (that of the Judges, the very end of the second millennium B.C.) or in some other period. It is, however, unlikely that this entire story would have been preserved in the biblical canon were it not for the incorporation of its two leading characters into the genealogy of David.

[14] Exod. 13:1f., 11ff.; 22:29f., 34:19f., Num. 18:17; Deut. 15:19ff. The Deuteronomic statement differs from that of the one in Numbers (the P version) only in that it permits the presenter of the animal to partake of its meat after the sacrifice whereas the P source reserves it completely for the priesthood.

[15] See my article "Genesis 31:38ff. and an Old Babylonian Herding Contract," *Journal of the American Oriental Society* **88** (1968): pp. 30ff. The setting of the story presumes that these practices prevailed in the region around Harran (Aram-Naharayim) in northwest Mesopotamia, where Laban dwelt, but we may safely assume that these details echo the usage and beliefs close in time and space in which the story took form, that is, in Palestine.

[16] Compare here LH §§15–20, which demand the death penalty for abetting escape of a fugitive slave or harboring him. In these contexts the biblical rules, except for the Deuteronomic statement, explicitly limit their concern to slaves of Israelite (or "Hebrew" as in Exod. 21:2) origin; elsewhere such specification is omitted. For example, Exod. 21:26f. enjoins the emancipation of a slave whose master had deliberately and permanently maimed him, while verses 20f. imply that blood vengeance may be exacted upon someone who flogs his slave to death. Regardless of whether the slave in these instances is thought to be Israelite or foreign, it is clear that the emphasis of these rules is on some measure of protection of slaves. How little any of these rules were observed—even when the slaves were native Israelites—is evident from Jer. 34:8ff.: King Zedekiah proclaimed a general emancipation for all natives held as slaves by other Judeans, presumably as a prudent act of penitence while the Babylonians were closing in on Jerusalem. Jeremiah's words (v. 14) imply that until this occasion the biblical prescriptions limiting such bondage were never complied with. Further, the effects of this emancipation—which was formalized in the most solemn ritual by all who complied (vss. 18f.)—were soon nullified: the former masters forcibly repossessed those who had been liberated.

I do not, of course, mean to imply that the general thrust of Mesopotamian law in this connection was invariably towards upholding the rights of owners over their slaves. Not only do we find the opposite tendency as well—as in LH §280, which ordains the release of a native Babylonian slave brought back from a foreign land—but the private documents reflect the considerable means and (relative) independence enjoyed by some slaves, as well as their frequent manumission and/or adoption as full family members. But I cannot pursue this subject further here. A comprehensive and analytical study of slavery is still a desideratum. As an introduction, Mendelsohn's *Slavery in the Ancient Near East* is still useful.

[17] Explicitly excepted are dwellings within walled cities, but even in such cases the seller is given the right of redemption for one full year from date of sale: Lev. 25:29f.

the same tendencies, as in Deut. 14 and 24:10ff., 19ff. In short, the concern over the consequences of social and economic inequality and personal distress, repeatedly expressed in the biblical law corpora, is in itself sufficient testimony that daily life in ancient Israel in the normal course of events operated in a pattern that was not so strikingly different from what we know about other societies in the ancient Near East.

Probably the largest single factor that creates for us the impression of a society so utterly at odds with what is found elsewhere in the ancient world lies in the simple fact that the Israelites recorded their mundane activities in a simple alphabet on papyrus and parchment. We have the literary testimony of Jeremiah, mentioned above, that the execution of such documents was routine,[18] but due to the climate of Palestine these records have disappeared almost without a trace.[19] This situation contrasts sharply with that of Mesopotamia, from which the epigraphic artifacts of the routine affairs of daily life are preserved in their tens (or even hundreds) of thousands.

It would be wrong to conclude from what has just been said that our situation with respect to Mesopotamian documentation is in some way "satisfactory," that is, that we dispose of at least a useful sampling of documents of varying kinds for the different periods and localities within the cuneiform tradition which would allow us to render an account of Mesopotamian society that is reasonably reliable. For this is certainly not the case. The bulk of the written remains from ancient Mesopotamia is accidental in the sense that all of it has been recovered by legitimate or illicit excavation. The resulting distribution of texts and text types is thus largely a matter of chance. Consequently cuneiformists are not in a position to identify first the subject or "problem" they wish to investigate and then proceed to search for relevant sources in the major archives or local records in the regions where their researches are to be concentrated. Therefore what is at times offered as a synthesis or survey of a given theme or problem in assyriology on closer inspection often proves to be at best an incoherent assemblage of data of widely disparate dates and provenance and at worst an apparently complete picture that has little resemblance to the reality of any given time or place.[20] Apart from these qualifications, the documents from ancient Mesopotamia are mainly contemporary and "disinterested."[21] By this latter term I do not, of course,

---

[18] As in Mesopotamia in certain periods, each document was in duplicate, one copy being rolled inside the other, the inner one being sealed. In Mesopotamian usage it was usually the outer text, or "envelope," which bore the seal impression. In either case the presumed reason for this practice was to assure the availability of an authentic and "undoctored" text in the event of future dispute. As in Mesopotamia, these documents too were kept in earthenware vessels (see Jer. 32:14).

[19] Ironically, epigraphic communications which were originally thought to have but ephemeral utility were often inscribed on potsherds (ostraca), and have thus been preserved; see, for example, the Lachish letters, written at about the same time that Jeremiah bought that field from his cousin. In general, epigraphic remains of any kind dating to the biblical period recovered by archaeological effort in Palestine and areas close by have been painfully rare.

[20] Up to a point, of course, such a procedure is not illegitimate. This is especially true in the realm of technology and the crafts. A good illustration of some of the points made here is the volume of cuneiform texts published by V. E. Crawford, *Sumerian Economic Texts from the First Dynasty of Isin*, Babylonian Inscriptions in the Collection of J. B. Nies **8** (New Haven, 1954). The texts comprising this volume, over five hundred in number, come from some unidentified site in Sumer that was part of the kingdom of Isin, the successor to the Ur III empire (*ca.* 2100–2000 B.C.). The tablets span a period of only thirty-six years of the first two kings of the Isin dynasty (*ca.* 2017–1982 B.C.), and represent almost all the private documentation extant not only for that time span, but also for perhaps another century or so. Yet the bulk of this material—obviously representing a single archive—concerns the processing and distribution of leather goods. As the author reports, the volume "contains far more texts related to the leather business than do all other published sources combined." Obviously, anyone proposing to write on leather-craft in the ancient world would be compelled to rely largely on this single archive, representing this relatively restricted chronological and geographical horizon, at least as regards ancient Mesopotamia. It is, of course, assumed that the technical terminology used in these texts would be accessible to the modern investigator; Crawford's doctoral dissertation, "The Terminology of the Leather Industry in Late Sumerian Times" (Yale University, 1948, unfortunately unpublished), is largely based on this corpus of material and addresses precisely this purpose. While it would not be invalid to generalize on the basis of this single source as to the leather technology available elsewhere in Mesopotamia and in other periods, it would *not* be valid to deduce from the fact that this archive is virtually all that we have from the early part of the Isin period that the majority, or even a significant part, of the population in the locality from which the archive derives was primarily engaged in the leather industry for its livelihood. That we are informed in such unexpected detail about the leather business in this one trove while remaining in almost total ignorance about anything else that went on in the same region in the same period is due entirely to the chance strike of some digger's spade in a very circumscribed area—perhaps no larger than a single room—which must have been the center of the leather business of the locality. Nor should this example be thought exceptional; indeed, it exemplifies the typical circumstances of extant cuneiform documentation. There are more striking examples still: Our knowledge of the affairs of the Old Assyrian kingdom (up to the end of the nineteenth century B.C.) is based almost exclusively on the excavated archives of a small Assyrian merchant colony in central Asia Minor while the site of the capital city, Assur, has—apart from a few short royal inscriptions—thus far maintained an almost complete silence for this period. Finally, there are long periods for which there is no extant documentation whatever. For example, the absence of sources from Babylonia for the first two centuries of the Kassite dynasty after the fall of the First Dynasty of Babylon in 1595 B.C. has caused that period to become known in assyriological literature as the "Dark Age."

[21] I exclude here certain historiographic or pseudohistoriographic writings. Although some of these may have been based on contemporary events, most are retrospective and are aimed at promoting a particular objective, or are otherwise tendentious or palpably propagandistic to the point of distortion of history. It is, in fact, in this category of texts that we can find compositions that in motivation and expression suggest useful comparison with certain portions of biblical narrative and prophetic literature.

mean that they reflect a deliberate effort to report facts accurately and impartially. It is rather that they are not reflective at all. They represent precisely what one would everywhere define as primary documentary evidence, and exhibit all the shortcomings of this kind of evidence in any area of historical investigation. In particular the documents are from the investigator's point of view almost invariably exceedingly laconic; they record the barest essentials of some transaction or correspondence among a number of parties, all of whom are fully cognizant of the details and ramifications of whatever happens to be the subject of the document or letter that by chance has been preserved for us, as we are not.

Once we are able to reconstruct the operation of some institution from the study of large numbers of related kinds of documents, however, we are on far more secure ground in discussing what actually went on in Mesopotamian society in some specific area in a limited time-span than we could ever hope to be with regard to Israelite society and institutions during the biblical period, or, for that matter, during the entire first millennium B.C. Further, when I assert, as I did earlier in this study, that a document such as the "Code" of Hammurapi is not a reliable source of information about the true facts of Babylonian law as it functioned even in Hammurapi's own time, that is a statement of an entirely different *order* than a comparable statement about the biblical law corpora vis-à-vis the true facts of Israelite law in pre-exilic times. For with regard to Hammurapi's "Code" we possess controls, limited as they may be in certain respects, that enable us to utilize that document with discrimination. We can discuss, for example, where it is being hortatory, where it merely confirms or amplifies a literary school tradition, where it approaches the standards of actual legal practice or confirms it, where it attempts bona fide reforms, and where it merely enunciates pious ideals. Above all, Hammurapi's "Code" is a contemporary work; we have the stela that was engraved in Hammurapi's own time, as well as tablet manuscripts—or rather parts of manuscripts—that date to his reign or at most a few years later.

Thus the "Code" of Hammurapi—and of course any cuneiform document of similar subject matter—is, within the constraints just stipulated, an infinitely more reliable witness for the prevailing legal standards of its place and time of origin than are the comparable biblical sources about whose very authorship, time, and documentary integrity basic disagreements remain. Discussions, then, of the extent to which the biblical material relates to the ongoing principles and practices of law in pre-exilic Israel must of necessity beg the question. It may, however, quite fairly be said that if we had for ancient Israel the same kinds of documents that we know from Mesopotamia, whether they belong to the prescriptive genre represented by the cuneiform law corpora and related kinds of texts or represent the primary documentation in the strict sense, we should most likely find that the conceptual and categorical gulf between the real world in which the pentateuchal law was written and the real world which was the home of the cuneiform law corpora was not as broad as is commonly believed, and as is even assumed as a basic premise of this essay. It is indeed my opinion that what the author or authors of the pentateuchal law corpora thought and proposed quite possibly bore as little relationship to the moral and conceptual categories that determined the form and practice of ancient Israelite legal institutions as did the cuneiform corpora to Mesopotamian legal thought and practice.

The problem which has engaged us can also be reformulated to emphasize a different contrast: Whereas ancient Mesopotamian cosmology, its categorical imperatives and its institutional concretizations have left no perceptible imprint on subsequent cultures or civilizations, biblical cosmology and its dependent imperatives have had quite the opposite effect. The Pentateuch gradually assumed the status of the "Law of Moses," that is, it essentially came to be viewed as a divine mandate. That process, which first began to have a vital effect in the post-exilic period, meant that individual prescriptions of this holy writ were accorded a measure of reverence they had never before enjoyed. In a real sense this reverence, or broadly based subscription to the belief that the Pentateuch was the national "constitution," correlated almost directly with the impossibility or impracticality of implementing its demands other than in areas of certain narrow aspects of religious observance. It was most likely in the early part of the Persian period[22] that the "Law of Moses" was accepted as the foundation for a cosmology and a categorical moral system by an entire people, rather than representing the particular perceptions of a minority group. But the Law of Moses served only as a most general guide and as the moral underpinning for the arrangement of real social institutions. The actual structure of those, which included all law affecting civil life as well as the substance of criminal law and procedure, was determined largely by practical considerations of the time and was strongly influenced by the law and institutions prevailing elsewhere within the realms of Persian, Hellenistic, and Roman administrations. The talmudical sages, in all their humanity, employed their knowledge and wisdom towards the end of reconciling the otherwise uncompromising biblical injunctions with the common usages of their day. The effect of their labors, by design as much as by an inner or instinctive loyalty, was to preserve the pentateuchal law as a moral force. At times this meant reversing the plain sense of the

---

[22] That is, from 500 B.C. to the beginning of the Roman period.

biblical "law" to its diametric opposite; I demonstrated such a reversal in the talmudical treatment of negligent homicide in the biblical law of the goring ox.[23]

In yet another sense the biblical legal corpora remain independent or unrelatable to any real social setting, in a manner comparable to the cuneiform law corpora of ancient Mesopotamia. As I have attempted to demonstrate in the introductory pages of this essay, the biblical legal material is characterized by a distinctive cosmological outlook which views the universe as a *hierarchy* governed by man. As I have also attempted to explain, in this view man the individual is subordinate to man the societal being. This societal being is not an abstract concept, but is a real corporate entity in which are embodied the ultimate qualities of man, which can be realized adequately only through society. God, the ultimate sovereign, is the personified abstraction of the sum of these qualities of man; he is the posited source of the series of imperatives which command the ordering of human society and the rest of visible creation in ways designed to give greatest effect to those ideal qualities. The biblical outlook, then, represents nothing more or less than a theory of sovereignty, albeit one couched in direct moral and religious rather than philosophical terms.

But this theory remained an ideal in the ancient Near East; it was never put to the test or given real effect until modern times.[24] In the pre-exilic era of ancient Israel, when for a span of almost five hundred years the Israelite people did enjoy total political independence, the all-encompassing conception we now observe in the Pentateuch (and, of course, throughout the historical and prophetic books of the Old Testament) had hardly been fully formulated, and was in any case far from having penetrated the consciousness of the broad base of the population. By the time that this world outlook had developed fully and its literary expression had become canonical and had permeated the consciousness of essentially an entire people, that people, the Jewish nation, was no longer a sovereign political entity as it had been prior to the Exile. Yet it was just because the highest political authority—and hence substantial areas of administration and law—lay beyond the responsibility of Jewish leadership for most of the time that the rabbis could for large areas of law freely pursue their ideals, since there was no imminent prospect that they would be called upon to implement their pronouncements.[25] Problems concerning the more serious

religious violations, of course, are among the most obvious subjects to fall into this category.

One further observation must be made here. It is not surprising that there was after the Babylonian Exile no real attempt in Jewish national life to abide wholly and literally by the biblical injunctions, even where the Bible was explicit.[26] To the Jewish sages Scripture, although commanding the most profound reverence, was not invested with the awesomeness of the strange and distant: the biblical injunctions were not perceived as the commands of a sovereign whose remoteness and power allowed of no questioning but required literal compliance. Instead, Scripture was something close and familiar to the Jewish teachers from the period after the Exile, and increasingly thereafter to the lay population. The rabbis were like sons attuned to the stream of commands of a stern father—and the implications and overtones of the concept of God as "Our Father in Heaven," which was the creation of the early rabbinic age, are in full accord here—who almost *instinctively* sensed when such commands were to be construed literally and when they could be treated hyperbolically.[27] The law concerning the ox that gored a person to death, as also many other biblical rules, was treated in that way. Indeed, the rabbis elaborated on the theme as a way of signaling their perception of the goring-ox laws as hyperbolical: If the biblical text appears to hold the animal guilty, then of course one must imagine circumstances in which the animal could not be held guilty. But if domestic animals were entitled to a "fair trial" to establish their innocence or guilt, then why not any animals, including the wild beasts, as Rabbi Aqiba proposed; and so on.[28]

To read a talmudic discussion of this type as either an attempt to "do away" with an inconvenient biblical law, or as a bit of levity or a mark of naiveté, is really to miss its point. That the rabbis' discussion of the goring-ox laws was serious is confirmed by the

---

beyond my competence. But we should nonetheless note that the issue of literal implementation of biblical prescriptions in the new circumstances of real independence lay at the heart of the greatest schism in Jewish history, that of the Sadducees—the "literalists," represented mostly in the political and priestly leadership—and the Pharisees, represented in the rabbinic and talmudic tradition. The conflict, which was periodically a bloody one as well as one of legal principles and practice, was resolved only in A.D. 70 when the Romans obliterated all traces of Jewish political sovereignty with the destruction of Jerusalem. The net result of this national catastrophe was, in effect, the triumph of the Pharisaic over the Sadducean conception of the "Law."

[26] Here we must again take into account the fact that the biblical law corpora, as already mentioned above, touch only upon a minute fraction of the institutions through which humans transact their daily affairs. The Talmud, or the "Oral Law" in its widest sense, was in large measure designed to "fill in" these lacunae, although what it in fact accomplished was infinitely more far-reaching.

[27] This does *not* imply that to construe any biblical law as hyperbolic or rhetorical was tantamount to dismissing it or treating it lightly.

[28] See above, p 32.

---

[23] See above, pp. 31f.

[24] For this theme, see *Temple Law Quarterly* **46** (1973).

[25] I am not ignoring here the century of political independence that was inaugurated by the Maccabean revolt in 164 B.C. and ended for all practical purposes in 63 B.C. with the Roman occupation under Pompey. To go any further into this subject would neither add to nor subtract from the thesis, and is in any event

fact that their primary intention was to abolish any possibility that the owner of the ox would be executed, no matter what the degree of his negligence. In arriving at a just alternative, however, they could not resist expressing concern that the animal—and thus all animals—deserved a comparable measure of consideration. It was certainly *not* the rabbis' view that animals should *actually* be tried in court for killing people or for otherwise causing injury or damage; their discussion of the "guilt" of animals in such terms is nothing but an extension in hyperbolic discourse of what they took to be the hyperbole of the original laws in Exod. 21:28ff. That I believe them to have been mistaken in that view, as I have argued earlier, is immaterial in the present context.

The situation became far different when, in the Middle Ages and even in contemporary times, animals —particularly domestic animals—were tried in common criminal courts. That subject will engage our attention in the second part of this study, but for the moment it is important to suggest the reason that this became possible. I believe that the phenomenon is attributable at least in part to the relatively "alien" nature of the Old Testament—especially the Pentateuch—in its European Christian milieu. The hiatus between early medieval Europe and the formative period of Rabbinic Judaism is more than a matter of chronology: the disjunction between the culture of which the books of the Old Testament were a part and the spiritual world of Christian Europe was total. Although the Pentateuch was studied earnestly in that environment, it was not perceived as something immediate and intimate. Its interpretation proceeded on a number of levels, which included also those such as the mystical which are part of the Jewish tradition as well; the "Law," however, was essentially read as literal.

We could say that whereas the talmudical authorities perceived the "Law" polychromatically, in medieval Europe it was seen with monochromatic vision. Thus, if an ox gored a person to death it had to be executed. To be sure, the biblical rule says nothing about trying the ox in a judicial procedure. But the medieval ecclesiastical authorities quite naturally assumed that such a procedure was plainly implied in the biblical prescription, and acted accordingly. There was, however, no question of weighing the animal's guilt or "innocence." The fact that the animal had killed a person was established by common knowledge and was the ground for its execution; there was no room for pleas of "extenuating circumstances." In adopting this view of the matter the medieval authorities acted, whether consciously so or not, upon a rationale that was indeed the same as that which dictated the stoning of the goring ox as prescribed in the biblical law: by killing a human being the animal

had violated the hierarchical order of the universe. Since by the design of Creation all animals were made subservient to man, man is entitled to kill oxen when it serves his purposes.[29] But the reverse act, the killing of a man by an ox, poses an implicit challenge to the hierarchical order which, if not summarily met, could be interpreted as a successful refutation of that order. The stoning of the offending ox—which in medieval Europe was appropriately translated into the burning or hanging of the offending animal— was therefore the only effective way of dealing with the *objective* danger to the universal order which its action had created. The direct analogy for this procedure today is the destruction of animals among which virulent disease has been discovered; neither the animals directly infected nor those destroyed out of precaution are viewed as "guilty" of any wrong. Their destruction—usually accompanied by a ban on the consumption of their remains for obvious reasons of health—is necessary because it serves a higher interest. The medieval courts which condemned to death animals that had killed humans represented nothing but a procedural device for gaining custody of the animal from its owner and assuring the restoration of the proper order of things by causing the animal's destruction.[30]

Finally, we may well perceive in the phenomenon of real animal trials in early Christian Europe one of the logical concomitants—albeit one manifested in a relatively trivial context and expressed in crude terms —of a uniquely biblical conception of sovereignty. This conception, which permeates almost every page of Holy Scripture, has cosmic links, as well as implications for the organization of human society. For historical reasons outlined above, this grand conception could not be implemented by the organization of a polity in pre-exilic Israel and post-exilic Judaea (nor, for that matter, in the Diaspora Jewish communities). But Europe in the "Age of Faith" turned out to be precisely that conjunction of time, space, and spirit in which the biblical world view could first be concretely realized in social and political life. We still live with the consequences of that fateful conjunction.

---

[29] This was set forth explicitly by one ecclesiastical authority in the seventeenth century, in the context of the trial of an insane man for homicide. In that trial the prosecution sought to prove the defendant liable to punishment by analogy to the law of the goring ox. See below, p. 70.

[30] I do not mean to deny altogether that these formalities may at the same time have served the sensible and practical purpose of ridding the local community of the real source of danger to life which a vicious animal could pose. We are concerned here, however, with the contemporary interpretation of the situation, which—as I propose to show further on—was not insignificant for later times and in entirely unexpected contexts.

PART II

"And Lord Man created the dog in His Own Image; in the Image of Man created He him."

VII. THE TRIAL OF ANIMALS: THE INTELLECTUAL BACKGROUND OF THE INQUIRY

Almost everyone, at least in the United States, is familiar with occasional items in the daily newspapers which report that some animal—typically a dog— was "on trial for his life" before some local court. Reportage of such incidents, which are hardly "news-worthy" in the conventional sense, is designed to offer some relief from the unvarying grimness of the main news on any given day, and to allow the reader a fleeting moment of respite in which he can even chuckle. Like the "comic" scenes in Shakespeare's tragedies, these "harmless" stories contribute also to providing a perspective that, for most of us, makes the real world bearable despite all. They point up, after all, certain human weaknesses that may be thought of as almost touching. They certainly are not meant to set us to pondering issues of cosmic import.

I propose, nevertheless, to do precisely that. The reasons for doing so will become clear in the course of the ensuing discussion. The topic, in any event, was suggested earlier, in connection with the talmudi-cal discussion about the propriety of executing the "goring ox": it will be recalled that in that context the rabbis broached the question of trying before a court any animal, including beasts of prey, that had been "charged with capital crimes."[1]

The theme of the trial and punishment of animals in societies outside the biblical world is a minor one in the ethnological literature of the formative decades of that discipline and is of miniscule interest to juris-prudence proper, although it will be demonstrated in the last part of this study that it is of greater relevance to contemporary Western law than is commonly realized. The typical discussion of the theme has taken the form of a series of examples of alleged instances of the phenomenon that has become, to all intents and purposes, a standard repertoire. From the late nineteenth century to the present day most discus-sions of the question have been unpretentious semi-popular efforts having little more point than to exhibit for the reader's amusement some foibles of the human intellect in times past, in barbaric societies, and as aberrations in our very own midst. All that pretend to some comprehensiveness in coverage of the sub-ject reflect a more or less explicit assumption of the unilinear evolutionary development of human intellect, rationality, moral notions, institutions, and the like.

I will begin our consideration of the topic by quot-ing from the most influential work of one of the great-est theorists of law in the twentieth century. In the introduction to his *General Theory of Law and State,* H. Kelsen declares:

> In primitive law, animals, and even plants and other in-animate objects are often treated in the same way as human beings and are, in particular, punished. However, this must be seen in its connection with the animism of primitive man. He considers animals, plants, and inanimate objects as endowed with a "soul," inasmuch as he attributes human, and sometimes even superhuman, mental facilities to them. The fundamental difference between human and other be-ings, which is part of the outlook of civilized man, does not exist for primitive man.[2]

I venture to suggest that the typical reader would concur with the import of these lines because they seem so patently commonsensical and self-evident. Kelsen states these assertions of "fact" with the pur-pose of providing a base of common consent—no one is expected to challenge such a trivial set of premises, which are clearly meant as "universal truths"—upon which he can then erect a more subtle theoretical structure. Had Kelsen looked for real substantiation for his statement, his search would have proved vain. What evidence there is demonstrates that the true state of affairs with regard to every item of Kelsen's as-sertion is the exact opposite of what he declared it to be.[3] Briefly stated, the authentic data from both historical and ethnographic sources provide no evi-dence that animals or inanimate objects were tried and punished in *any* non-Western society at any time. *Only* in Western society, or in societies based on the hierarchic classification of the phenomena of the universe that is biblical in its origins, do we see the curious practice of trying and executing animals as if they were human criminals. As I intend to demon-strate below, the belief in the propriety of such a procedure is not yet totally extinct today, even in the United States.[4]

---

[1] See above. p. 32.

[2] H. Kelsen, *General Theory of Law and State* (trans. A. Wed-berg; New York, 1961), pp. 3f. (The earliest American edition was published as Twentieth Century Legal Philosophy Series, 1 [Cam-bridge, Mass., 1945].)

[3] While it is true that the first version of Kelsen's major work on the "Pure Theory" of Law (*Reine Rechtslehre*) dates to pre-World War I days, revised and much altered versions appeared even in German, decades later. Kelsen (who died in 1973), was himself much concerned with even the latest translations of his works into English (*The Pure Theory of Law*, 1971).

[4] See below, pp. 83f.

Professor Kelsen was only one of the most recent commentators in a long and prestigious line of social theorists reaching back to the late nineteenth century who have espoused and disseminated views about the "natural" evolution of human thought and society which, however much they are discredited by the mass of empirical data now available, continue to exert a decisive force on much thinking today, and that not only in jurisprudence. The source of these views is to be found in that nexus of evolutionary theory and social science commonly referred to as "social darwinism," which was associated with theorists such as Spencer and Tylor, and was carried to universal and encyclopedic extent by such figures as Frazer, Hobhouse, and Westermarck. Kelsen's brief statement amounts almost to an epitome of the import of the work of these last three, and we shall see further on that exactly the same set of beliefs underlies the structure of Oliver Wendell Holmes's *The Common Law.*

My purpose here is not to take issue with Kelsen or with others whose approach to legal institutions is much in the same vein. Rather, I wish to stress here, as I did in the Introduction to Part I, how the failure to become conscious of one's unconscious premises, and to subject them to the most searching scrutiny, effectively undermines the grandest schemes. Kelsen worked in a climate of legal and social thought we call "positivism." Kelsen's legal positivism, like its English counterparts and its antecedents, is rooted in the premise of the existence of a vested "sovereignty." Like Austen's classic statement that "law" is no more and no less than "the command of the sovereign," Kelsen's "Grundnorm" is rooted in the idea of law as a pyramid-like structure with the sovereign as its capstone. The idea of the sovereign, the existence of a visible or palpable sovereignty, is crucial to the whole structure. There can be no quarrel with this scheme so long as it is clearly understood that "sovereignty"—for our purposes best defined negatively by the non-existence of any authority beyond it that can exert coercive force to control conduct—is a feature that is distinctly Western, that is, biblical, in origin and connotation. Societies and civilizations, ancient and contemporary, that lie outside this tradition may or may not have persons or groups of persons whose native titles we may or may not render by such terms as "king, monarch, oligarchy," and so on. It cannot, however, be *automatically* accepted that any such individuals or groups are at the same time "sovereigns" with all the specific legal and legislative associations of that peculiarly Western term. It must first be ascertained whether functions that define "sovereignty" are *exercised* by such persons and groups. The simplistic position which required that any society was bound to have a "sovereign" was long ago shown to be untenable by abundant evidence of the existence of numerous societies in Africa and elsewhere in which the telltale indicia of "sovereignty" were absent. This fact led some to deduce that such societies lacked "law" as well, though it was not implied that they were "lawless." Yet that such societies did have effective legal institutions, that is, that they had operative law which facilitated a significant measure of social control, was really too obvious to be denied. It is now a commonplace, among most social scientists at least, that "sovereignty" is *not* a universal prerequisite for the exercise of law.

Considerations of the sort just broached are involved in the implied background to Kelsen's statement cited above, even if they are not apparent at first sight. To begin with, it is clear that Kelsen desires to set up a sharp dichotomy between the "primitive mind" of the savages, which he perceives as having an undifferentiated view of man and the world outside man, and that of "civilized man," that is, *rational* man, who is aware of the categorical difference between the two, and acts accordingly. It is characteristic of this kind of approach, which holds that the "primitive mind" confronts the world external to man in a way that is fundamentally different from that of "civilized" (read: "Western") man, that it should dismiss the concepts of the "primitive mind" as "animism." That term, in Kelsen's use of it, connotes little more than classificational anarchy. Whether Kelsen was conscious of it or not, his view is tantamount to saying that there could be no law—or no law worth talking about—in primitive society. For if you could try anything as well as anybody by a single procedure, then the term "law" with reference to such a procedure does not serve any demarcating function. It may all equally well be characterized as magic or as a non-rational process designed to correct, without discrimination, any sequence of events felt to have upset the social equilibrium. According to the classic conception of the social evolutionists, the social "evolution" of primitive man towards the state of a "civilized" society is accompanied by a corresponding sharpening of the distinction between man and the natural universe. In this process the quality of the distinction must serve as an index of the level of civilization attained. At the same time, law, "real" law, is increasingly differentiated from the realm of magic and the irrational, ultimately coming to serve as the exclusive mechanism of social control.

Intimately bound up with the idea that "animism" characterizes the "primitive" mind's understanding of the powers to be experienced in the natural universe is the concept of "totemism." The term "totemism" was applied by late nineteenth century Western thinkers to an almost limitless array of phenomena reported from non-literate societies that suggested to the observers—and more particularly to the synthesizers of the observed data—that the very fabric of the social structure, the institutions, and the beliefs of such societies can be explained only in terms of the all-but-universal belief that special relationships exist between various groupings of humans and different species of animal, vegetable, mineral, meteorological, and a host of other phenomena, as well as various topographical features. If "animism" was no more than an abstract term denoting a mode of thought, a way of apprehending man's environment, "totemism" was thought of as concretely and comprehensively denoting palpable realities in a society's experience, such as marriage, kinship, tribal structure, eating customs, and other carefully observed rules of conduct. Totemism was seen as the master key which enabled scholars to reduce the bewildering diversity of primitive beliefs and institutions to something approaching a systematic order. The social darwinists of the end of the nineteenth century seized upon this tool as upon no other single concept in their aim to demonstrate the progressive development of human thought and practices in general. Frazer's encyclopedic *Totemism and Exogamy*[5] is the grandest monument to this endeavor.

"Totemism" as a mental construct of Western thinkers of a certain orientation—predictably those affected most strongly by the Christian progressivist ethos or its secularized evolutionist counterpart—had no correspondence in reality as far as it could be verified in field study, and the rubric "totemism" soon disappeared from all reputable textbooks of anthropology. In more recent times C. Lévi-Strauss has resurrected the term, but towards ends that are far different from those envisaged by the writers who first coined and used it. "Totemism" as originally conceived incorporated within its domain just about everything in non-literate society that had a bearing on the sense of relationship between humans and the non-human world. Modern authorities like Lévi-Strauss start from the presumption that such manifestations are rationally rather than irrationally based, even if they are poetically expressed. It is therefore important to them to strip away the old conceptual encrustation in which the "totemistic" phenomena had been encased, and "totemism" is now understood as a mode or idiom for encoding and expressing, usually in an entirely logical way, a wealth of interpersonal and intergroup relationships as well as the interaction of persons with the environment. "Totemism" is therefore "firstly a projection outside our own universe . . . of mental attitudes incompatible with the exigency of a discontinuity between man and nature which Christian thought has held to be essential."[6]

There is today little dispute about the restricted sense in which the notion of "totemism" is to be understood. The differences of opinion in contemporary ethnology center about reducing to a more simplified and manageable structure the widely disparate and intricate single totemic systems that have been developed by individual societies that use totemic language to express their views of the world of man and their interrelationship with the world outside man. The aim of modern scholarship is, in effect, to construct a paradigm that will convey the commonality of all totemic systems without distorting the data of any single system.

I have offered this précis of the matter because statements such as that of Kelsen quoted earlier are implicitly grounded upon conceptions of the primitive mind and its expression of the bonds between man and nature which have long since been discredited; among these "totemism" figures largely.

Let us for the moment drop the issue of Kelsen's introductory statement and its assumptions and implications, and cast a glance at a work of very recent vintage, *Human Law and Human Justice*, by Julius Stone.[7] If we are to take the title of the work seriously, as the author presumably intended, the coverage, or the applicability, of what is set forth should be of global dimension. The bibliography is indeed extensive, even exhaustive. But both the work itself and the bibliography take account only of the legal phenomena and the literature of law of Western civilization. No mention is made of the legal phenomena of the great societies of East and South Asia, or of the vast field of law in Islamic society. Neither is there a single reference to any work dealing with legal phenomena in nonliterate contemporary societies. It is as if the ethnography of law, or legal anthropology, either does not exist or has no relevance for the theme of "human law and human justice." Insofar as Professor Stone considers anything at all outside the Western tradition of legal thought in the stricter sense, he limits himself to a cursory glance back to the classical sources and to biblical and post-biblical traditions—in other words, the universally recognized twin fountainheads of our own Western cultural tradition.

Yet in one sense I have as little to quarrel over with Stone as with Kelsen: the quality of what he has to say may, for all I know, be quite unexceptionable. But the label on the package grossly misrepresents the content, and this in itself is not a trivial matter. It is possible, to be sure, that Stone *is*, by implication, proposing that the legal experience in Western civilization and the traditions in legal and political philosophy surrounding it, provide a reservoir of practice and theory in the realm of law that is of sufficient variety and depth to serve to explain the legal phenomena of non-Western societies more meaningfully than could be done by appeal to their respective internal categorical systems. I doubt, however, that this was his intention; but even if it was, no

---

[5] (London, 1910), supplemented by *Totemica* (London, 1937).

[6] C. Lévi-Strauss, *Totemism* (trans. R. Needham; Boston, 1963), p. 3.

[7] (London, 1965). Even the earlier version, *The Province and Function of Law* (Sydney, 1946), is of comparatively recent date.

support is offered on its behalf. What is really implicit in Stone's choice of a title for his work, as it is also in Kelsen's opening statement, is a twofold view: (1) The thought and institutions of non-Western and non-literate societies are inherently incapable of casting any light on the legal experience and thought of Western societies. This, of course, is a kind of occidentocentric vision of the world; it could also be characterized as a kind of intellectual imperialism. (2) The first presumption leads to another, by which it is deemed legitimate to make sweeping assertions about the legal phenomena of non-Western, especially non-literate, societies, as if these were the most self-evident truths, and hence pose no obligation on those who make them to substantiate them in any way. These presumptions, I must emphasize, have been hallowed by an impressive intellectual tradition and are reinforced by the stature of those who still espouse them today. It is not an idle pursuit, however, to seek a more accurate understanding of the thought and institutions of non-Western societies for understanding's own sake.

Before turning to consider earlier evidence and authorities, it is useful to confront one further assertion in Kelsen's statement that concerns the "primitive's" sense of his relationship to the universe of extra-human phenomena. In Kelsen's way of reasoning, the idea that primitive man will try animals and things as if they were human is only a consequence of a more general notion imputed to primitive thought, namely, that each of these non-human entities is "endowed with a 'soul' *inasmuch* (emphasis added) as he attributes human . . . mental faculties to them." The key presumption, on which the rest depend, is that whatever sense of will is ascribed to animals and things by the "primitive mind"—presumably in any time or place—is adequately to be comprehended by the notion of "soul." The term "soul" is not further defined,[8] but inherent in the statement cited is the view that whatever special power or vitality the "primitive mind" imputes to non-human entities beyond their manifest physical attributes is to be measured by and within the highly charged field of notions and beliefs comprising that realm of Western metaphysics

surrounding the idea of the soul, a quality or "entity" which, in Western thought, is precisely what sets man apart from the rest of creation. Since Western thought (or, in Kelsen's equivalent, "civilized man") associates the idea of the soul with the notions of rationality and morality as the basis upon which man can be held accountable for his conduct, *eo ipso* the primitive mind which, in this view, imputes the same or comparable faculties to animals and things will accordingly also hold them accountable for their conduct, and therefore will bring them to trial and punish them for their "misdeeds."

What Kelsen has misunderstood here—and in this he is typical of most Western commentators—is the sense, widespread in primitive societies (as, indeed in civilized societies of non-Western derivation), that the extra-human universe is *autonomous* and that this autonomy or integrity is a quality inherent in every species of thing. To give expression to this sense, however, requires resort to metaphor: what animals and things are by nature and what they "do" can be expressed *only* in terms of human speech and human thought processes.[9] This is not the place to attempt to render account of the vast literature, both historical and ethnographic, on the expression of the sense of interrelationship between man and society

---

[8] It is obviously presumed that the term "soul" required no further definition, even though in an exclusively "civilized" context, as Kelsen would surely have agreed, it would be futile to proceed without defining more precisely what one is talking about. I am not certain what Kelsen intended to convey by putting the word "soul" in quotation marks. Did he want to stress that the primitive notion of the soul—at least insofar as it is imputed to non-human entities—is not quite identical with what the primitive mind conceived of as the human soul, or did he mean to imply that the idea of the soul in primitive thought is, in general, not quite the same as what "civilized man" means by the term? It may even be that Kelsen meant that the notion of the "soul," even among "civilized men," has no place in scientific discourse in general and must therefore be demarcated from concepts rooted in reality by the use of quotation marks when the context of an exposition requires reference to it.

[9] The fallacies involved in any other approach to the problem are best exposed by turning the question around: What would an ancient Mesopotamian or a traditional Chinese thinker make of George Orwell's *Animal Farm* in the absence of any acquaintance whatsoever with the whole cultural and historical nexus out of which that "fable" took shape? Most of us have recourse to similar kinds of metaphors in daily discourse, and we do not make a point of indicating that we do not mean it literally when we refer to someone as a "fox," "goat," "pig," "lamb," or "rock." And is it too much to say that a significant number of "civilized" people actually believe that the animals associated with certain human traits—particularly the less flattering ones—actually possess those traits and are for that reason to be reviled and, when such behavior becomes acutely offensive—or when it results in actual harm to people—even "punished"? Is it not likely that an observer from some alien culture would find some of this "irrational"? Or, again, what would such a visitor conclude about Western categorical thinking upon observing the almost incredible manifestations of our pet culture: highly competitive campaigns promoting pet foods, pet "hotels" (see below, 85 n. 26.), pet schools which offer courses and award diplomas (below, p. 85), pet hospitals (other than veterinary medicine provided for the care of animals that are crucial to the economy or that are used in commerce), and, finally, pet cemeteries fully set out with gravestones inscribed with the tenderest sentiments? A careful non-Western observer would first want to gain a better grasp of the total cultural and ideological framework before concluding from such data that the Western view of the universe does not clearly demarcate the boundary between the human and non-human, at least insofar as *some* classes of animals are concerned. It does not, however, occur to a considerable number of Western observers that "primitive thought"—all characteristically combined into this amorphous category—equally requires fuller and closer analysis before it can be properly characterized. As another observer recently stated it: "It needed the arrogance of late-nineteenth-century materialism to reduce the poetry of primitive thought to the status of a childish superstition." Edmund R. Leach, *Claude Lévi-Strauss* (New York, 1970), pp. 133–134.

on the one hand and the almost endless catalog of the universe of non-human phenomena on the other as it is attested for non-Western societies. Apart from other considerations, the present writer is not qualified to do so, assuming that it can be done at all. We must, however, consider some general observations and a more or less random sample of illustrative data from both non-literate and non-Western literate societies.

The ways in which the ancient Mesopotamians expressed their feelings about the place of man in relation to the phenomena outside man were reviewed in the Introduction to Part I of this study. We need not rehearse any of that discussion here except to observe that, in comparison with the summary kinds of dismissal which have been accorded "primitive" thought and institutions, Mesopotamian cosmological thinking has been shown a considerable degree of respect. To be sure, much of the early learned literature on the subject came to a large extent from bible scholars, theologians, and the like. These, being blind to their own religious bias, vented their disparagement of Mesopotamian polytheism, magic, divination, and so on, in disingenuously plain language. Some of that attitude can still be observed today; this kind of hostility is properly to be ignored. Similarly, when Lévy-Brühl's theory concerning primitive mentality was in vogue, there was something of a fad among certain students of ancient Near Eastern thought (including that of Egypt as well as of Mesopotamia) to interpret the data within that theoretical framework.[10]

The manner in which non-literate societies apprehended the world of nature has in recent decades attracted great interest far beyond the borders of ethnology proper, largely as the consequence of the theoretical work of C. Lévi-Strauss. From the standpoint of our own theme, the issue of the merits or shortcomings of certain parts of his system for "decoding" native statements relating to man and his natural environment—and these are the focus of much controversy among ethnologists and other social scientists—are of little concern. The main value of Lévi-Strauss's work for us is that it has recalled to our attention the fact that statements in non-literate societies about the phenomena of the natural universe in their relationship to man, and the connection between such views and certain institutional arrangements, are a code—more exactly, a multiplicity of codes. The idea itself is hardly a new discovery, but never before has so much and such widely dispersed evidence been brought to bear on the theme, nor have we ever before had a more convincing exposition of the thoughtfulness, the insight, and the almost infinite imagination and ingenuity with which the "primitive mind" has contemplated man and nature and given

verbal and institutional expression to the various facets of "the truth" that it has perceived.

It would be pointless to catalog here the infinite variety of ways in which non-literate societies give expression to their perception of nature and man as a single continuum, a continuum, moreover, of which the several constituents—species, individuals, various phenomena, and so on, as context requires—lie in a horizontal plane of equipollence rather than in a vertical line of hierarchy. I offer here a few examples to illustrate the point. These are not to be thought of as typical or strictly representative of the diverse ways in which the idea is expressed; they are a random selection based on unmethodical reading, and derive from the experience of the North American Indians. This in itself is somewhat accidental, but is also a result of the fact that the sense of identity with the world of nature is manifested in Indian thought with an intensity, intellectuality, imagery, and eloquence that is probably not equaled elsewhere in non-literate thought. It is no accident that the demolition of the nineteenth-century conceptual structures about the development of society, language, morals, law, and so on, was largely due to early ethnological work among various American Indian groups. It must, indeed, be pointed out that a considerable part of that research was already in print when the social evolutionists were elaborating their grand designs of the unilinear progress of human thought and institutions.[11]

It has often been remarked that the Indians referred to animals and birds as "people," that is, as "four-legged people" or as "winged people" in contrast to themselves as "two-legged people." It is easy enough to draw from this usage the conclusion, echoed in Kelsen's opening statement, that it reflects an inability of the primitive mind to distinguish between the different orders of being; all have "souls," whether they be two-legged, four-legged, or winged creatures. Let us consider first some excerpts from the rituals connected with building the Sun Dance Lodge, narrated and described by a Plains Indian. The construction required the felling of a specially selected cottonwood tree and the preparation of fresh buffalo hides:

[The buffalo] represents the people and the universe and should always be treated with respect, for was he not here before the two-legged peoples, and is he not generous in that he gives us our homes and our food? The buffalo is

---

[10] On the discrediting of this school of thought, see E. E. Evans-Pritchard, *Theories of Primitive Religion* (Oxford, 1965), pp. 78ff.

[11] For example, it was Franz Boas who, already in 1888, first exploded the idea that the grammar of non-Western languages (essentially limited to the inflecting Indo-European and Semitic families) can be comprehended within the categories of Latin and Greek; see Roman Jakobson, "Franz Boas' Approach to Language," *International Journal of American Linguistics* **10** (1944): pp. 188ff., especially pp. 190f. And it was A. A. Goldenwieser who, in 1910, first exposed the fictitious character of "totemism"; see Lévi-Strauss, *Totemism*, pp. 4ff., and Evans-Pritchard, *Theories of Primitive Religion*, p. 12.

wise in many things, and, thus, we should learn from him and should always be as a relative with him.[12]

"You are a kind and good-looking tree; upon you the winged peoples have raised their families; from the tip of your lofty branches down to your roots, the winged and four-legged peoples have made their homes. When you stand at the center of the sacred hoop you will be the people, and you will be as the pipe, stretching from heaven to earth. The weak will lean upon you, and for all people you will be a support."

Several reasons are given to explain why the cottonwood tree was considered to be very sacred; among these are:

Even in the slightest breeze you can hear the voice of the cottonwood tree; this we understand is its prayer to the Great Spirit, for not only men, but all things and all beings pray to Him continually in different ways.[13]

Proceeding from the tree to the buffalo, the peroration continues while the chief priest holds the skin of a buffalo calf: "It is from this buffalo person that our people live; he gives to us our homes, our clothing, our food, everything we need."[14] At another stage in the ritual, the priest offers the hide images of a buffalo and of a man, and prays:

Behold this buffalo, O Grandfather, which You have given to us; he is the chief of all the four-leggeds upon our sacred Mother; from him the people live, and with him they walk the sacred path. Behold, too, this two-legged, who represents all the people. These are the two chiefs upon this great island; bestow upon them all the favor that they ask for, O *Wakan-Tanka*.[15]

Much later in the ceremony the priest prays again to *Wakan-Tanka*:

"*O Wakan-Tanka*, behold us! Next to the two-leggeds, the chief of all four-leggeds is *tatanka*, the buffalo. Behold this dried skull here; by this we know that we, too, shall become skull and bones, and, thus, together we shall all walk the sacred path back to *Wakan-Tanka*. When we arrive at the end of our days, be merciful to us, O *Wakan-Tanka*. Here on earth we live together with the buffalo, and we are grateful to him, for it is he who gives us our food, and who makes the people happy. For this reason I now give grass to our relative the buffalo."[16]

About the hunting and fishing Naskapi of Labrador, F. G. Speck reports in a similar vein:

The killing of animals, then, entails much responsibility in the spiritual sense. Since the animals' spirits at death are foregathered in their proper realms to be reincarnated

later, the slaying of them places the hunter in the position, theoretically, of being their enemy. But he is not that in the ordinary sense of the term, because it is the ordained manner of procedure and one to which they are adjusted and inured. Requirements of conduct toward animals exist, however, which have to be known and carried out by the hunter. . . . His wilful disregard of them . . . is sin.[17] . . . So, blessed with a feeling that they owe a debt to the animal world for its sacrifice of life in their behalf, they have developed a system quite profound and rational in the spiritual sense.[18]

A further aspect of the Naskapi's relationship to the animal world is revealed in connection with their beliefs with regard to fishing. The moose-fly, a ubiquitous and fiercely-biting insect, is considered to be the "Master of the Fish," the one who oversees success in fishing. "Wastefulness is an offence to him, hence a cause of failure in taking fish."[19]

The moose-fly is observed to appear upon the scene when the fish are taken from the water in the summer, and he is then regarded as coming to witness the treatment of his subjects by the fishermen—his inclination to torment them by his stings . . . being an indication of custody over the fish and warning against wastefulness of the flesh. Then, to the observant and economical fish catcher the ration of flesh will be continued, while wasteful fishermen will sooner or later be punished by deprivation. Such warning is seldom merited by the Naskapi in respect to his source food.[20]

The "statement" of the moose-fly, as dictated, deserves quotation:

Məsᵊna'k I am called, the one who is master of the fish. I support them. You Indians will be given fish; you who do as is required are given fish, not him who wastes them. He who takes fish and wastes them will not henceforth secure anything. And likewise he who laughs at the fish on account of his big eyes here, will not catch fish. And he who ridicules the way the fish are formed will not be happy for they will not be given my fishes. Whoever wants to take fish must do right; after this fish will be given him.[21]

The beliefs of the early Indian groups in Pennsylvania were quite similar. These beliefs included the idea of the "Keeper of the Game," a being who was half-human and half-animal (either a bear or a deer), who "sent forth the animals which were the hunter's quota."[22] Complementing this being was a legendary Iroquois being, the "Good Hunter." He

[12] Joseph Epes Brown (ed.), *The Sacred Pipe: Black Elk's Account of the Seven Rites of the Oglala Sioux*, The Civilization of the American Indian **36** (Norman, Okla., 1953): p. 72.

[13] *Ibid.*, 74f. The informant here, of course, expounds the formal "apology" to the tree in terms which, he feels, will be more easily understood by the members of his white audience, or his readers.

[14] *Ibid.*, p. 78.

[15] *Ibid.*, 78ff.

[16] *Ibid.*, p. 90.

[17] Frank G. Speck, *Naskapi: The Savage Hunters of the Labrador Peninsula,* The Civilization of the American Indian, **10** (Norman, Okla., 1935): p. 77.

[18] *Ibid.*, pp. 77f.

[19] *Ibid.*, p. 117.

[20] *Ibid.*, p. 118.

[21] *Ibid.*, p. 119.

[22] J. Witthoft, "The American Indian as Hunter," *Pennsylvania Game News*, **24/3** (March, 1953): p. 16. This is part of a series of illuminating articles on the theme that are not easily accessible; they are reprinted as *Reprints in Anthropology from the Pennsylvania Historical and Museum Commission* **6**. I am indebted to Floyd Lounsbury for bringing them to my attention.

was an exemplary Indian male, who conformed to the ideal of the hunter. He only killed when he needed food, and always left the entrails of his game for the carnivores of the forest. He always left some of his food at his camps for the animals, he was kindly, soft-spoken and patient. As a result of his good behavior, the animals considered him a friend and came gladly to his bag.[23]

The Indian attitude toward game animals is rooted in religious beliefs:

The Indian considered the animal as an intelligent, conscious fellow member of the same spiritual world as himself. His own destiny was linked with that of the animals by the Creator, and he felt that both he and his victim understood the roles which they played in the hunt; the animal was resigned to its fate.[24]

The relationship the Indians sensed to the non-human world can be expressed in the following terms: "Man held no feudal lordship over animals, nor did the supernaturals hold vassalage over him; rather, he held a reciprocating, mutually beneficial relationship with each type of being."[25]

A more personal and eloquent summary of the nexus between man and nature is this earlier statement by an Indian:

I can recall days—entire days—when we roamed over the plains, hills, and up and down streams without fear of anything. I do not remember ever hearing of an Indian child being hurt or eaten by a wild animal. . . . We did not think of the great open plains, the beautiful rolling hills, and winding streams with tangled growth, as "wild." Only to the white man was nature a "wilderness," and only to him was the land "infested" with "wild" animals and "savage" people. To us it was tame. Earth was beautiful and we were surrounded with the blessings of the Great Mystery. Not until the hairy man from the east came and with brutal frenzy heaped injustice upon us and the families we loved was it "wild" for us. When the very animals began fleeing from his approach, then it was that for us the "Wild West" began.[26]

---

[23] *Ibid.*, p. 22.

[24] *Ibid.*, p. 16. This attitude on the part of the Indians is there cited in contrast to that of the white man, who "saw game animals as meat which he found, as mere objects to be taken."

[25] *Ibid.*, p. 17.

[26] Chief Standing Bear, *Land of the Spotted Eagle* (Boston and New York, 1933), p. 38. In this connection one immediately recalls the passage in the Old Babylonian version of the Gilgamesh Epic which describes Enkidu in the state of nature, romping and feeding together with the wild animals of the steppeland, unconscious of any distinction between himself and them, as the animals were not aware of danger in his presence among them. As soon, however, as he was seduced by a harlot who was sent with that specific mission by the hunters (whose animal traps Enkidu had been tearing up), Enkidu suddenly found the animals running from him in fear; nor was he any longer capable of keeping pace with them. It is the dawn of his consciousness: he has come to know that he is "different." He turns back to the harlot who promptly instructs him in human ways of eating, and the wearing of clothes. Transformed by custom, appearance, and consciousness, his regret for lost innocence submerged in exultation over his newly acquired

There is little reason to belabor here the point that if the few examples of Indian beliefs and attitudes just cited have any bearing at all on the kind of statement about the "primitive mind" of which that of Kelsen is representative, their testimony amounts to a refutation of it in every detail. In their statements about the phenomena of the natural world about them the Indians manage to convey, with an economy of expression, and certainly not in an irrational way, certain truths about their society's interaction with these phenomena. It is rather we in the West who are deficient in perception in this regard: We have come to equate truth, and especially the search for and the exposition of "truth," with the atomization of phenomena—which all people sense directly as a simultaneity of many facets—into a sequential and *prosaic* analysis. We then proceed to apply this literalness to non-Western statements that attempt to express a number of complete and concurrent truths— which is another way of denoting "reality"—by means of poetry. We further compound this fundamental error by rendering the native terms and notions into ostensibly comparable terms in our own

---

"wisdom," he marches off to Uruk, the archetype of a civilized community, ultimately to experience death, the dark reverse of the coin of consciousness. See *ANET*[3], pp. 73ff.

In contrast to Chief Standing Bear's reminiscences we should note the complaint of a California ranger, who expresses his exasperation over the wanton destruction of wildlife (and the rest of the ecosystem) in the desert area under his supervision by organized clubs of "varmint hunters" who track down coyotes, foxes, and similar species: "There is a very delicate balance of nature between varmints and other types—the varmints weed out the weaker animals. . . . But for some reason *these people feel they have a religious duty to kill varmints.* I just don't understand them." (*New York Times*, April 11, 1971, p. 54, emphasis added). In this connection I recall a news broadcast some years ago which reported a federal agency decision that canceled the construction of a new airport for Miami because it would have had disastrous consequences for the wildlife in the adjoining Everglades. The newscaster, expecting that the federal ruling would lead to a mass sell-off of real estate, interviewed land speculators who had invested heavily in the region leading to the proposed airport. One speculator expressed bland unconcern over the ruling, stating also that her sentiments were representative of her colleagues. According to her, the federal action was only a temporary decision, a sop to conservationists. With the pressure of population growth in the region the airport would inevitably be built. As she put it (the quotation is approximate): "If it's a question of the needs of animals and the needs of man, the animals will simply have to give way."

This confidence was borne out in a different context. Not much later the conflict arose over the construction of the Alaska oil pipeline from the Arctic zone southward, a project that would inevitably disrupt the foraging route of the caribou herds. In response to this objection the mayor of Fairbanks—which was anticipating an unprecedented boom through the oil exploitation— was quoted in the press in the following way (more or less): "God put that oil there and he intended it for use by man; the caribou must take second place." As a consequence of the recent international oil crisis the decision to build the pipeline became inevitable; the problem of the caribou's welfare has merited little further consideration.

languages. But such a procedure at best distorts the evidence. Even ignoring such a patently loaded term as "soul," mentioned earlier, the examples cited clearly show how as relatively simple a word as "people" can lead to misunderstanding. Surely nothing could be further from the truth than to conclude from the Indians' use of a term for "people," which at least in some contexts can include birds (as "winged people") and animals (as "four-legged people"), that the speakers using that terminology perceive the boundaries between humans, animals, and birds only in terms of the number and function of their loco-motive limbs. But we hardly need press this argument any further.

While it would be pointless for us to track down every instance in which a non-Western usage had been misconstrued by the social evolutionists and their heirs as evidence of boundary confusion, animism, totemism, and the like, it is another matter when the question is that of putting animals on trial and punishing them as if they were human felons. For the central thesis of this entire essay would fall to the ground if a single clear and unambiguous in-stance of such a procedure could be adduced from a non-Western source. I will enter but a single caveat here, namely, that the cases I propose to review are those that have come to my attention through the secondary literature on the subject, both historical and ethnographic. Should there be primary data that have not previously been cited in studies devoted to the present theme, they will be absent here as well.

The earliest of the modern studies of the subject of the trial of animals is that of Karl von Amira, "Thierstrafen und Thierprocesse."[27] Though he ex-hibits the evolutionary notions of his time, von Amira was a legal historian of repute, and his study is still the most reliable and judicious evaluation of the data. The most exhaustive treatment is that of E. P. Evans, *The Criminal Prosecution and Capital Punishment of Animals.*[28] The work is inferior to that of von Amira; it is full of evolutionary pronouncements of the crudest sort[29] and of a chaotic mélange of notions derived from human and animal psychology. But Evans's industry was commendable and his effort is independently valuable since it includes a long bibliog-raphy of the subject, going back to the sixteenth century, and a full register of European cases and of pertinent original documents, going back to the ninth

century. All subsequent studies—including the pres-ent one—are heavily dependent on these two works, at least for the data they provide.

Another authority who addressed himself to the theme of punishing animals was W. W. Hyde, who published a study "The Prosecution and Punishment of Animals and Lifeless Things in the Middle Ages and Modern Times."[30] For most aspects of the varied data Hyde acknowledged dependence on the two studies cited above; he also shared the evolutionary prejudices of the age. He was, however, primarily a classical scholar, and provides the fullest informa-tion bearing on the data presumed to show that the punishment of animals and inanimate objects was known in classical Greece. I shall therefore in this study concentrate on his explanation of the classical sources.

The last large-scale publication to deal with the theme of the trial and punishment of animals is Sir James Frazer's "The Ox That Gored," a chapter in the third volume of his compendious *Folk-lore in the Old Testament.*[31] Frazer collected from the secondary and ethnographic sources available to him the bits and pieces bearing on our theme.[32]

The thesis which suggested to Frazer the idea of assembling under the rubric of the Goring Ox all the heterogeneous information having to do with real or alleged trials and punishment of animals and inanimate things is the same as that which underlies the state-ment of Kelsen cited at the beginning of this chapter. It is the familiar evolutionary doctrine that at a certain stage of social and intellectual development all dis-crete human societies did not discriminate between reasoning beings, that is, humans, and other entities, especially living ones, such as animals, which the modern mind knows to be incapable of reason but which the primitive mind could not differentiate from reasoning beings. It was also inevitable on a number of counts that for Frazer the biblical laws of the goring ox in Exod. 21:28ff. should serve as the touchstone of all that was to follow: of all the extant ancient statements which condemn an animal to be executed, the biblical formulation was—and remains—the clearest in that it occurs in a textual context which permits of no doubt that the animal was viewed as a felon guilty of a capital crime. Further, as has so frequently been observed, almost all social evolu-

[27] *Mitteilungen des Instituts für österreichische Geschichtsfor-schung* 12 (Innsbrück, 1891): pp. 545–605.

[28] (London, 1906).

[29] For example, "The childish disposition to punish irrational creatures and inanimate objects, which is common to the infancy of individuals and of races has left a distinct trace of itself in that peculiar institution of English law known as deodand," Evans, *Criminal Prosecution of Animals*, p. 186. I shall take up the deo-dands later in the present study.

[30] *University of Pennsylvania Law Review* **64** (1915–1916): pp. 696–730.

[31] Sir James George Frazer, *Folk-lore in the Old Testament: Studies in Comparative Legend and Law* 3 Pt. IV: The Law. Chapter VI: The Ox That Gored (London, 1918): pp. 415–445.

[32] For authentically relevant data, Frazer is completely depend-ent on earlier studies; what he adds to the corpus can, after careful sifting, be found to be nil. In terms of classificatory discretion and in the use of theory—even within the framework of evolutionary theory—his effort actually constitutes a retrogression.

tionary studies in the late nineteenth century had their roots in theology and in the Old Testament background of the Christian faith, or in reaction against it. Frazer himself belonged to the latter category, but his entire life's work was set in motion by the earlier (and far more profound) work of W. Robertson Smith, who remained a devout Christian theologian.[33] Finally, and obviously, the title of Frazer's work required this approach.

The contents of *Folk-lore in the Old Testament* are not, of course, what the title might suggest. It is rather that the Old Testament, and more specifically those passages within it that Frazer interpreted as embodying folkloristic motifs, served as an organizing principle for assembling data from all over the world and from all ages. He thus used the Old Testament to demonstrate the universality of particular sets of beliefs, practices, and so on, each of which could be referred to an appropriate motif. The arrangement is itself a function of the second consideration mentioned above, which dictated that almost any social phenomenon deserving study in historical depth should take its point of departure from the Bible. Not only did the Old Testament, together with the classical Greek sources comprise the richest mine of data on the earlier "stages" in moral and institutional development of human society, but the data are the more valuable in that they lead directly to our own Western institutions and values.

Frazer's account of "The Ox That Gored" shows a curious omission: Hammurapi's treatment of the theme in his laws is nowhere mentioned. Yet, as I noted earlier,[34] the "Code of Hammurapi" was discovered and promptly published in 1902. Within a year S. A. Cook published his compendious volume comparing biblical law with Hammurapi's promulgation.[35] D. H. Müller's study, prompted by a similar interest—as shown by his translation of the Akkadian of Hammurapi's text into the biblical Hebrew idiom side-by-side with his German rendering of the text—appeared in the same year.[36] By 1904 further editions of Hammurapi's text and translations into many Western languages had already appeared, and the secondary bibliography on the subject had become extensive. By 1918, when Frazer's work appeared, it was enormous.[37]

Frazer was not unaware of the impact that Hammurapi's "Code" was having upon the study of biblical law and upon Old Testament scholarship in general. He in fact cited the text elsewhere in his work, and referred also to the study by Cook.[38] There is, however, no real mystery about Frazer's failure to utilize an original document of great extent which describes, and prescribes for, the social institutions of a society that is about a thousand years earlier than the biblical translation and has obvious affinities to it. Hammurapi's text was plainly an embarrassment to him. It was the oldest "code of laws" known to mankind at the time and it was almost entirely devoid of the kind of evidence that by Frazer's criteria could be characterized as backward or primitive. In contrast to the Bible, in which Frazer detected many references to beliefs and usages "that can hardly be explained except on the supposition that they are rudimentary survivals from a far lower level of culture . . . preserved like fossils,"[39] the far earlier text of Hammurapi appeared all too rational (again using Frazer's test for high marks on the evolutionary scale). In the case of the laws of the goring ox, where the literary associations between the biblical laws and the Laws of Hammurapi (§§250–252) are closer than in any other comparable groups of rules—and possibly anywhere in the biblical text as a whole—Frazer's silence is eloquent indeed. For the difficulty which confronted him was precisely that Hammurapi's laws pay no attention whatever to the fate of the ox. Hammurapi's silence on that subject, of course, has far-reaching implications for the evolutionary picture Frazer was creating.

The difficulty was seen by T. H. Gaster, who has recently attempted to resurrect Frazer's work by way of a drastic abridgment of the original supplemented by observations based largely on sources that have come to light in the fifty years since the appearance of Frazer's work.[40] Noting that the Laws of Eshnunna also devote a series of rules to the goring ox,[41] and that there too, as in Hammurapi's rules, nothing at all is said about the disposition of the animal, Gaster comments:

It will be observed that in neither of these earlier systems is there any question of *punishing* the offending beast. This, therefore, puts a question mark against Frazer's suggestion that the Hebrew law is a relic of ancient usage embodying

---

[33] In this connection see Mary Douglas, *Purity and Danger* (London, 1966), pp. 10, 17ff.; she also touches in general on the then current interaction between theology and anthropology.

[34] See above, 15 and n. 4.

[35] *The Law of Moses and the Code of Hammurabi* (London, 1903).

[36] *Die Gesetze Hammurabis.*

[37] To gain some impression of the effect of the discovery of Hammurapi's laws on biblical and ancient Near Eastern scholarship of the time—and, indeed, on the informed laity at-large—we need think back only to 1947, the year in which the first of the Dead Sea Scrolls came to light, and consider the effect this discovery has had on scholarship and publication in these and related disciplines right from the start up to the present moment. In the

case of the Dead Sea Scrolls, of course, new documents were added to the treasure trove every few years; many of them have not yet been published.

[38] But of all the hundreds of rules set down by Hammurapi, Frazer saw fit to comment on only one, §282 (the very last one in the text), which prescribes the cutting off of the ear of a slave who denies his master, a trivial and obvious provision, of very little intrinsic interest, and substantively associated with no biblical rule whatever. And this in a volume in which almost four hundred pages go under the title: "The Law"!

[39] Quoted from Frazer's Preface, *Folk-lore* 1: p. vii.

[40] *Myth, Legend, and Custom in the Old Testament* (New York, 1969).

[41] See above, pp. 20 and 21f.

that principle. If he is right, the Hebrew rule would have been a peculiar atavistic survival of what had been discarded centuries before in the sister systems.[42]

Frazer was, of course, not "right" in the first place, and the gratuitous recourse to "atavistic survivals" testifies only to the desperation to which surviving adherents of social evolutionary doctrine have been reduced. Curiously enough it does not appear to have troubled Gaster that Frazer had kept silent about Hammurapi's rules in his discussion of "The Ox That Gored." Having committed himself to a salvage operation, Gaster proceeds:

While, in the Hebrew legislation as elsewhere, stoning was indeed a method of executing criminals,[43] in this case it may well have served a purely utilitarian purpose: obviously, one could not risk getting sufficiently close to a habitual gorer as to be able to dispatch it in the the normal way by slitting its throat! The further provision against eating its flesh would then be nothing other than the normal Hebrew prohibition against eating of any animal that had not actually been slaughtered.

Gaster's retreat to the threadbare old utilitarian-materialist explanation of ancient custom—the attempt to show that beneath the "irrational" surface of a quaint primitive practice there is sure to be found a sensible and functional purpose—fortified in this instance by an appeal to an allegedly more general food taboo does not really warrant point-by-point refutation. It should be noted, however, that Gaster's explanation exhibits at least two glaring errors. First, the biblical law prescribes the stoning of the ox in *every* instance in which it caused a human death, even inadvertently, and not only if the animal had already had a record as "a habitual gorer." Thus the utilitarian explanation that stoning was the only safe way of getting rid of the animal falls to the ground. The ox was to be stoned even if it had no such record.[44] Second, the appeal to the Jewish rule about kosher slaughtering as an explanation of why the animal's carcass may not be eaten—which is basically only a slight variant of the utilitarian explanation itself—involves Gaster in a plain anachronism. The biblical laws about the slaughter of animals and fowl otherwise permitted as food are far from being identical with the laws of kosher slaughtering as known today; the latter were formulated only in Rabbinic Judaism of a much later time. As far as biblical law is concerned only two rules must be observed: (1) The blood (and

fat) may not be consumed (Gen. 9:4; Lev. 7:23–27,[45] 17:10ff.[46]; Deut. 12:15–16, 22–25,[47] and 15:23). (2) The flesh of animals that had died naturally or carcasses of animals killed (and partially eaten) by beasts or birds of prey is not to be consumed.[48] But the prohibition is a very mild one; eating such flesh brings only an impurity that automatically disappears the same evening,[49] whereas the eating of the blood incurs the dire divine punishment of being "cut off from the people." If the purpose of stoning the ox to death had been simply to rid the community of a menace by the safest means and nothing more, then a way could surely have been found to incapacitate the animal so that it could be given the coup-de-grâce in a manner that would have preserved the fitness of its flesh for human consumption well within the bounds of the biblical requirements. For the destruction of an ox was no trivial matter in a small agricultural community, and could easily have amounted to an economic disaster for its owner.[50] Then to be deprived as well of the consolation of eating the animal's flesh, if the prohibition against doing so had *not* been an ordained and intrinsically necessary part of the procedure—as Gaster suggests—would have been felt acutely as a cruel, pointless self-denial and an unconscionable waste.[51]

---

[42] Gaster, *op cit.*, p. 250.

[43] As noted above, pp. 26ff, execution by stoning was reserved for only certain specified capital crimes, and was *not* the mode for executing criminal homicides.

[44] Of course, Gaster might concede that his specification of the animal as "a habitual gorer" was unnecessary and still maintain that stoning was nevertheless the only safe means by which a population that was being extra-cautious in light of the event could dispatch the ox. There is no way of *categorically* refuting the utilitarian explanation at that point.

[45] Lev. 17:3–5 is a separate issue; its purpose is not to stress the blood taboo *per se*, but to prevent the spread of slaughtering which—as one might expect from the Priestly source which has formulated the rule—is interpreted as a deliberate attempt to deprive the priests of what they considered their rightful share of the meat.

[46] In verse 13 the emphasis is on animals and fowl that are caught by hunting (and trapping), which are not fit for sacrificial offering but are otherwise of the permitted species.

[47] In this passage the biblical author takes a much more reasonable approach to private slaughtering than did the Priestly source (note 41, above), reserving priestly slaughtering only for animals intended as bona fide offerings.

[48] Lev. 11:39–40, 17:15.

[49] It would seem that in this case the "hygienic" principle is really a factor, since the return to the normal state of cleanliness is signaled not only by the washing of one's clothes, but also by the passing of the waste of this food out of the body.

[50] An ox often commanded the same price as a slave; see also the Decalogue.

[51] In this connection it has often been observed that Arab bedouin will slit the throat of a camel when it appears that the beast is about to die; this renders the flesh consumable under Muslim law. The camel is permitted food in Muslim law, but not in biblical law; *cf.* Lev. 11:4, where it heads the list of explicitly prohibited animals. In respect to the blood prohibition and the eating of the flesh of beasts that had died naturally, however, Muslim law is essentially the same as the biblical rules. A similar example concerns the consumption of the hindquarters of kosher-slaughtered animals. It has become part of the *kashruth* practice among Western Jewish communities that the hindquarters of permitted animals are *intrinsically* unkosher, and hence are not to be eaten by the orthodox. This is *de jure* not accurate: late rabbinic ruling held the hindquarters of permitted animals fit for consumption after the excision of certain parts of their musculature. (This stipulation was somehow traced back to the enigmatic statement in Gen. 32:33 that concludes the episode of Jacob's wrestling with the mysterious stranger who touched him on the thigh and apparently so dis-

Quite simply, the requirements that the ox be stoned and that its flesh not be eaten are deliberate and cannot be separated. Both derive from the same rationale: the animal had transgressed against an inviolable hierarchical order and must suffer the same form of execution as human beings who commit crimes that are similarly to be interpreted as violations of the order. Stoning is the token of the penalty for such transgressions. The ox therefore must be stoned. That the ox is not "morally" guilty is irrelevant; the guilt in such cases is objective, for it is as dangerous and as polluting as a contagion. It must be eradicated in the most public way, and the public must participate in the act of eradication as a demonstration that it is consciously and effectively restoring the order that had been disturbed. That the flesh of the ox was not to be eaten is an inevitable consequence of the rationale that dictated the procedure.

VIII. THE CLASSICAL SOURCES AND THE ETHNOGRAPHIC EVIDENCE

A. The Prytaneion at Athens

Following the biblical rules of the goring ox, the oldest evidence regularly adduced as demonstrating the universality of the idea of punishing animals were certain customs alleged to have been practiced in the Prytaneion at Athens.[1] The Prytaneion seems to have

been primarily a ceremonial center. In it the common hearth of the city was maintained, and the functions that took place within it included the reception of foreign embassies, and the mounting of special entertainments.[2] No substantive governmental activity seems ever to have been carried out there. It is not mentioned as the scene of any judicial activity except for the following instances of murder and accidental death: 1. if the murderer was unknown or could not be found; 2. if death was caused by an inanimate object; 3. if an animal had been the cause of death.[3]

The classical sources for trials held at the Prytaneion and for the trial of animals are as follows:

1. *Demosthenes 23 (Aristokrates) 76 (352 B.C.)*
There is yet a fourth court in addition to these, the one at the Prytaneion. What is this court? If a stone or a piece of wood or iron or something of that kind strikes a man, and one does not know who threw it, but knows and holds that object which caused the death, a lawsuit is brought against such objects in the Prytaneion.[4]

2. *Patmos scholiast on Demosthenes 23.76*
At the Prytaneion: in this court they are tried for homicide whenever a person is known to have been killed but the person who committed the homicide is missing. One delivers the written accusation to the basileus, and the basileus makes an announcement through the herald and forbids this man who killed so-and-so to set foot in holy places and the land of Attica. Also, if an inanimate object falling on someone hits him and kills him, a trial is held for it in this same court and it is cast beyond the frontier.[5]

3. *Pollux 8.120 (2nd century A.D.)*
The court at the Prytaneion gives judgment concerning homicides even if their identity is not known; it also gives judgment concerning inanimate objects which have fallen on someone and killed him. This court was presided over by the phylobasileis, whose duty it was to remove beyond the border the inanimate object which had fallen upon the man.[6]

---

located or otherwise damaged a muscle that Jacob was left with a permanent limp. This is not the place to pursue this interesting combination of patriarchal tradition and aetiology, however.) Since there was no way of identifying for certain which muscle was affected, it became traditional to demuscle the hindquarters of butchered animals entirely before they could be sold as kosher meat. But this was apparently an act of butchery that required great skill and patience. It was practiced in relatively impoverished Jewish communities such as those of Eastern Europe, where labor was cheap and there was time to spare, and where the slaughter of a head of cattle—most typically a calf or an aging cow—was an uncommon occurrence. It would have been unthinkable in such circumstances to be deprived of half of the carcass (and the half with the choicer meat at that!) because of some obscure story that in itself implied no sanction. That hindquarters of cattle and sheep are "unkosher" today is due solely to the pointlessness of subjecting those parts to the costly process of demusculization (assuming that that art is not totally lost) in an age when beef and lamb production is an assembly-line industry and there is plenty of naturally kosher forequarter meat available at reasonable cost.

[1] [*Editor's note*: This is the only section of the volume in which I have added to the original draft; elsewhere I have limited myself to editorial reorganization and deletions, except for a few bracketed notes. The original manuscript of this section cited only Hyde's interpretation of the classical material (*University of Pennsylvania Law Review* 64 [1915–1916]: pp. 696–730). While Hyde's topical study remains the chief focus of the discussion in this chapter, I thought it useful, especially for readers not at home with the classical sources, to provide in the volume itself a catalog of those sources that bear on the topic. The present version therefore includes an abstract of the available statements by classical authors, and several standard references for the Prytaneion. Homer A. Thompson and R. E. Wycherley, *The Agora of Athens: The History, Shape and Uses of an Ancient City Center*, The Athenian Agora, 14 (Princeton, 1972): pp. 46–47: "The Prytaneion,"

describe the Prytaneion and its functions. The literary sources bearing on the Prytaneion (which has not actually been recovered in modern times) are conveniently available in R. E. Wycherley, *Literary and Epigraphical Testimonia*, The Athenian Agora 3 (Princeton, 1957): pp. 166–174: Prytaneion: testimonia nos. 541ff. D. M. MacDowell, *Athenian Homicide Law in the Age of the Orators* (Manchester, 1963), pp. 85–89, discusses the judicial function of the Prytaneion. He considers that Aristotle, *Ath. Pol.* 57.4, although it does not mention the Prytaneion by name, probably also refers to it, and adds it to the documentary evidence for the functions of the Prytaneion, as does Wycherley, *Agora* 3: p. 167, note to no. 548. This last reference, in fact, provides the only ancient classical evidence for the trial of animals, at the Prytaneion or anywhere else.

In the discussion which follows, references to the three works listed above added by me to the original manuscript are placed in square brackets.]

[2] [Thompson and Wycherley, *Agora* 14: p. 47]

[3] [*Ibid.*; MacDowell, *op. cit.*, pp. 86–87.]

[4] [Wycherley, *Agora* 3: p. 167 no. 548; see also MacDowell, *op. cit.*, p. 85.]

[5] [Cited from MacDowell, *op. cit.*, p. 85. The passage is not excerpted by Wycherley, *Agora* 3: pp. 167–174.]

[6] [Wycherley, *op. cit.*, 170 no. 560; see also MacDowell, *op. cit.*, p. 86 (cited there as Polyd. 8.120).]

4. *Pausanias I.28.10–11 (2nd century A.D.)*

What is called the Court in the Prytaneion, where judgment is given on iron and similarly on all other inanimate objects, began I believe on the following occasion. When Erechtheus was king of Athens, for the first time the ox-slayer killed an ox at the altar of Zeus Polieus. Leaving the axe there he went out of the country into exile. The axe was at once tried and acquitted; and a trial is held every year to the present day.[7]

5. *Aristotle, Ath. Pol. 57.4*

When one does not know who did it, one brings a case against "the doer." The basileus and the phylobasileus try also the cases of inanimate objects and of animals besides.[8]

MacDowell included this last citation with the Prytaneion references, although that place is not mentioned. It does not in fact matter for us whether or not the Prytaneion is to be inferred as the locus of the trial—on the basis of the involvement of the basileus —since we are indeed interested in the trial of animals, rather than in the functions of the Prytaneion as such. The excerpt from Aristotle is the only explicit reference to the trial of animals in the classical sources; but it must be noted that interpreters of the classical data—including Aristotle in this reference— have usually rounded out the list "unknown killer," and "inanimate object as the cause of death" by "death caused by an animal."

Thus the sources that mention the Prytaneion as a place of venue for trials. In ancient Athens there were no less than five regular courts which heard homicide cases. The kinds of cases listed above that were said to have been held in the Prytaneion were never held in those courts.[9] But were trials of the type mentioned ever actually held in the Prytaneion? What little is known concerning what took place there is, of course, derived from the works of late Greek authors; there is no primary source material, and therefore no direct evidence that any such trials actually ever occurred.

The classical sources for the alleged trials of animals were studied in some detail by Hyde, and I will use his work as the basis for the present discussion.[10] Hyde assumed that all the trials associated with the Prytaneion "were of a ceremonial character," but that they "were carried on with due process

of law,"[11] and conjectured that the procedures, including the preliminary investigations, paralleled those that were known to have been followed in real instances of homicide. The sharp demarcation between the kinds of cases alleged to have taken place in the Prytaneion and the procedures followed in real instances of homicide, however, should have indicated to Hyde that two different kinds of procedure were involved. I shall next examine the three different kinds of cases associated with the Prytaneion, and Hyde's interpretation of them.

1. *The "trial" of unapprehended murderers.* There is no documentation that unapprehended murderers were ever "tried": all that is mentioned about such instances is that public proclamation was to be made in order to notify the unidentified murderer that he should avoid the land of Attica and such sacred public places as temples, altars, and agoras, so as not to spread the blood-pollution to the community at large. Nothing is said about any trial.[12] Hyde explains the custom as "merely another manifestation of the *lex talionis*, the oldest and deepest rooted of all human laws, axiomatic in all primitive societies, and traceable . . . even in the most advanced." This is total nonsense, though Hyde is not to be blamed for it. *Lex talionis* is not by any means the same thing as blood feud, even assuming that blood feud is or was as universal as the evolutionists declared it to be (some went so far as to claim for it the status of the source of all law). Indeed, where the *lex talionis*, or some practices that might be so characterized, is found, it uniformly marks a change *from* an earlier practice whereby deliberate injuries and even most homicides could be compounded between the guilty and aggrieved parties in pecuniary terms.[13]

---

[7] [Wycherley, *op. cit.,* p. 169 no. 555. The passage is not excerpted by MacDowell, *op. cit.,* pp. 85–89, but he does cite, in addition to the references excerpted here, Pausanias 6.11.6 (and Ais. 3.244) for objects banned beyond the borders.]

[8] [Cited from MacDowell, *op. cit.,* p. 86; the passage is also adduced by Wycherley, *op. cit.,* p. 167, note to no. 548 (Demosthenes).]

[9] [For Athenian court procedure, see in general MacDowell, *op. cit.*]

[10] [While Hyde's study is quite old, it may be noted that the climate of opinion in which he worked is still somewhat reflected in more modern—if not so exhaustive—statements on the subject. See, for example, MacDowell, *op. cit.,* pp. 86ff., who, incidentally, cites death caused by a goring bull as an example for the trial of animals.]

[11] Hyde, *University of Pennsylvania Law Review* **64** (1915–1916): p. 696.

[12] See Hyde, *op. cit.,* p. 697 and n. 5.

[13] I cannot pursue this theme in detail here; it deserves an independent and comprehensive study. For a general exposure of the fallacies in this widely-believed and still very influential notion, see E. A. Hoebel, *The Law of Primitive Man* (Cambridge, Mass., 1954), pp. 329ff. Like the notion of the punishment of animals and the biblical rule of the goring ox, much of the "theory" of the *lex talionis* (more correctly to be referred to as the rule of the *talio*) took its point of departure from the "eye-for-an-eye" formula in Exod. 21:24–25. The evolutionists were delighted, and apparently vindicated, when the same principle was found in the "code" of Hammurapi, §§195ff. But there was much puzzlement when the earlier—and equally Semitic—Laws of Eshnunna showed that the penalties for bodily injuries were strictly pecuniary (§§42–48. Note Goetze's comment: "This archaism in the Laws of Hammurapi is remarkable," *Laws of Eshnunna,* p. 122 n. 9). When the still earlier Sumerian "code" of Ur-Nammu similarly showed pecuniary penalties for these offenses, various attempts were made to reconcile this irrefutable evidence with the cherished evolutionary doctrine. One of these involved making a distinction between the more "civilized" Sumerians and the "barbaric" Akkadians or Semites in general (ignoring the Laws of Eshnunna). It was suggested that the later but "crueller" law of the *talio* was attributable to the harsh circumstances of existence in the desert—the presumed original home of the Hebrews as well as

2. *The trial of inanimate things.* The sole item of evidence that inanimate things were "tried" in the Prytaneion is a ceremony held in the Prytaneion in Roman times, in which "an axe was ceremonially tried and acquitted[14] each year"; the ceremony was understood to be "in commemoration of the traditional first slaying of an ox on the Acropolis"[15] in prehistoric times. According to Hyde, "this peculiar . . . ceremony goes back to the earliest times, and is probably to be explained as a survival of totemism," while "also the animistic conception of nature which must have underlain such trials of things . . . belong[s] to the infancy of races as well as individuals."[16] This "explanation" contains, without documentation, what were some of the commonest clichés of social evolutionism, and reflects what was accepted orthodoxy, to which anyone might proclaim allegiance without the slightest feeling that it might be in need of justification. As I have shown earlier in the case of Kelsen, that attitude still persists.

3. *The trial of animals.* Hyde concedes that there is no evidence, even from the secondary traditions of later classical authors, that trials of animals were actually ever held in the Prytaneion; he merely *assumes* this to have been the case by analogy with the case of inanimate objects.[17]

The question will inevitably arise whether the events described above, said to have occurred in the Prytaneion, are in any meaningful sense to be treated under the rubric of law or judicial process. Even if we grant that the "trials" which Hyde tells us took place in the Prytaneion actually did occur there, it is obvious, even from his own statements, that these procedures belong to the realm of magic and ritual rather than to that of law.[18] That the procedures of one realm *imitate* — often in an exaggerated manner — the processes characteristic of another realm, the realm where they are at home, should serve as a signal to the observer that he had better look for the special circumstances that might have commended recourse to such an imitative process. It certainly does not give him a license to confound the two summarily. This warning should have been especially obvious in the case of the Prytaneion and the "trials" alleged to have been conducted there, since neither the place, nor the court, nor the kind of "defendant" is the same as that convoked in cases with real human defendants. This distinction will be crucial when we take up below the alleged cases in which animals are said to be "tried" in certain contemporary nonliterate societies, and especially when we analyze the two different kinds of procedures followed in medieval Europe for trying domestic animals on the one hand and "pest" animals and insects on the other. For the moment however, it will suffice to keep in mind a word of caution expressed by Sally F. Moore. Of the often perplexing problem which confronts a legal ethnologist who is trying to decide whether an action he is describing is "civil" or "criminal," she wrote:

It is not solely on the investigation of the process or the impartiality of proceedings that analyses civil or criminal should be focussed, if one is trying to decide whether a matter is one of private or public involvement. The question is what kinds of networks, groups or administrative structures are set in motion and what kinds of things they do.[19]

It is *a fortiori* the case that the distinctions must be observed when there is total discrepancy between two allegedly similar social phenomena, where not a single constituent entity is shared in common.

B. The Mad Dog of Zoroaster

The next item in the standard repertoire, both of the earlier evolutionist authorities mentioned above and of those whose concern was with animal trials specifically, is a datum derived from ancient Iranian sources. It is alleged that these show that dogs were punished for attacks upon sheep and persons by being mutilated in a prescribed fashion. Together with the biblical goring ox, the story of the Prytaneion, and a fixed list of ethnographical citations, the mad dog of Zoroaster became a canonical litany of "evidence" for primitive notions on the subject of punishment, to be recited whenever the theme was sounded. One

---

of the Amorites (the stock from which Hammurapi descended, and which had formed a strong element in the Babylonian population for hundreds of years before Hammurapi). Thus Hammurapi's law of the *talio*, as also the biblical expression of the principle, was adjudged a retrograde step in the inexorable evolution of human society towards greater "humaneness," "moral perception," and so on. It is only slowly beginning to sink in among commentators on ancient Near Eastern law that they may have been looking at the evidence through the wrong end of the microscope. It is, however, too much to expect that the implications of this "new discovery" will finally eradicate traces of the earlier vision; that was too neat a formula and offered too comforting a sense of smug satisfaction with the high moral level of our own contemporary legal notions to be easily abandoned.

[14] According to Frazer (*Folklore* 3: p. 421) the ax, or knife, was always declared guilty, condemned, and cast into the sea. The disposition of the ax is hardly material to the present discussion, however.

[15] Hyde, *op. cit.*, p. 699. [See the Pausanias citation, item 4 in the source list above.]

[16] *Ibid.*, p. 699.

[17] *Ibid.*, p. 698.

[18] [MacDowell, (*op. cit.*, p. 89) does cite the Prytaneion court as "an outstanding example of the operation of ritual in Athenian homicide law." But he saw its function as being (a) to take note of the manner of such deaths, and (b) to take steps to prevent such deaths in the future; he concludes by comparing the court of the Prytaneion in some of its functions with a modern coroner's court. MacDowell does not discuss the question of whether such trials as are attributed to the court of the Prytaneion ever actually took place.]

[19] In M. Gluckman, ed., *The Allocation of Responsibility* (Manchester, 1972), p. 74.

can only conclude that each of these authorities, in turn, relied on his predecessor for the veracity of the evidence, and did not trouble to look up the source for himself. There can be no other explanation for the astounding misrepresentation of the "evidence" in this case.

The source in question is to be found in a chapter of the Zend-Avesta entirely devoted to extolling the virtues of the dog—the most honored animal in Zoroastrianism—and to assuring its protection and well-being under all circumstances. The section is known as Fargard 13 of the part of the Avesta known as the Vendidad.[20] Anyone who kills or otherwise harms a dog, especially a shepherd dog or watchdog, is to suffer severe penalties. Starting with §29,[21] the subject is that of dogs who have lost their voices or have gone mad, and what is to be done about them. Such dogs are to be collared and muzzled, in order to protect people from them. If this is not done and if such a dog then attacks a sheep or person (presumably killing the sheep and wounding the person), a sequence of "punishments" is prescribed for the dog: its right ear is to be cut off after a first attack, the left ear after a second attack, a gash is to be inflicted on the right (fore?) leg after the third attack and on the left (fore?) leg after the fourth attack, and its tail is to be cut off after a fifth attack.

It is plain from this sequence of "punishments" that the aim of the prescription is twofold: (1) to inflict such pain upon the dog as to deter it—on a crude "Pavlovian" principle—from further attacks, without permanently crippling it. The gashing of its legs for third and fourth attacks may have had the additional purpose of hobbling the dog so as to give any future victim a better chance of escaping; (2) to so mark the dog—again without inflicting crippling injuries—that people would be able to identify it as dangerous before it came too close and so could give it a wide berth. A dog with severely clipped ears and lacking a tail could immediately be recognized as dangerous, thus giving people a chance to get themselves and their flocks out of its way. §§35ff.[22] make it clear that these precautions are based on solicitude for the dog, rather than for people or sheep. These paragraphs discuss what is to be done with a dog that has lost its sense of smell or has turned mad. First, one must make every effort to cure its condition, as one would do for a believer. Should this prove unavailing, then the dog is to be collared, muzzled, and tied, lest—as Ahura Mazda explains to Zoroaster—a dog without a sense of smell

should fall into a stream or well, or from a precipice, and be injured. Such an event would bring great sin upon its owner.

Despite the fact that the context makes it very clear what the "punishment" of the dogs is intended to accomplish, this passage has become the basis for such statements as: "Many cruel punishments were inflicted upon animals in the code of the Zenda-vesta,"[23] or "If a mad dog bites without barking, smite a sheep or wound a man, 'the dog shall pay for the wound of the wounded as for wilful murder.' "[24] The passage is in general adduced as part of the standard source list for the trial and punishment of animals. But there is not, of course, the remotest suggestion in the entire passage that a judicial procedure is involved. The dog was not to be "tried" by either a real or even a quasi-judicial court. The treatment to be accorded the dog is "punishment" in the same sense that the methods used by some people to "house-train" pet dogs today are punishment. It is also comparable to the "punishment" of children by parents and schoolmasters as a way of inducing more acceptable social behavior. It may be "punishment," but it is not "law." Yet even von Amira, who acknowledged the special character of the section as related to the sacred status of the dog in Zoroastrianism, refers to its prescriptions relating to mad or dumb dogs as "eine echte Thierstrafe."[25]

It can only be laid at the door of the reiteration of this piece of "evidence" by "authority" after "authority" that it ultimately came to be included, as an example of the punishment of animals, in such a

---

[20] J. Darmesteter, *Le Zend-Avesta* 2, Annales du Musée Guimet, **22** (Paris, 1892–1893): pp. 192ff. The earlier English version in the series *The Sacred Books of the East* (ed. F. Max Müller; 1893), a reworked translation from Darmesteter's French text, is inaccurate and should be avoided. I am indebted to my colleague Stanley Insler for elucidating this material for me.

[21] Darmesteter, *op. cit.*, pp. 201ff.

[22] *Ibid.*, p. 202.

[23] L. Hobhouse, *Morals in Evolution* 1 (London, 1906): p. 95, following directly upon a reference to the biblical goring ox. With reference to the Avestan dog, Hobhouse adds this gratuitous note: "Entirely, no doubt, under the influence of magical ideas." Far more than scholarly integrity is involved here. It really does not deserve the dignity of a characterization, and is best simply quoted without comment.

[24] E. Westermarck, *The Origin and Development of the Moral Ideas* 1 (London, 1906): p. 254. This misrepresentation of the original was apparently due to the English rendering of Darmesteter's French, which itself amounts to willful distortion. There is nothing in the original to support it. The French at that point reads: "il sera puni pour la blessure du blessé de la peine du *baodhô-varshta.*" Darmesteter notes (*op. cit.*, p. 202 n. 37) that the term *baodhô-varshta* is obscure, which is why it is left untranslated. I am mystified by the ability of Westermarck (as well as the other evolutionists) to render it confidently as "wilful murder." I might also note here that where Darmesteter writes—with regard to gashing a dog's leg—"on lui fera une entaille au pied droit/gauche," the English renders this as "they shall cut off his right/left paw." Apart from this gross misrepresentation—to characterize it merely as a mistranslation is inadequate—it would create the nonsensical sequence in which the loss of its tail would be the culminating "punishment" for a dog that had already had two paws cut off. Apparently this reversal of logical progression was precisely what appealed to the evolutionists; it appeared to confirm their lowest estimate of primitive thought processes.

[25] Von Amira, "Thierstrafen und Thierprocesse," p. 575.

serious work of jurisprudential scholarship as Glan-
ville L. Williams's *Liability for Animals*.[26]

C. The Ethnographic Evidence

In a number of fundamental respects what I have to
say under this subheading presents certain difficulties
that are frustrating, yet the conclusion to which the
evidence leads appears to me inevitable. I am not an
anthropologist, and therefore do not command all the
published data which might be relevant to our present
theme. There is also the further difficulty that the very
kernel of this theme—the trial and/or punishment of
domestic animals—does not itself constitute a rubric
or item that ethnographers are wont to index as such
(or in such ways as would indicate that data bearing
on the theme are to be found in the text). For this
there is a very good reason: such evidence, as near as
I can determine, simply does not exist!

Yet sweeping generalizations about how the primitive mind cannot distinguish between man and the
lower forms of life (and non-life), and how, as a consequence, primitive society frequently will put beasts
and things on trial and punish them, remain a common
coin of jurisprudential literature, or are assumed as
axiomatic truths even if not stated with the boldness
and assurance that characterized Kelsen's declaration, which I cited earlier. I do not for a moment
entertain the delusion that this state of affairs will
be materially altered by the recitation here of evidence
that exposes the baselessness of that widely held
belief. But I nevertheless consider it necessary to
offer at least a sampling of this evidence, all of it
negative. My aim is not so much to demonstrate the
falseness of those assumptions about primitive
thought and practice, as to provide the background
for the overwhelming *positive* evidence that it is the
Western system of categories that has been uniquely
hospitable to such notions about animals and things
as have indeed resulted in their trial and punishment, in the present as well as in the past.

The ethnographic evidence bearing on the theme of
the trial and punishment of animals forms one category in the Human Relations Area Files kept at Yale
University. Somewhat startlingly—but, on reflection, inevitably—the rubric under which material
relevant to the topic is filed is entitled "The Ox That
Gored." The collected evidence is most meager, and
all the specific examples—with a single exception to
which I shall return below—quite plainly illustrate
owner responsibility for damage, injury, and death
caused by domestic animals, rather than the punishment of the animals, the element that above all others
lends to the biblical "ox that gored" its unique
character.

The treatment of injury or death caused by a
domestic animal as a wrong for which the owner of

the beast is liable is often merely a function of the
total character of killing as a private or civil wrong.
This includes intentional homicide, which results
either in a manifestation of blood vengeance or—
as is more likely to be the case—in composition
with the kin of the deceased in a form which amounts
to a wergild. In this context it is also quite common
to find that the degree of "moral" culpability on the
part of the one held liable is, at most, only marginally
relevant to the amount of damages due for the death.
The loss is the preeminent concern, and the loss
remains the same whether the death was caused by
willful murder, negligence, mischance, or by action of
someone's property, such as an ox, camel, horse, and
the like. The target of any action following death
caused by an animal is therefore inevitably the person
or group responsible for the animal, never the animal
itself. This position appears to be illustrated among
some of the tribes of the Northeastern Bantu in
Africa.[27] Yet other tribes do make a careful distinction, in terms of the amount of damages to be
awarded, between intentional and accidental killing
such as that caused by one's animal. In some instances the award could include the animal that had
caused the death; it might also be limited to the surrender of the animal to the kin of the deceased.[28]

A. Musil observed a generally similar procedure
among the Rwala bedouin of Arabia. When a herds-
man was killed by a camel, the deceased's family
seized the owner's entire herd. This must, however,
be understood as a formal or symbolic act inasmuch
as it was accompanied by the tying of the clothing
of the deceased to the camel that had caused the
death. Once the owner of the herd had sworn an oath
that that animal alone was the sole bearer of responsibility for the victim's death the judges awarded the
camel to the father of the deceased.[29] Whatever the
formalities in which they are embedded, the substance
of the different ways in which the problem was
resolved is the same: it is the noxal surrender which is
familiar from Roman and early Germanic law.[30] Other

---

[26] (Cambridge, 1939), p. 265.

[27] J. Middleton, *The Central Tribes of the North-Eastern Bantu*
(London, 1953), p. 44. The information there is in large part
excerpted from earlier authors rather than derived from first-hand
observation, since the work is part of a large series of surveys and
was not intended as primary ethnography. See note 28, below.

[28] T. O. Elias, *The Nature of African Customary Law* (Manchester, 1956), p. 139; see also below. As for the prevailing
practice among the (A)kikuyu to which both Elias and Middleton
refer, there appears to be some discrepancy with respect to the
issue of whether or not a distinction is observed between intentional and accidental homicide. There is, however, no question at
all about the attitude towards the animal: it is mere property.

[29] A. Musil, *The Manners and Customs of the Rwala Bedouins*
(New York, 1928), p. 499.

[30] Musil (*Rwala Bedouins,* p. 499) reports the case just sum-
marized under the rubric of "vengeance." It is, of course, nothing
of the sort. In the instance reported, vengeance—or better, the
implied *threat* of vengeance—was at most a symbolic act, a formal
gesture, the signal given to the immediate community that its
impartial adjudicative power, represented by its informal but

examples exist. There is little point to discussing them in any detail, but we may cite a few. Among the various Mongol tribal confederations, fatalities caused by cattle (as well as by minors and mental incompetents) were the responsibility of the owner or, as the case may be, the legal guardian; as might be expected compensation was assessed in terms of horses.[31] In Imperial China the penalties for accidental killing of persons by horses (whether these were being ridden or not) or by cattle were inordinately severe, and included physical punishment and lifelong exile. Negligence seems to have been assumed *a priori* and the cases are treated as criminal rather than civil.[32] But the punishment was only for the person legally responsible; nothing at all is said about the animal that caused the death. The idea that an animal should be punished would presumably have struck a Chinese official as particularly absurd.

Among the cases entered in the Human Relations Area Files, however, there is one that demands our attention. The case concerns the trial of a crocodile among the Nupe of the Niger valley; the custom is adduced in the early ethnological literature, but was last reported at first hand by Nadel.[33] The wider context of the practice will put this "trial" in fuller perspective. The Nupe of the vicinity of Mokwa, it appears, believe that disease and drought are caused by a malevolent spirit, named Bukpe. These evils are associated with crocodiles in general, but the spirit Bukpe proper is believed to be incarnate in a particular crocodile inhabiting a local stream.[34] The people of Mokwa believe that they can neutralize the evil potential of Bukpe effectively by means of a treaty that is renewed annually; the ritual has the same name as the spirit, Bukpe. "It is part of the pact that the people of Mokwa must never kill or annoy this or any other crocodile, while they in turn will not be harmed by any member of the species."[35] Nadel observes,

however, that "this belief is not willingly put to the test." As it happened, a child was killed, apparently by this particular crocodile, during Nadel's stay in the area. A "trial" was accordingly held, in which the crocodile was charged with violation of the treaty; it was sentenced to death.[36] In point of fact, however, the crocodile was not put to death. The local people told Nadel that the crocodile had died. Nadel relates that he saw the same crocodile in the stream after the trial and reported this to the local people. Their response to him was that he was mistaken; he was assured that the crocodile he had seen was a "different one."

The point need not be belabored that this instance does not represent the trial and punishment of a domestic animal. Indeed, Nadel does not report the incident as an authentic instance of a juridical procedure. It is a ritual, and is analogous in every fundamental respect to the quasi-judicial ecclesiastical procedures that were invoked in medieval Europe against harmful pests, which are discussed below. The effectiveness of the ritual depends on some supernatural intervention for neutralizing the source of the harm, rather than on a direct societal action. The "death" of the crocodile obviously was nothing more than the solemn pronunciation of some curse against it. The ritual pact represented for the local population a way of maintaining their confidence and self-esteem. The Mokwa people prided themselves on their power to curb the destructiveness of crocodiles through the ritual pact; other villages in the region which did not enjoy such powers were presumably at the mercy of the crocodiles. The fiction of the power of the ritual pact was therefore maintained at all costs, although Nadel does intimate it was not quite fully believed. In reality, of course, no other alternatives were available, any more than there were to the medieval Europeans to use against the devastations by vermin and pests to which they were periodically subjected.

Von Amira long ago commented on the paucity of evidence for the trial and punishment of animals in primitive societies.[37] Similarly A. H. Post, whose compilations on law in primitive and non-Western societies were the most comprehensive works of their kind in the nineteenth century, could cite no evidence

---

traditional judicial personnel, is to be invoked for the purpose of resolving the trouble by assessing appropriate compensation. It is undoubtedly true that in isolated instances circumstances could be such as might precipitate a vengeance killing; this would typically involve a background of smoldering hostility between two families against which a killing, even if obviously accidental, serves as the spark that ignites the whole. But such a situation can hardly be taken as representing the norm. "Blood-money" is the norm, computed in terms of whatever might be the local measure of wealth: camels, cattle, horses, and so on. Vengeance is the exception, and signifies only that for certain special reasons the usual adjudicative processes of settling disputes were not called into action.

[31] A. Riasonovsky, *The Customary Law of the Nomadic Tribes of Siberia*, Indiana University Uralic and Altaic Series **48** (Bloomington, 1965): pp. 118, 137, 147.

[32] D. Bodde and C. Morris, *Law in Imperial China* (Cambridge, Mass., 1969), pp. 284ff., 350–352.

[33] S. F. Nadel, *Nupe Religion* (London, 1954), pp. 27ff.

[34] Nadel (pp. 27ff.) even supplies a photograph of this crocodile in the stream (pl. 2 opposite p. 22).

[35] *Ibid.*

[36] *Ibid.*, p. 28. The specific procedure of the trial is not reported.

[37] "Bei Naturvölkern hört man von Thierstrafen auffallend wenig," "Thierstrafen und Thierprocesse," p. 579. He also noted that there was no punishment of animals in early Germanic law, but rather the equivalent of the noxal surrender (*noxae deditio*) of Roman law. He nevertheless came to the conclusion (pp. 587ff.) that this amounts to a form of "private vengeance" against the animal, and that the practice is to be ascribed to the kind of notions about persons, animals, and so on that are common to all "primitive people"—a clear capitulation to the orthodox evolutionist doctrine that was then in the ascendant. Yet apart from this relatively harmless generalization von Amira's study is both scrupulous as regards the evidence and perceptive in his judgment of it.

for juridical procedures against, or the punishment of, domestic animals. He reports rather briefly and matter-of-factly that damage, injury, or deaths caused by animals are the responsibility of the owner, or some other person who could be held liable for an animal's destructive action, as for example a shepherd.[38] The ethnographic information of more recent decades bearing on this issue has provided overwhelming confirmation of these earlier observations. Societies of non-Western derivation and primitive peoples *did not and do not* attribute "human" will or "human" personality to animals or things, and *never* have tried them or punished them as they did human offenders. The notion that trials and punishments of irrational creatures and of inanimate things are a valid legal procedure occurs *uniquely* in Western society. The evidence for the rationale of the procedure will be discussed in the next chapter.

IX. ANIMAL TRIALS IN MEDIEVAL EUROPE

The medieval European data for the trial and punishment of animals will be found to show a clear distinction between the treatment accorded two classes of non-human life. This phenomenon was already observed by von Amira,[1] and is revealed also by Evans's chronologically arranged case register, though Evans did not formally separate the types.[2] The cases range in time from the ninth century onward.

Only a handful of instances are cited for the period from the ninth to the mid-thirteenth centuries. These are all procedures against pests such as moles, field-mice, insects, eels, and "serpents" (the last is quoted simply as "9th cent."; it may have been an imaginary infestation). The earliest cited case involving a domestic animal is the execution of a pig in 1266 in France; it was burned for having eaten a child. Thereafter attestations become more frequent, and Evans's register continues with a single chronological sequence of instances involving pests and vermin as well as domestic animals. In the latter category pigs are most frequent, but it includes also cows, oxen, bulls, goats, horses, asses, and dogs. I am at a loss as to how to classify a case against dolphins in Marseilles in 1596 and one against turtledoves in Canada ("end of the 17th cent."), though I should imagine that these may somehow have been thought of as pests (they may have interfered with the work of fishermen and farmers, respectively). It is also possible that these cases resulted from fevered imaginations, as happened in the instance of the cock tried in Basel in 1474 for having laid an egg; for that unnatural crime it was burned at the stake.[3]

The earliest of the modern commentators, von Amira, carefully directed attention to the "sharp distinction" which must be observed between those cases in which civil procedure (*weltliche Verfahren*) is applied, and those in which ecclesiastical (*kirchliche*) procedure is invoked. Civil procedure, he noted, was limited to cases involving domestic animals, and was invoked solely for the crimes of killing or injuring persons; the mode of execution was specified in the sentence.[4] In the occasional instances of trials for bestiality—which only tangentially touch upon the phenomenon of animal trials—the animal was executed along with the person.[5] Von Amira pointed out that ecclesiastical procedures are the earliest attested, and were directed against insects, vermin, pests, and the like, and called attention to the fact that the sentences in all such cases were exorcistic; they took the form of anathemas, maledictions, and even excommunication of the offending creatures. It is significant that these ecclesiastical trials were conducted with solemnity, and with a most solicitous attention to the fine points of judicial process such as was never accorded to domestic animals or to human prisoners brought before the courts.[6] It must be pointed out here that, despite the fact that von Amira's study is regularly quoted in the work of succeeding commentators, who moreover appeal to essentially the same body of evidence, there was a rapid blurring of all distinctions between cases in later studies on the topic. In the end all of the material was simple grist for Frazer's mill, and even Hyde so misstated the facts that he could say that "Beginning with the ninth century we have records that domestic animals, such as swine, dogs, *etc.*, were tried in the ordinary criminal courts like men."[7] Evans's register of cases, which is Hyde's main source, clearly shows that this was not so.

We must now dispose of the entire stream of medieval (and even later) European cases in which pests and wild creatures were allegedly put on trial, for they have no relevance whatever in any discussion

---

[38] A. H. Post, *Grundriss der ethnologischen Jurisprudenz* 2 (Oldenburg and Leipzig, 1894): p. 692.

[1] See the discussion below.

[2] Evans, *Criminal Prosecution of Animals*, pp. 313ff.

[3] *Ibid.*, pp. 162ff.

[4] Von Amira, "Thierstrafen und Thierprocesse," pp. 550ff. He noted also that in the earliest documents such cases were limited to instances in which the victim was killed. The specified modes of execution of the "guilty" animal included hanging, burning, beheading, and stoning—the last attested mainly in Slavic countries, and in explicit compliance with the biblical law of the goring ox, Exod. 21:28.

[5] *Ibid.*, p. 556.

[6] Evans (*op. cit.*, pp. 18ff.) describes how at Autun, at about the beginning of the sixteenth century, an ecclesiastical court appointed the jurist Chassenée—famous for his forensic abilities—to defend some rats that had destroyed a barley crop. Chassenée seems to have delayed the proceedings permanently on the plea that the court, having summoned the defendants, could not guarantee their safety on their journey to the court against the peril of the cats who were lying in wait for them at every corner. While some of this may be fanciful, Evans (pp. 41ff.) cites sufficient authentic evidence for the elaborate care with which the ecclesiastical trials of this sort were prosecuted.

[7] *University of Pennsylvania Law Review* 64 (1915–1916): p. 703.

centering on actual, *bona fide* legal procedures by which animals were "tried" and executed. That trials of rats, insects, and other vermin were *not* proper trials but were ritual procedures intended to invoke supernatural powers is plainly indicated in the extant reports. We have already seen that the courts in such instances consisted of ecclesiastical personnel only, and that their judgments or "sentences" consisted solely of the pronunciation of anathemas and the like; there was *never* any punishment in the accepted sense. The circumstances of certain of these trials as they have been recorded in the same sources provide further evidence in this respect. Thus it is reported in a number of cases that before the dread anathema was pronounced as a last resort the population of the infested region was exhorted to penances and to propitiation of the pests themselves. In other words, the pests were to be viewed as instruments of divine punishment for sin[8]—although at other times they could be thought of as incarnations of Satan; there was thus an initial change of roles, with the people the defendants and the pests as the "agents" of the divine prosecutor.[9]

In sum, the proper view of these ecclesiastical proceedings against infesting pests is that they are ritual appeals for non-human intervention to rescue a helpless society from an enemy beyond human reach. The Church was the *only legitimate* intercessor in these cases. If it did not succeed in ridding the locality of the pest, its ineffectiveness could always be laid at the door of the great sinfulness of the people themselves. And if the pest should disappear (as it would sooner or later), then the Church would be credited with great efficacy in its ministrations or its curses.[10] In other words, the procedures followed in these cases, though they were *at times* cast in the form of a judicial trial, are nothing else but what would—when observed in the "occult" practices in pagan and non-literate societies—be characterized (and dismissed) as

"magic" or "sorcery." This interpretation is only reinforced by the elaborateness with which these procedures were performed. It was of the utmost importance that these harmful vermin—who were yet creatures of God and as such had a rightful place on earth—be treated with the greatest respect. For apart from the common human trait that requires the most cautious conduct when one is confronted with an adversary against whom one is defenseless, there was also the underlying belief that the pests were sent as a plague for the sins of human society. They therefore were accorded every "legal" courtesy and right. The plight of domestic animals, not to speak of humans accused of felonies, provides an enlightening contrast; short shrift was made of whatever defense might have been offered in their behalf. The reason is obvious: in those cases the accused were identifiable *individuals* liable to apprehension and subject to effective and direct sanction by society. There was no need to fall back upon supernatural authority, whose effectiveness was uncertain at best.[11]

The use of judicial forms and formulas as a vehicle for a content that is intrinsically magical is quite common, and is by no means limited to societies that trace the lineage of their moral categories back to the Bible. All societies, whether ancient, modern, Western, or non-literate, mediate disputes by forms which amount to "judicial process." Such forms—which externally may in some instances amount to nothing more than the designation of a respected elder to serve as arbitrator—lend a specific quality of solemnity to the proceedings. This, in turn, is designed to elicit honesty, truth, and the like, and to afford some assurance that the disputants will abide by the outcome of the proceedings; this last is an important consideration in societies without regular agencies of enforcement. These formal procedures are not invoked in *every* kind of situation that threatens the social peace. Certain troublesome situations may be resolved by private self-help: the wronged party may exact "vengeance" against the wrongdoer(s), usually with the tacit approval of the society. Others may be resolved through summary action by the society against

---

[8] The appointed defenders of the infesting pests often argued eloquently, and sometimes successfully, on behalf of their "clients" that in eating crops and vines, and so on, they were only executing the mandate enjoined upon them by God in Gen. 1:30, which permits "all things that creep upon the earth" (together with the other animals) to eat "all green vegetation." At times this led to a standoff in the proceedings, and amusing attempts at "compromise" between the court and the defendants ensued, such as "permitting" the pests to feed to their hearts' content in a specially reserved area if only they would quit other areas! See Evans, *Criminal Prosecution of Animals*, pp. 38–50, for the protracted case of the worms that ravaged the vineyards of St. Julien in 1587. The final outcome of that case is not known because the last of the twenty-nine folio leaves on which it was recorded is worm-eaten!

[9] See Evans, *op. cit.*, pp. 52f. and 124f. In the last case (which occurred in the mid-sixteenth century), the Bishop of Constance ordered abstention from dancing on Sundays and feastdays and "from all forms of libidinousness, gambling with cards or dice and other frivolities," in response to complaint by the population of torment by "gadflies."

[10] *Ibid.*, p. 111.

---

[11] The contrast serves also as a commentary on the relative strength of formally recognized individual rights in any age, when confronted with the *power* of society. It can hardly be denied that the meticulousness with which the medieval ecclesiastical courts observed every legal nicety in their prosecutions of rats and insects was nothing but mimicry—even if exaggerated—of procedures which they knew as appropriate in authentic judicial situations. Yet in such authentic situations those procedures remained largely in the realm of the ideal, because of the overriding authority of social power. The ramifications of this theme in the context of sovereignty, and power versus law and justice, are taken up in the last part of this study. It is, nevertheless, important to note that at a very early stage in Western thought knowledge of and subscription to certain ideas about individual rights and of formal procedures designed to guarantee them is attested although these rights and procedures were in practice denied to those for whom they had obviously been intended.

the individual whose action or conduct is seen as an intolerable threat to that society's well-being. Such a person would be eliminated without formal proceedings either by an open killing—which would, in our terms, be called a lynching—or by a tacitly sanctioned covert killing, that is, an assassination. With these we are not concerned at the moment because the operative principle in those instances is *power*, not *law*.

The formal processes of law are characteristically invoked if there is no clear overriding popular interest that would indicate the summary disposition of the trouble-source by the unleashing of naked power, or if it is felt that a consensus—reached by means of a more or less formal set of procedures designed to establish publicly the facts of the case—must be established before such power is to be exerted. It is *a fortiori* clear that if this power is non-existent a "higher" power must be appealed to for the resolution of the problem. The formalities of judicial process are ready to hand as the mechanism which can activate this "higher" power. Here, then, is another reason for the great care taken in the conduct of trials of insects and vermin. They are magical rituals; and like all magical rituals their efficacy depends on exactitude in performance. In contrast with regular trials, in which form is incidental and certainly never more than secondary to the substantive matter at issue, in the ritual quasi-trials the form is the very essence of the procedure. The whole process—and sometimes the ritual trials went on for many months—was deliberate, conscious play-acting, even if the solemnity was not feigned.

We have seen that the alleged trial of the crocodile in Nupe territory also belongs in this category.[12] No different is the East European Jewish tradition of the "Dybbuk," which prescribes the exorcism of the spirit from the possessed.[13] In the classic enactment of the ritual the exorcism was accomplished through a rabbinical court, organized for this special occasion within the synagogue since the presence of the sacred scroll of the Law was felt to be necessary to effect God's immediate intercession. The procedure was called a *dīn Torah*, that is, a judicial process in accordance with biblical-rabbinic law; the same term denotes the process used by rabbinical courts for civil and domestic litigations within the Jewish communities. In ancient Babylonia the formal procedure that initiates an act of extispicy—the systematic examination of the entrails of sacrificial animals (usually sheep) in order to determine the fortunes of the petitioner—is cast as a trial. Shamash the sun-god—the divine judge *par excellence*—and Adad the weather-god—the

patron deity of divination—are invoked as the "court" who are to "judge the case" of the petitioner. The substance of the "case" consists of the evidentiary "facts" represented by the marks and configurations of the organ being examined, each set having (from the standpoint of the petitioner) a plus or minus value, according to an established code. When all the evidence is tabulated there is a "decision": the sum of all the evidence is a decision either favorable or unfavorable to the petitioner. The word for "decision" in this usage is exactly the same as the word that denotes the verdict or sentence delivered by a real judge in a real court for human litigants. The very word, *purussū*, is a technical term at home in the realm of legal vocabulary. The structure of the lengthy manuals for interpreting the ominous data—whether they concern extispicine or astro-meteorological phenomena, or fetal anomalies, or whatever—is modeled on the structure of the legal codes. Thus, "If the facts/observed phenomena are thus-and-thus, the decision (that is, the resolution indicated by the configuration of the given facts) is thus-and-thus." But this does not mean that we can equate such divinational procedures with proper legal trials. Nor were they thought of as such by the ancient Babylonians. The experts in divination techniques—and, as in most Mesopotamian professional life, there were specialists adept in each kind of procedure—were not court judges.[14] Finally, if whatever events related to the present topic that took place in the ancient Athenian Pyrtaneion were more than the figments of later ancient or contemporary authorities, they must be considered as magical ritual in the loose guise of a legal process. They are not in the remotest sense to be cited as evidence that the ancient Greeks, even in their dimmest prehistoric past, put animals and things on trial.

To sum up, when it is necessary to appeal to supernatural powers for intercession in human affairs—and such intercession is sought precisely when a troublesome situation arises that is not amenable to resolution by society—it is almost inevitable that the ritual forms will imitate with greater or lesser exactitude just those procedures to which society has recourse when it does have the power to resolve troubles, namely the processes of a legal trial. But legal trials, the end of which is a human verdict and a social action, must not be confounded with superficially similar procedures which from society's point of view depend for their effectiveness on divine or supernatural participation in the process and for the resolution of the problem on a manifestation of divine or superhuman power.

We may now turn to authentic trials of animals in medieval and post-medieval Europe. The evidence I

---

[12] See above, p. 63.

[13] Literally, "possession" in the etymological sense of "cleaving," typically of one body to another; in this special usage it denoted the "possession" of a living human body by an alien, and hence malevolent, spirit.

[14] A divination "priest" may occasionally be found among a panel of judges in a particular case, but as a dignitary among other local dignitaries.

shall cite here will necessarily be selective; to do otherwise would entail the recapitulation of the bulk of the source material given in detail by von Amira, and especially by Evans. My aim, however, is to include such data as will shed light on the categorical issue and its ramifications, the theme which is central to my present purpose. I must first of all restate briefly that the trials of animals with which we will be concerned from here on are those involving domestic animals only. These are the only ones in which, in *all* essential aspects procedures are indistinguishable from those implemented against persons accused of serious crimes.[15]

Certain general observations must be made at the outset about the date, provenience, and nature of the evidence. These will suggest certain questions to which I can offer no answers other than to suggest avenues for further inquiry which I am not qualified to pursue. We will thus see, first of all, that geographically the bulk of the evidence seems to derive from the south and east of France and adjacent parts of Switzerland, Italy, and Germany. A scattering come from more distant localities, with a small concentration in the Slavonic regions; the latter were collected mostly by von Amira. There is one questionable case of the trial of a dog in England in 1771,[16] and one very dubious case, also involving a dog, is reported from Scotland in the first half of the sixteenth century.[17]

The earliest of the authentic cases is the trial of a pig in a village near Paris in 1266. By far the largest number of reported trials of domestic animals from then until the end of the sixteenth century involved pigs. There were some thirty-three such cases—some of the trials involved more than one pig—which is about twice the total number of reported trials of all other domestic animals for the same period. Thereafter only two more trials of pigs are reported, one in 1613 and another in 1641, both in France. There is one further instance in which a pig that had bitten off the ears of an infant was executed in Pleternica, Yugoslavia, in 1864; its carcass was thrown to the dogs.[18] For the three centuries down to the beginning of the twentieth century the total number of cases of all kinds—including in this count those which are of the magico-ritual kind which Evans does not differentiate from the others—is a mere fraction of the number reported from the three previous centuries. We might have expected that the ratio of cases of the ritual variety to authentic trials of domestic animals would have dropped with increasing secularization, but that does not appear to be the case: three cases of trials of "locusts" and "grasshoppers" are re-

ported in the late nineteenth century, as is the trial of a wolf(!) in Calabria. The latter case—if authentic—would also belong to the ritual-trial type.

In discussing these summary data I am not proceeding on the assumption that all of them are authentic—for I suspect that at least some of them are not. Rather, I feel that, raw as the data may be, they will be adequate for our purpose. This assumption is based on the following considerations: First of all, a considerable part of the evidence is beyond suspicion. Evans in his appendices quotes *in extenso* from primary documents and related materials going back to the fourteenth century. All but one are from various French antiquarian publications of the eighteenth to mid-nineteenth centuries.[19] Von Amira appears to draw the conclusion that this body of evidence is representative of the geographical and temporal limits within which the phenomenon was known,[20] but I find that hard to believe. It is a known fact, for one thing, that archival documents in general are relatively scarce for medieval Europe for the ages earlier than about the mid-thirteenth century. Second, from observation of the sources used by the authorities who have written on the subject—and I refer here not to the secondary authors I have mentioned by name, but to the antiquarians who first brought the documents to light—it does not appear that any systematic search of all archives was ever undertaken for the purpose of recovering primary documents bearing on this theme, assuming—which I do not—that such an undertaking is at all feasible even for one entire country such as France. The fact that the greater portion of the known evidence derives from France, and at that is concentrated mainly in the eastern half of the country, may signify nothing more than a fortuitous conjunction of greater accessibility of documents and the initiative of local antiquarians. Indeed France, in general, has been the primary focus for research in medieval society for precisely those reasons. Another factor which must be taken into account concerns the proportion of literacy in the countryside: the phenomena that concern us appear to be typical of a village rather than a town setting, as one might expect of matters centering upon domestic animals. A limited incidence of literacy, or the sparing use of writing

---

[15] There are certain inevitable adjustments, which will be noted.
[16] Evans, *op. cit.*, p. 333.
[17] *Ibid.*, p. 325.
[18] *Ibid.*, pp. 137, 334.

[19] Appendices G to Q. R is an irrelevant excerpt from Racine's *Les Plaideurs* which describes the trial of a dog for having stolen a chicken; it belongs in the realm of fable. Appendix S, the last document cited, is from the register of a parish near Leipzig. Published in 1880, it records the decision of the Law Faculty of the University of Leipzig in 1621 by which a cow was condemned to death, executed, and buried whole (that is, "without being skinned"), for having killed its own mistress. The expert advice of the Law Faculty was required in this instance because such an attack by a cow was an "unerhörte[r] Fall"—presumably, if the attacking animal had been a bull, or some other beast, the local officials would confidently have proceeded without legal advice.

[20] Von Amira, *op. cit.*, p. 559.

for recording affairs of daily life, therefore affects the use of extant written sources as an index of institutional usage. The punishment of domestic animals in Eastern Europe is a case in point. There, especially in Slavic areas, the execution of animals by stoning proves how deliberately the practice was made to conform with the prescriptions in Exod. 21:28f. Yet from those areas there do not appear to be any records relating to this practice which antedate the nineteenth century.[21] It will surely not be maintained that in those cases the practice was an innovation of such recent date. The late date of the documentation in those regions must rather be attributed to the relatively late date for the widespread use of writing for mundane purposes; the custom itself was probably many centuries older. I would therefore suggest that the punishment of domestic animals[22] was a phenomenon more frequent and more widespread in medieval and later Europe than the currently known and authentic data would appear to indicate.

I do, however, make one exception, which I consider significant; it relates to the almost total absence in British records of trials or punishment of domestic animals.[23] Indeed, I believe that the custom never took root in Britain. The line of thought which on the Continent led to the actual punishment of animals in England took a different course; it expressed itself in the institution of the deodands,[24] to be discussed in greater detail below. For the moment it will be sufficient to note that the deodands practice was already well established in England by the time of Edward I: a statute defining the deodands procedure was enacted *ca.* 1280.[25] It quickly turned the consequences of wrongful death to the fiscal benefit of the Crown—and the accidental killing of a person by an animal was only one form of wrongful death. Thus what in continental European practice was dealt with according to folk ideas and customs in England became subject to royal enactment. Both the deodands and the punishment of animals were strongly inspired by the goring-ox laws of Exod. 21:28f. But these two methods of dealing with such contingencies were, in effect, mutually exclusive. The strength of the deodands—a matter to which we shall return in the final part of this study—is an index of the relatively advanced state of the political power of the Crown in England

in comparison with the powers of continental European kings at the same time. There is evidence of an attempt to initiate a similar confiscation procedure in Burgundy in the twelfth century:

> If an ox or a horse commit one or several homicides, it shall not be condemned to death, but shall be taken by the Seignior within whose jurisdiction the deed was perpetrated . . . and be confiscated to him and shall be sold and appropriated to the profit of the said Seignior.[26]

But there is no evidence that this "law" was ever effective; had it been, it would have amounted to a variety of deodand assessed locally. The fact that in English law it was the king who soon became the exclusive beneficiary of deodands forfeitures[27] was the crucial factor in the effectiveness of the system. The fragmented state of legal jurisdiction in France prevented such a centralized system from developing. Instead the execution of animals who had caused a death was a concession to local popular sentiment, and was in effect a kind of formal lynching of the unfortunate animals; it benefited no one. Biblical hierarchical classification may, in a vague way, have been originally responsible for the existence of such sentiments among the village folk. There is, however, no question that the more formal aspects of the execution of the beasts—which seem to have increased in Western Europe until the general disappearance of the custom towards the end of the seventeenth century—were inspired directly by the biblical law of the goring ox of Exod. 21:28f. To this point we may now return.

The most significant single aspect of the punishment of domestic animals in the Middle Ages in Europe is that, apparently right from the start, it was explained and justified by appeal to biblical prescriptions. These included the law in Exod. 21:28f. which condemns to death by stoning the ox that had gored a human being to death and bans the consumption of its flesh as food, and also the more general principle enunciated in Gen. 9:5 which holds that animals are accountable for the shedding of human blood.[28] The practice of punishing animals apparently was an innovation that was introduced some time before the thirteenth century. Before that, on the Continent as well as in England, fatal attacks upon persons by domestic animals were regarded largely as civil injuries, to be remedied by pecuniary means. The animal itself became the subject of noxal surrender. This practice, which had its base in Roman and Germanic law, dictated that the offending instrument (in this instance

---

[21] *Ibid.,* p. 572; Evans, *op. cit.,* p. 334. Note especially that the custom went so far as to require that the owner of the animal was to cast the first stone at it; for this see Deut. 13:10f. and John 8:7.

[22] I shall return below to the distinction between the "trial" of domestic animals and their "punishment."

[23] Von Amira, *op. cit.,* p. 559 and nn. 5–6 expresses skepticism about the authenticity of the two cases involving dogs, one English and the other Scottish, which were alluded to above.

[24] Scottish law differed somewhat, but the difference is more terminological than substantive.

[25] See below, p. 76 n. 18.

[26] See Evans, *op. cit.,* p. 165.

[27] Theoretically the deodands may have been destined for the Church as an expiatory offering, then to be distributed as alms, but this seems in practice never to have been observed. See below, p. 76 n. 18.

[28] See von Amira, *op. cit.,* p. 574; also Evans, *op. cit.,* p. 12.

the animal) be surrendered to the surviving kin of the victim. On the Continent the institution of noxal surrender was displaced when the increasing influence of Canon Law in many areas of daily life caused biblical principles of classification to become dominant over those characteristic of pre-Christian Europe.[29] The early Burgundian law cited above apparently was an attempt to reconcile the biblical law with the earlier noxal surrender, an aim successfully attained in England through the institution of the deodands. This is clear from the wording of the Burgundian rule: "If an ox or a horse commit one or several homicides. . . ." Since attacks by oxen upon humans were extremely rare—especially when compared with the frequency with which pigs were punished for homicide—it is hardly open to doubt that the biblical rule was the inspiration of the law.[30]

Earlier in this chapter I touched upon a misconception concerning the process by which domestic animals were condemned to death; we must dispose of it here. It concerns the idea that animals were "tried" and convicted by judicial process in the same manner as that ostensibly accorded human criminals. Von Amira went to great lengths to demonstrate

that this was not the case. He emphasized and reiterated the necessity of maintaining a complete distinction between animal trials (*Thierprocesse*) and punishments of animals (*Thierstrafen*). The former were restricted to pests and vermin and resulted in the pronunciation of anathemas. As noted earlier, it was only in such cases that the full panoply of prosecution and defense, formal charges and rebuttals, and so on, was invoked. The cases of domestic animals that had killed persons were not trials at all. The judicial process in those instances consisted at most of a plain statement of the essential facts and the pronunciation of a verdict setting out the precise manner in which the animal was to be executed.[31] There was no formal defense.[32] The confusion of the two separate kinds of procedure, against which von Amira expressly warned, began with Evans, although he clearly understood von Amira's thesis and appears not to have disagreed with it. The mixture then became firmly set and was used to support the animistic notions about primitive mentality propounded by the evolutionists. It has persisted to this day.[33]

---

[29] See von Amira, *op. cit.*, p. 591f. I am speaking here, of course, not of ideologies adopted and championed by those social strata that wielded temporal and spiritual authority, but of the ultimate effect of these ideologies once they had permeated the perception of deeper and broader bases of society. This process of transformation was gradual and took centuries to complete. Indeed, by the time the masses of Europe were successfully christianized—that is, "biblicized" in cosmological outlook—the intellectual and spiritual segments of society that had initiated that process from the ninth century onward had "rediscovered" the virtues of classical pre-Christian literature and thought. In doing so they precipitated the movement that can, with some justice, be characterized as a "resecularization" of society, although that change, of course, has as yet by no means fully succeeded in areas such as Spain, Portugal, Ireland, and in some respects even elsewhere in Western society. I do not, of course, mean to imply that together with this "resecularization" there has been a concomitant reorientation of cosmology towards the pagan pluralistic perception of the universe. Indeed, I perceive the concept of the national state, whose ideological bases were already being laid as early as the late eighteenth century, when the ideology of "resecularization" was reaching its zenith, to be a reinforcement of the monotheistic perception. It is this ideology—whether under a socialist-materialist banner or under the national flag (it is not insignificant that the design of a national flag is a top priority item for populations, however minute, that are "emerging" as independent nations)—which is now sweeping all before it beyond the borders of Western society, the homeland of the monotheistic cosmology. I do not, however, wish to be understood by these remarks as championing the ideological factor at the expense of other forces that are at work in altering the affairs and outlooks of human society. For this theme see *Temple Law Quarterly*, **46** (1973).

[30] The addition of the "horse" is derived from the realities of medieval village life to add verisimilitude. In biblical times the horse was used exclusively for military purposes, first in chariotry, and later—in the first millennium B.C.—for cavalry. It was never harnessed in the ancient Near East either for field husbandry or for overland transport.

[31] The one issue that can be disposed of summarily is whether or not the execution of homicidal domestic animals is to be interpreted as a police action (deliberately or in effect), as was suggested by Gaster (see above, p. 57) and others before him. A police action—understood as a summary and judicially unsanctioned disposal of a nuisance or a source of physical danger—would not have required the elaborateness with which the execution of these animals was carried out. Aspects of the execution included hanging on the public gallows, the payment of the hangman, the maintenance cost of the condemned animal (especially the pig) in prison before execution, and so on.

[32] There were, however, occasions when special pleas of mercy were put forward. Thus in one instance that took place in 1379, three sows attacked the child of the swineherd, and two entire herds rushed to join in the attack. The child was fatally injured. All the swine were "arrested as accomplices" and were doomed to execution in addition to the three sows that had precipitated the attack. But on the petition of the owner of the herds (a local prior), the Duke of Burgundy (Philip the Bold) "pardoned" the full herd, and only the three sows directly responsible for the child's death were executed; see Evans, *op. cit.*, pp. 144f. and Appendix K. In this instance, however, the question was not so much one of mercy, as of common sense prevailing in view of the great financial loss that would be involved. Pleas were also entered on behalf of animals condemned to death in cases of bestiality, a matter which does not directly concern us here.

[33] In addition to Kelsen's statement with which I began this section, we might also note a piece by J. P. McNamara in the *Notre Dame Lawyer* **3** (1927–1928): pp. 30–36; the author was at that time the editor-in-chief of that journal. The article is entitled "Animals at the Bar," under the general rubric "Curiosities of the Law," and was intended as a light-hearted glimpse into the backwaters of ancient and modern law. But, like much other writing in this vein, it reflects more of a sense of smugness than of real understanding or compassion. The author manages to convey the maximum amount of misinformation about the subject in the shortest possible space. He not only confounds entirely the trials of pests and insects with the execution of pigs and other domestic animals, but also avows that the Babylonians who, according to the Laws of Hammurapi, required pecuniary compensation for killing by goring oxen later "came to the Hebrew view of the matter. This is found in Exodus 21, 28sqq. where the Hebrew law requires that . . . the

The medieval authorities who ordered the execution of homicidal domestic animals did not do so mindlessly. They rationalized the procedure in very much the same vein as did the talmudical authorities in the Roman period who, as we have already noted above, included the goring ox among the class of felons condemned to stoning and discussed the possibility of exceptions. However crude the popular perception of the condemned animal as having killed with homicidal intent may have been, the learned sector of society, largely ecclesiastical, was under no such delusion. An eloquent illustration is provided by a case that occurred in Berne in 1666, in which an obviously insane man was tried for murder. The prosecutor attempted to prove the liability of the accused by appealing to the biblical law of the goring ox, which according to him demonstrated that absence of moral responsibility—it being clear that no one believed that the execution of the animal was based on any imputation of criminal intent—was no bar to the imposition of the capital penalty. The argument was rejected by the ecclesiastical court on the ground that

although God enacted a law for the ox, he did not enact any for the insane man, and the distinction between the goring ox and the maniac must be observed. *An ox is created for man's sake, and can therefore be killed for his sake; and in doing this there is no question of right or wrong as regards the ox*; on the other hand, it is not permissible to kill a man, unless he has deserved death as a punishment.[34]

To be sure, this case occurred late in the period with which we are here concerned. The court, moreover, is reported to have declared that the biblical law of the goring ox "is not binding on other governments (that is, non-Jewish ones), and is not observed by them. . . ." But this was true only in the technical sense that there were no statutory laws enjoining the execution of homicidal domestic animals; the *ad hoc* practice of putting such animals to death was still widely known if not reported as frequently as for earlier centuries.[35] The court in Berne also made

clear, in theological terms, that the execution of the goring ox was not punishment for sin:

Even if the Jewish law should be really applicable to all men, it could not be appealed to in the present case, since it is not permissible to draw an inference *a bove ad hominem*. Inasmuch as no law is given to the ox, it cannot violate any, in other words, cannot sin and therefore cannot be punished.[36]

In short, the court clearly perceived that the execution of the ox is not grounded on any idea that the animal was "morally" guilty or that it committed a crime in the normal legal sense, since as an unreasoning being it was incapable of doing so. The ox is to be executed, not because it had committed a crime, but rather because the very act of killing a human being— voluntarily or involuntarily—had rendered it an object of public horror. This horror is engendered by the implications of such a killing: the animal was seen as a living rebuttal of the divinely ordained hierarchy of creation; by an action that itself could not be judged on a moral standard the ox turned into an instrument that undermined the moral foundations of the universe. The ox, the visible object embodying this threat, had therefore to be disposed of without trace. The authorities of the Middle Ages and later who thus rationalized the execution of domestic animals got at the heart of the biblical law of the goring ox with unerring accuracy,[37] as the talmudical authorities did ages before.

The same rationale is more distinctly visible in connection with executions for bestiality. For the crime of engaging in sexual congress with animals the tribunals of the Middle Ages and thereafter, as also those of the Puritan colonies of Massachusetts and Connecticut in Colonial America in the seventeenth century, imposed the death penalty both on the person and on the animal (or animals) that he had used in the act. It has never been doubted that the sense of public outrage engendered by this act was rooted in the biblical laws on the subject, Exod. 22: 18, Lev. 18:23, and especially Lev. 20:15–16, which explicitly ordain the execution of both the person and the animal. Although the biblical laws say nothing about it, it was frequently the practice in Europe to

---

ox was to be stoned,—and by way of further punishment, to the ox we suppose,—the flesh thereof was not to be eaten" (p. 31). Of course, no authority is cited for this bald untruth. And the last bit about the biblical proscription of the carcass of the ox as food is typical of the snide "humor" throughout the piece. A further uncomprehending popular review of the subject—but without the snideness—is a short piece by F. A. Beach, "Beasts Before the Bar," in *Natural History* for October, 1950. I imagine that there may be other, even more recent, publications on the subject that have not come to my attention. It is probably as well; all of the evidence, without exception, ultimately derives from von Amira, but is grossly distorted and (mercifully) uncredited.

[34] Evans, *op. cit.*, p. 171, emphasis added.

[35] Evans's tabulation does not, in fact, list occurrences of the phenomenon in Switzerland—though ritual trials of vermin did occur there, including an alleged one against "rats and bloodsuckers" in Berne in 1451. It is, of course, not impossible that the court in this instance was truly ignorant of the practice, of which instances continued to be recorded in the nearby regions of eastern France, and in Germany.

[36] *Ibid.*, p. 170.

[37] On this point von Amira was clearly mistaken, for he interpreted the biblical prescription for the stoning of the ox as a ritual procedure, distinguishing it from executions within the temporal, criminal process, and asserting that the medieval authorities had misunderstood the biblical law in this connection. Apart from the arbitrariness that has characterized differentiations of the sacred and the profane, civil and criminal, and so on, in social phenomena in the ancient world and elsewhere, the context within which the goring-ox laws are embedded, which is that of the law of persons (see above, pp. 26f, 38ff), compels us to view the stoning of the ox as a secular punishment, not one whit different from the same punishment when imposed upon certain human offenders. All stonings are "ritual" in the sense that they required formal public participation. But this is equally true for human and animal victims.

burn the corpses after the execution,[38] which was usually done by hanging.

In the strict sense, the "execution" of animals used in acts of bestiality ought not to be treated under the rubric of animal punishment, for it is clear that in such cases the killing of the beast is purely ancillary to the execution of the human culprit. It is no real contradiction of this view to find that, on the popular level, the treatment of the animal occasionally depended upon whether it was a willing or unwilling partner.[39] But the formal attitude towards bestiality, particularly as regards the fate of the animal involved, illuminates for us the principle that underlies the punishment of domestic animals that had killed persons. The Mishnah, discussing the reason for condemning an animal to death when it had been merely an uncomprehending instrument in an act of human depravity, concludes that it must be done out of consideration for human dignity. To let the animal live would have amounted to perpetuating visible evidence of a degradation that affects all humanity. The destruction of the animal is the only way of obliterating this taint.[40] The same rationale was given by legal authorities in Europe in the sixteenth and seventeenth centuries for the execution of both the human and animal participants in acts of bestiality.[41] Bestiality offends against divine creation in two respects. First, it violates the hierarchical order of the universe, in which man occupies an exclusive and superior position vis-à-vis all other terrestrial life. Second, it aims directly at the very principle of Creation: the separation of species and even of such phenomena as day and night, the waters above the "firmament" and the waters below it, the seas and the dry land, and so on. Creation consists of separation, the marking off of borders. The blurring of these borders is a reversion to Chaos. Creation of living things consists of the divine order that propagation shall be "each after its own kind" (Gen. 1:21–25). "Kind" encompasses function as well as attribute. Biblical law goes to extraordinary lengths to insure the inviolability of these boundaries. Thus even fibers used for clothing must be kept distinctly apart; it is forbidden to wear an article of dress in which wool (animal fiber) is combined with linen (vegetable fiber).[42] The civilizations of the ancient Near East had no laws governing such behavior. The only surviving rules which bear on the subject are the closing sections of the Hittite laws; there only intercourse with a pig is classed as a capital crime, and even then both the offender and the animal may be pardoned by the king. Sexual intercourse with equids is explicitly stated not to constitute a punishable offense.[43]

Beyond these considerations there is the special biblical aversion to abnormality of any kind, both physical and functional. Again in contrast to all other civilizations in the ancient Near East (and almost all others anywhere and anytime), homosexual practice is a capital crime (Lev. 20:13) as it is an "abomination." Even transvestitism is "an abomination to the Lord" (Deut. 22:5), though the punishment for it is not specified.[44] In the Mesopotamian view the abnormal, whether it be in the realm of physical attributes, of behavior, or of occurrences, may be aberrant and ominous, but it is not "unnatural." It is recognized by the simple fact of occurrence, and one must come to terms with it in one way or another. In the biblical view there can be no autonomous "nature." The world and all that is in it are created by Will, and every category of thing

---

[38] See Evans, op. cit., pp. 147–152. In the American Colonies the reference to the biblical law was explicit since the earliest criminal codes of Massachusetts and Connecticut were little more than restatements of the laws of the books of Exodus and Leviticus. Thus, the report of the conviction and execution in Massachusetts in 1641 of the sixteen-year-old boy Thomas Graunger relates: "first the mare, and then the cowe, and the rest of the lesser catle, were kild before his face, according to the law, Levit. 20:15, and he him selfe was executed." E. Powers, Crime and Punishment in Early Massachusetts (Boston, 1966), p. 303. For a similar case in New Haven, Conn., in 1662, see Evans, cited above, p. 148f.

[39] Evans, op. cit., pp. 150f. cites a French case of 1750 of bestiality with a she-ass. In that case the death sentence was imposed on the human partner, but the animal was acquitted after testimony by the local curate and many parishioners that the ass was "a virtuous and well-behaved" beast and was in this instance the unwilling victim of a violent attack.

[40] Tractate Sanhedrin 7:4, Danby, op. cit., p. 392.

[41] Evans, op. cit., pp. 151f. The specific context is the provision for the mitigation of the punishment if the act was not fully consummated. In such cases "the human offender was publicly scourged and banished, and the animal, instead of being killed, was put away out of sight in order that no one might be scandalized thereby" (emphasis added).

[42] In Lev. 19:19 the prescription occurs in a sequence which prohibits the pairing of domestic animals of different species and the planting of mixed species of seed in the same field. In Deut. 22:11 it follows a rule prohibiting the harnessing of an ox together with an ass to draw a plough. The mixed-fiber clothing prohibition is still observed today among certain groups of ultraorthodox Jews.

[43] See §§199–200 of the Hittite Laws in ANET³, pp. 196–197. The Hittite rules cannot be construed as a generalized bestiality law, but must be understood in the wider context of the specifically defiling nature of the pig in the Hittite beliefs about purity and sanctity, an attitude which the Hittites assimilated from other Near Eastern societies. In this connection it may also be noted that the Hittites exhibit a marked sense of purity and defilement, affecting the entire population as well as the priesthood and royalty. That sense is not found in the societies of ancient Mesopotamia, and can only be compared in the ancient Near East with the biblical laws of purity, though the latter are far more comprehensive.

[44] Only in the Assyrian laws are there rules about homosexuality, and they are limited to situations in which someone is defamed by a public accusation of being the passive partner in such acts—the punishment for such defamation is scourging, penal labor, and shaving of the head—and to the more serious crime of the rape of one man by another. As punishment for that crime the rapist is to be subjected to a homosexual attack and then castrated! See Driver and Miles, The Assyrian Laws, p. 391, §§19–20. In other words, homosexual acts per se are not punishable, though it is clear that persons playing the female part in such acts were widely held in contempt. The subject is not discussed at all in Hammurapi's laws.

is testimony to that Will which had by design ordained
the features and attributes defining the category.
Deviations from the standard are therefore not only
abnormal but appear to challenge the order of Creation in varying degrees. They might even be viewed
as embodying the frightening implication that the
Creator, the personification of Will, did not quite
do as perfect a piece of work as was claimed and
believed. It is for this reason, rather than as a question
of aesthetics, that members of the priestly families
with visible physical defects are disqualified from
officiating at the altar, and that the animals to be
sacrificed must also be free of any physical blemish.[45]
For to allow less than perfectly formed officiants to
perform the central act symbolic of communion with
the Creator, or to permit the offering to be less than a
perfect specimen of its kind, can be interpreted as a
subtle way of mocking and rebuking the Lord of
Creation for his handiwork. It is therefore essential
to keep such embodiments of imperfection out of
sight; at the very least, they must not be flaunted
in the Creator's face.

Against this background the gravity with which
biblical law views the perversions of bestiality and
homosexual acts stands out in full relief. Here it is
not merely a matter of physical deformity—that,
after all, is a curse with which one is afflicted rather
than a condition adopted by choice—but a calculated
act of human will. To engage in such acts is to present
a deliberate challenge to the Creator. The implication
of the act is the negation of the fundamental principle
of Creation. No mercy can therefore be shown to the
perpetrators. They must be promptly rooted out and
executed. And the animals that served unwittingly
in the perversion of bestiality and thereby became
visible testimonies of human infamy similarly had
to be destroyed.[46]

We may conclude our review of the "trials" of
domestic animals in medieval and post-medieval
times by stating that these animals were never "tried"
in the strict sense. The destruction of such animals—
whether for having killed a person or for having been
used in acts of bestiality—was mandated by the
simple fact that the deed had taken place. That there
were occasional acts of "mercy" by which the animal
was spared (as far as the record shows these were
limited to condemnations for bestiality) testifies only
to the human terms in which these occurrences were
perceived by the local populations, since they were
invariably phenomena of local village life. The angry
cruelty often vented upon the animals condemned to
destruction for having killed a person represents the
opposite side of the same coin. Thus in 1386 a pig
that had mangled an infant and caused its death was
mangled in precisely the same manner before it was
publicly executed (dressed in human clothing) by
the official hangman.[47] It is wrong, however, to infer
from such manifestations—and numerous other
details of an anthropomorphic nature surrounding
the execution of homicidal animals[48]—that malice,
will, or intention were imputed to beasts generally.
One must rather picture these solemn executions
of animals as a kind of drama, in certain respects not
so far removed from the simple morality plays enacted
in medieval Europe for the unlettered folk on other
occasions. Certain moral and even civil points were
brought home through them. Sometimes the message
was full of commonsense and obvious. Thus, in
pronouncing a sentence of hanging upon a pig that had
killed and partially devoured an infant in 1567, the
court (in Senlis, France) warned the local population
against letting their swine run free on pain of physical
and pecuniary punishment.[49] In an earlier instance of
the execution of a pig for killing an infant (near
Chartres, in 1499), the owners of the animal were in
fact fined for culpable negligence and imprisoned
pending the payment of the fine.[50]

For the most part, however, the message of such
executions was simple and implicit, and concerned
the gravity of the offense of killing a human being.
In the case of the pig that was led to execution in
human clothing this message verged on the explicit.
Its import is precisely the opposite of the construction
that Evans (and all the others who found this somewhat amusing) placed upon it. The animal was dressed
in clothes, *not* because the people imagined that the
condemned pig suddenly became a rational and therefore a morally culpable being, but rather because the
authorities decided to use the execution of the animal
as a vivid lesson to the public. It was surely meant
to teach people, rather than other pigs, the consequences of homicide. The dressing up of the pig in
this instance, and the various details of other public
executions of homicidal domestic animals, all were

---

[45] Lev. 21:17ff. and 22:19ff.; also Deut. 15:21, referring to the
first-born of cattle and sheep. See, in general, Douglas, *Purity
and Danger*, chap. 3, and especially pp. 51f.

[46] The question of the economic loss caused by the destruction of such animals was, of course, a serious problem. It posed
no difficulty when the person was convicted of bestiality with his
own animals, or those of his family, as seems to have been the
case in the instances cited above. When, however, the act was
committed with animals belonging to a third party, that person
was in effect caused to suffer a financial loss for a crime in which he
was in no way implicated. This is an important question of justice
that has not been resolved to this day. Its full import will become clear in the discussion of the confiscation of "guilty automobiles," *Temple Law Quarterly, op. cit.,* pp. 213ff. The potential injustice was foreseen in a German ruling of 1635, which
provided for the compensation of the owner of the destroyed
animal out of the estate of the executed felon, or out of the public
treasury if the latter had no property; see Evans, *op. cit.,* p. 151.

[47] Evans, *op. cit.,* p. 140.

[48] There is no point in recounting them here, amusing as some
of them might appear to be; they are related by Evans, *op. cit.,* pp.
140–170.

[49] Evans, *op. cit.,* p. 160.

[50] Evans (pp. 154f.) assumed that the fine was in no way related to
their responsibility for the animal, but was rather for the infant that
had been placed in their care. Such a distinction, however, is
arbitrary.

directed at drilling the public in respect for the sanctity of human life, in dramatic and unsubtle ways. As already noted above, these manifestations ceased by the end of the seventeenth century, although occasional destruction of vicious animals (as opposed to formal public execution) continued beyond that date. The "age of rationalism" was not without some minimum effect even upon the lowest levels of society.

When all is said and done we are left with the incontrovertible fact that for a period of hundreds of years it was thought necessary and appropriate in Europe to execute formally domestic animals that had killed persons. The justification of the procedure rested squarely on the law of the goring ox in Exod. 21:28ff. It is, however, vital for us to perceive that the medieval rationale for the execution of homicidal domestic animals is not the consequence of any confusion in Western thinking about the capacity for will or intention in animals or in inanimate things, even though there have been times, as we have seen, when such ideas did become manifest on the folk level. On the whole, however, the reverse is true: there is an unbridgeable gulf between mankind and the rest of creation, and there is beyond that an acute sensitivity towards boundary breaching between kinds within the world of living things. This is indeed the key to this strange and apparently irrational practice. Animals that have killed persons were to be extirpated because the very fact of their having done so disturbed the cosmological environment in a way that could not be tolerated: the act appeared to negate the *hierarchically* differentiated order of creation by which man was granted sovereignty in the physical world. The visible evidence of the breach of this order had to be removed—and removed in solemn public procedure—in order that the cosmologic equilibrium would be widely recognized as having been restored. The law in Exod. 21:28f. which requires that an ox that gored a person to death be stoned and its flesh not eaten is the earliest expression of this deeply felt sense.[51] It also served as the paradigmatic example and the justification for all later trials and punishment of animals in European and American society, as well as for certain additional doctrines in Western law. These doctrines on the surface appear to bear little relation to the biblical law of the goring ox, but their rationale was nevertheless expressly anchored in it. They revolve about the idea of sovereignty as this notion has developed in Western thought, and about the exclusive prerogatives that such sovereignty is thought to enjoy in the realm of law.[52]

---

[51] In consonance with the biblical rule it was customary also in medieval (and later) animal executions to prohibit the consumption of the animal's flesh and hide. The carcass of the dead beast was usually either burned or buried.

[52] These ramifications are explored in the last part of this study; see *Temple Law Quarterly, op. cit.*, pp. 227ff.

X. THE DEODANDS IN EARLY ENGLISH LAW

We have already noted that the phenomenon of the solemn execution of animals for having caused the death of a person appears not to be attested in the records of early English law. There, instead, we find the procedure by which any chattel that served as the instrument that had caused the death of a person was to be "given to God," Latin *deo dandum*. In theory the object or animal *itself* was presumably to be given to the Church, or some pious foundation. In fact, however, this happened only by way of exception and in unusual circumstances. Instead the *value* of the object or animal was assessed, and the sum then became a forfeiture or fine. Nor was this sum normally given to the Church; it became due to the king, that is, to the royal exchequer. The object itself was called *deodand*; when its value had actually been paid into the exchequer it presumably was no longer *deodand*, and was again suitable for normal use.

The institution of the deodand had an extraordinary history in the course of the development of English law. In certain significant respects, the institution of the deodand has also had an impact on modern American law that is quite palpable, even if not widely recognized. The history of the deodands and its consequences in later law, especially from the nineteenth century onward will be reserved for the final part of our study. We must limit our attention here to the earlier manifestations of the institution.

Almost any work dealing with the history of the English Common Law has a reference or two to the deodands. More often than not the subject is dismissed with a note of contempt for the primitiveness of the kind of thinking that gave rise to such an institution and permitted it to flourish for so many centuries. There is usually also a sense of relief that the disappearance of the deodands had rid the otherwise noble legacy of English law of an aberration and a source of embarrassment. Beyond such casual allusions to the deodands one is hard pressed to find in the literature any references to the actual functioning of the institution in its early phases. To my knowledge there exists not a single modern study of the deodands that has any significant depth or perspective. The most reliable statement on the subject remains that made by Maitland almost eighty years ago. In a single paragraph he only hinted at the importance of the deodands in early English law without reporting more extensively on the varied ways in which it was enforced and interpreted, matters upon which he was evidently very well informed.[1]

My own inquiry into the subject is limited in terms of both my competence and the purposes of the present essay. The sources used here are limited to those that have been translated out of the Latin of the

---

[1] F. Pollock and F. W. Maitland, *The History of English Law* 2 (2nd. ed.; Cambridge, 1898): pp. 473f.

original rolls, and that have been provided with indices.[2] The overwhelming number of published references to the deodands appear to be concentrated in the thirteenth century. I can venture no opinion on whether the absence of earlier documentation in the published sources bespeaks a general paucity of court records or the predilections of those who publish or edit sources of this kind. Since, as we shall see, the deodand is documented at least as early as 1203, it must be presumed that the institution was in force for some considerable part of the twelfth century, if not earlier. The incidence of deodand forfeitures in the published records becomes sparse after the fourteenth century. Again, it would be unwise to draw any inference from this fact concerning the frequency of recourse to the deodand procedure in these later centuries, since this decline in documentation could be due to desuetude, to the preferences of the judges of the assizes (which came to replace the eyre in the fourteenth century), or even to the preferences of modern scholars in choosing source materials for editing and publishing. It will be sufficient to note that the deodands do reappear in the court reports in the first half of the nineteenth century, and were apparently assessed in cases with a frequency not adequately reflected in the reports.[3] It was precisely this traditional recourse to the deodands as a remedy for wrongful death that led finally to their abolition of 1846. It is improbable that the coroner's juries—whose duty it was to assess the deodand sum that was to be forfeited to the Crown—had deliberately revived a usage that was long defunct, especially one which they themselves obviously thought distasteful.[4] Our assumption must therefore be that the deodand continued to be enforced with greater or lesser frequency at different points throughout its long history.

Apart from the obscurity of its origins, the operation of the deodand, the methods by which the sums were assessed, and the disposition of the money due to the crown as a forfeiture, are the subject of much misunderstanding, contradiction, and *ex post facto* rationalization by the English legal commentators from Bracton in the middle of the thirteenth century down to Blackstone in the eighteenth. It would appear, further, that the later the authority the less reliable the explanation. Bracton is the earliest commentator and lived during the period from which the greatest number of attestations of the deodand come; he also served as a justice during most of his career. He

therefore is the most trustworthy of the commentators, but even he cannot be relied upon for a fully satisfactory analysis of the institution. His explanation of the deodand amounts to drawing an analogy between the instrument which caused a human death through misadventure and a human murderer: "If a man by misadventure is crushed or drowned or otherwise slain, let hue and cry at once be raised; but in such a case there is no need to make pursuit from field to field and vill to vill; for the malefactor has been caught, to wit, the bane";[5] the latter term translates the old Saxon (and general Teutonic) word for "killer, murderer," which had come to denote specifically inanimate instruments that caused death.[6] Neither Bracton nor any of the later commentators addressed themselves to the obvious question of how a "thing" which had become dangerous and abhorrent as a result of having caused a human death is instantaneously divested of its noxious quality by virtue of the forfeiture of its monetary value to the king. We never hear of the destruction of the thing itself—and I presume this never happened; yet this is a consequence we might have expected if, as we are consistently told, the deodand is rooted in the "primitive" belief that vengeance for a killing may be wreaked upon some inanimate object as well as upon human murderers. While the continental execution of homicidal animals may indeed be seen in this light, the deodand cannot be explained in the same way. Thus, in contrast to the frequent execution of pigs for having killed children, which we reviewed earlier, we may cite a case that occurred in England in 1218 (or a few years earlier). "A boy was dead from a pig's bite. No one is suspected." The judgment was misadventure (*infortunium*), and the price of the pig, 6 pence (deodand), "whence let Gilbert fitzRenfrey (the sheriff) answer."[7] We must presume that in the normal course of events the pig in question was confiscated and sold for the assessed sum. There is no requirement that the animal even be slaughtered for meat, and it is apparent that once the sum was realized no further "guilt" attached to the pig. Clearly then, explanations of the deodands based on the idea of the "guilt" of the death-dealing object are inadequate. While a notion of this kind might have played *some* role in the development of the institution, a number of additional, and probably more influential factors,

---

[2] I am not qualified to survey or examine the primary sources for English legal history, nor have I any way of estimating the extent of the sources that bear on the institution of the deodands.

[3] See *Temple Law Quarterly, op. cit.*, p. 172 and compare 171.

[4] *Ibid.*, on the practice of such juries to assess as low an amount as possible on the deodand object.

---

[5] Translated in Pollock and Maitland *op. cit.*, p. 473 and n. 2.

[6] The term remains alive in the English language in such words as "baneful," and also in its original sense of "killer" in words like "ratsbane, henbane," poisonous plants that kill rats and fowl, respectively.

[7] D. M. Stenton (ed.), *Rolls of the Justices in Eyre, Being the Rolls of Pleas and Assizes for Yorkshire in 3 Henry III (1218–19)*, The Selden Society **56** (1937): p. 250 no. 667. For which "the sheriff answers" means that the sheriff of the time is to account for the deodand sum and to see that it is paid into the royal exchequer.

gave the deodand its distinctive character. These factors, moreover, are probably those which helped keep this otherwise "irrational" institution alive up to the middle of the nineteenth century.

Two primary cultural traditions are to be perceived in the origins of the deodands, the pre-biblical, comprised of Saxon and Roman legal usages, and the Christian or biblical tradition.[8] To be sure, by the time of our earliest evidence for the law of Anglo-Saxon England there is little that can with any confidence be thought to be uncontaminated by the biblical tradition and its distinctive moral categories. The Laws of Alfred the Great (*ca*. 900 A.D.) were prefaced by a translation of chapters 21–22 of the Book of Exodus, and Christian—that is, biblical—moral notions permeate much of the statement of the laws proper even if the substance of the rules themselves may be thought to be largely pre-Christian in origin.[9] It may nevertheless be conceded that the rule in Alfred chapter 13, which provides that within thirty days after the accident the kin of the victim are to take the tree that fell upon and killed their kinsman as a result of an accident caused by a fellow workman, is a fair reflection of the early and widespread usage commonly designated as the "noxal surrender" (*noxae deditio*). This surrender of the instrument of death when there was no malicious intent on the part of any person involved in the circumstances of the death was not understood as a true restitution for the damage done (that is, the economic loss to the family of the victim caused by the latter's death). It was a ransom by the owner of the wrongdoing chattel, designed to forestall further action by the injured party. Only a refusal to surrender that wrongdoing agent (which could have been a person's slave, beast, or inanimate chattel) might have exposed the owner to suit for full composition.[10] The custom of noxal surrender was practiced in pre-Christian European societies and was also an established usage in Roman law.[11] It is also known in the customary law of African tribal societies, as the following statement indicates:

Among the Akamba, accidental killing was always compensated by only half the amount of blood-money for intentional killing. This is called *mbanga*, which is a word also used by the Akikuyu to signify the killing of a man by some article or the animal belonging to another. Both the Akikuyu and the Akamba would award the article or the animal causing the death to the deceased's relatives.[12]

That the deodands are in part a continuation of this institution of noxal surrender has not been in dispute. But, as many authorities have already observed,[13] the effect of the way the deodands law functioned was far from the intent of the noxal surrender. Obviously, the assessment of a deodand upon an instrument with which the person who owned it accidentally killed himself can by no stretch of the definition be explained as a noxal surrender.[14] Further, while the noxal surrender was strictly an arrangement between the private parties involved, the deodands belonged to the realm of Crown Pleas, that is, that branch of delicts that became the kernel of the criminal law. The beneficiary of the deodands assessment was neither the party that had suffered the loss due to the death, nor the Church (as has often been asserted), but the king. It is true that one occasionally finds in the records instances in which the justices (acting for the king) ceded the money due for some particular deodand to a charitable purpose "for God's sake" (*pro deo*), or even to the victim's survivors.[15] But as a rule the deodand, like every other kind of fine or forfeiture, was due to the king. The very reason for holding the periodic judicial commissions known as eyres,[16] and the assizes that succeeded them in the fourteenth century, was to insure that the exchequer received all that was due it from all kinds of fines and forfeitures in the several counties, as well as the rents and various revenues due to the Crown from the local jurisdictions. Indeed, once the eyre or assize was concluded, a separate roll was drawn up listing the amounts due; the sheriffs were then held responsible for seeing to it that these monies actually went into the exchequer twice yearly.[17] The eyres and assizes were in effect *de facto* fiscal audits carried out by the highest justices on behalf of the Crown's financial interests; questions of justice *per se* were relatively incidental. The occasional allocations by the justices of the deodand award towards some local charitable purpose must be understood as tokens of the king's

---

[8] I am here not speaking of chronological priorities in general terms. It is rather a question of the sequence in which these two traditions affected and left their imprint on English law; no one would question the priority of the Saxon and Roman traditions in this context.

[9] See Williams, *Liability for Animals*, p. 267 and n. 1, with reference to F. Liebermann, "King Alfred and the Mosaic Law," *Transactions of the Jewish Historical Society of England* 6 (1912): p. 21.

[10] See Williams, *Liability for Animals*, p. 270.

[11] *Ibid*.

[12] Elias, *The Nature of African Customary Law*, p. 139. Elias calls attention there (note 3) to the deodands as a parallel.

[13] For example Williams, *op. cit.*, p. 270.

[14] This example from the year 1243 is typical: "A carpenter named Roger accidentally wounded himself with his axe while working, and died of the wound. Judgment: misadventure. Value of the axe 8d., for which the sheriffs are to answer." Helena M. Chew and Martin Weinbaum (eds.), *The London Eyre of 1244*, The London Record Society 6 (1970): p. 67 no. 167.

[15] See Pollock and Maitland, *op. cit.*, p. 474 and n. 5, reporting a case in which the price of a cart which had killed the man who owned it was ceded to his children *pro deo*, and a horse that had apparently killed its owner was turned over to a poor man that had formerly been its owner.

[16] The word means a journey or itinerary in circuit.

[17] See the Introduction to *The London Eyre of 1244*, pp. xvi ff.

grace and sense of compassion. They were not warranted by right, nor were they relics of an earlier age when deodands were alleged to have regularly been put to such pious or charitable uses.[18]

The justices in eyre, to be sure, had a certain amount of discretion in the disposition of the deodands, and practice could vary greatly from shire to shire. Thus in an instance from the early fourteenth century, the justices directed that "the weapon by which any be slain, and deodand not exceeding sixpence halfpenny, go to the clerk; and those exceeding the value of sixpence to the king. It is his fee, and shall be given to him forthwith."[19] The revenues from the deodands are here explicitly stated to be the king's property as a matter of right. The same source provides one of the earliest formal definitions—which is at the same time an implied explanation—of the law of deodands: "Everything that moves along with that particular thing through whose movement a man is killed is deodand to the king or the fee of the clergy."[20] This, with a greater or lesser amount of elaboration, is essentially the same explanation offered for the deodands by all later English legal commentators. However, the belief that in order for a thing to become deodand it must have been in motion when it caused a human death or that it must be capable of being in motion is as ill-founded as the belief that the proceeds of deodands were at one time devoted to pious or charitable purposes. Yet already in the thirteenth century Bracton thought it an abuse of the law that objects which were motionless at the time that death ensued were indiscriminately declared deodand together with objects or animals that were in motion.[21] Thus it is

reported in the Warwickshire Eyre of 1221 that "Simon of Coughton fell dead from his horse in drunkenness." In this instance the township was held by the justices to be "in mercy" because it did not "present his death at the county [court] nor to the coroners. . . . The horse's price is one mark, for which the sheriff must account."[22] There are some even more striking examples from the London Eyre of 1244: In 1231 a person fell into a vat of hot mead and was scalded to death. A deodand was declared on the vat, which was valued at two shillings.[23] Two other accidents with tubs of hot mash were reported for 1244. In both cases the victim was scalded to death, and a deodand was declared to the king for the value of the tubs.[24] The same source reports no less than four cases in which a person was killed by falling down steps; in each instance the steps were assessed as deodands.[25] In the first of these, which occurred in 1231,[26] the local officials, including the chamberlain and the sheriffs "falsely presented the plaint and concealed the bane"; that is, they were apparently loath to declare the steps deodand. In view of this flouting of proper procedure "the king is to be consulted because no inquest has been correctly held" and "the justices in eyre preferred judgment against the chamberlain, and the citizens against the sheriffs." In 1237, the same eyre reports,[27] a man fell from a beam inside a house; the beam was declared deodand at the value of sixpence. Numerous instances of the same kind could be found in other records of the time. The implication of all this is plain: there never appears to have been, in actual practice, any distinction between objects in motion or motionless, or things which were intrinsically incapable of motion—such as steps or fixed beams—when it came to the laying of deodands.[28]

The sum of this brief review of the early history of the deodands law is that the deodand was of a new and unique character and that it was only in a minor respect a descendant of the pre-Norman noxal surrender. Its distinctive features were the absoluteness of the criteria for forfeiture: the object which was the instrument of a human death was forfeit whether or not that object was animate and moved of its own accord (such as a horse or an ox), or inanimate (such as a cart or a boat, or even a tool), or fundamentally

---

[18] This explanation, accepted by almost all authorities, including Maitland, apparently is based on the literal interpretation of the term *deodandum*, "given to God." It must be emphasized that no evidence has ever been adduced to support this view, though the justification for making the king the beneficiary of the deodand was in one instance formulated as residing in the praiseworthy purpose of purchasing masses for the poor soul of the deceased which, having "been hurried out of this world, outweighs the claim of the dead man's kinfolk." (Pollock and Maitland, *History of English Law* 2: p. 474). The anonymous author of an article on the deodands in *The Law Magazine*, N.S. 3 (1845)—written à propos of the parliamentary debate of the measure that was to abolish the institution (see chapter XII below)—is the only authority I know of who expressed skepticism that the deodands had ever been intended for pious purposes (p. 198). He also mentions (p. 189 n. 1) a statute prescribing the deodand procedure that was enacted at the time of Edward I (*ca.* 1280). This statute, which was cited in the judgment of one of the last deodand cases (*Regina* v. *Great Western Railway Co.*, 3 QB 341), provided that the value of the deodand, assessed by a coroner's jury, was laid upon the township in which the accidental death had occurred; it was to be paid to the king.

[19] F. W. Maitland, L. Harcourt, and W. C. Bolland (eds.), *Year Book of the Eyre of Kent, 6 & 7 Edward II (1313–1314)*, 1, The Selden Society 24 (London, 1909): p. 139.

[20] *Ibid.*, p. 89.

[21] Pollock and Maitland, *op. cit.*, p. 474 n. 4.

[22] F. W. Maitland (ed.) *Select Pleas of the Crown A.D. 1200–1221*, The Selden Society (London, 1887): p. 100 no. 156. Drunkenness was a major cause of fatal accidents involving boats and horses and carts; see Pollock and Maitland, *op. cit.*, p. 474 n. 4.

[23] *The London Eyre of 1244*, pp. 26f. no. 65.

[24] *Ibid.*, nos. 170, 174 (in the latter instance the tub fell on the woman and killed her).

[25] *Ibid.*, nos. 60, 78, 99, 138.

[26] *Ibid.*, no. 60.

[27] *Ibid.*, no. 111.

[28] This was already known to Maitland; *cf.* Pollock and Maitland, *op. cit.*, p. 474 n. 4.

immobile (steps, beams, and the like). For it to be necessary that a deodand be declared it did not matter whether the victim was himself to blame for his death (through negligence, drunkenness, and so on). Even when the instrument of the death belonged to the victim and was in use by him at the time of the accident, and when no one else was involved, the deodand was required. Above all, the peculiarity of the deodand was that, although the object was invariably "guilty," it was not confiscated or destroyed. Instead, its value was assessed in money, and this money became a forfeiture due and payable exclusively to the king, that is, to the royal exchequer, even though some discretion was permitted in assigning the proceeds on occasion to some charitable purpose.

The quintessential quality of the deodands, that which sets the institution apart from all that had preceded it in early Europe such as the noxal surrender of Saxon and earlier times, as also from the execution of homicidal domestic animals in medieval and even later ages in Europe, lay in the notion of "objective liability." Though the turn of phrase denoting the idea is of recent jurisprudential vintage, the principle is an old one: its original manifestation is to be seen in the biblical law of the goring ox. The homicidal ox was to be stoned to death, but not because it was thought to be "at fault" or "guilty" in the same sense that a rational human being might be held guilty, or "at fault" in some moral sense (even if only for negligence). Rather, it was to be extirpated because the death of a human being of which it was the unwitting instrument precipitated a condition in the social environment that was held to be dangerous —like that caused by a virulent disease—and its traces had to be completely eradicated. The only circumstance in which this principle of objective liability was to be followed was one in which a transcendent value was thought to be harmed or jeopardized. By contrast, wrongs committed by humans were subject to remedy calibrated along the axes of the gravity of harm caused by the conduct and the moral culpability of the agent of that harm, though in the case of homicide there always remained a residue of objective liability by virtue of the transcendent nature of the harm that ensued. The execution of the ox, however, was not a confiscation or forfeiture to some entity thought to represent the corporate society. What Yahweh—the projection and the apotheosis of the corporate sense of transcendence—decreed was the excision and the obliteration of the offending beast; it would be inaccurate to conceive of the compliance with this rule as even a form of atonement in the strict sense.

It is one thing, however, for a society to purge itself of taint in response to a command from an incorporeal authority that ultimately is but the personification of the collectivity. But it is quite another

matter when that authority became vested in a single human being, namely a king, in whom the collectivity was asserted to be incarnate. The transformation of the biblical ox condemned to death by stoning into the deodand of medieval England cannot be severed from the broader nexus of the political theology which developed around the king's person in medieval times. It may be true, as Kantorowicz's famous study has shown, that the doctrine of the "King's Two Bodies," fully elaborated in Elizabethan times, was a fiction bordering on the absurd.[29] But there were potent antecedents for this notion extending far back into the early Middle Ages. Thus the unidentified Norman cleric now referred to as "The Norman Anonymous"[30] wrote at around the turn of the twelfth century A.D.:

We thus have to recognize in the king a *twin person*. . . . Concerning one personality, he was, by nature, an individual man: concerning his other personality he was, by grace, a *Christus*, that is, a God-man.[31] The power of the King is the power of God. This power, namely, is God's by nature, and the king's by grace. Hence, the king, too, is God and Christ, but by grace; and whatsoever he does, he does not simply as a man, but as one who has become God and Christ by grace.[32]

In almost the same terms, and about the same time, Hugh of Fleury wrote in a tractate about royal power vis-à-vis the church hierarchy, which he dedicated to Henry I of England (1100–1135):

Verily, the king, within his realm, seems to take the place of God the Father, and the bishop that of Christ. All the bishops, therefore, appear to be rightly subjected to the king, just as the Son is found to be subject to the Father.[33]

Finally, about a century later, Bracton himself propounded similar views about the nexus of God-King-Law: the royal judges sit in the place of Jesus Christ but the king himself sits in the place of God the Father.[34]

I do not mean to imply through these citations that the rise in England of institutions such as the deodands and similar royal prerogatives are to be attributed to the deliberate propagation of certain doctrines about royal power. The authority for such institutional innovations is to be sought, in the first instance, in the practical exercise of power. The rationalization for the assumption of authority, while serving as a legitimation of power and as a means to its consolidation, is commonly a secondary manifestation, though one far from unimportant both to the contemporary scene and in historical perspective. In this sense, therefore, one must look for the roots of the

---

[29] E. H. Kantorowicz, *The King's Two Bodies* (Princeton, 1957).
[30] *Ibid.*, p. 42.
[31] *Ibid.*, p. 46.
[32] *Ibid.*, p. 48.
[33] *Ibid.*, p. 161.
[34] *Ibid.*, pp. 155–160.

deodands, as also for almost every other feature of English law, in the unique experience of the Norman conquest of England in 1066. Maitland stated it simply: "The Norman Conquest is a catastrophe which determines the whole future history of English law."[35] The Domesday Book was only the first stroke in a slate-cleaning process that enabled the Conqueror and his successors to erect a political and social order that was as different from what had preceded it in Anglo-Saxon England as it was from that of France and elsewhere on the Continent. From the very beginning, and with increasing force, the king in England personified, and was in fact, the centralizing and central governmental authority. He thereby placed himself—or rather the principle of monarchic sovereignty—in opposition to the diffused sovereignty of the feudal system on the one hand and the more universal dominion claimed by the Church on the other. Very little time was lost in creating the institutions that gave teeth to the scheme, which was soon to make the royal authority immediate in every English shire and hamlet. It was Henry I who first gave permanent form to the Curia Regis, which before the end of the twelfth century developed into the formal structure of the king's courts, displacing the local independent courts. Henry I also founded the Exchequer to look after royal accounts and the income due to the Crown from whatever source. The royal courts and the Exchequer thereafter worked in complementary fashion to insure both the king's interest in the dispensing of justice, and the revenues from fines, forfeitures, amercements, and so on, that fell due to the king in connection with the dispensing of that justice. The English Norman kings accomplished this arrogation of powers long exercised on the Continent by independent barons by the opportune use of power. Ideological and moral justification for this new order was brought forward only when it was already well on its way to entrenchment.

The spiritual and ideological factors in the equation should not, however, be overlooked in any accounting for the character of the temporal authority of the English king as exemplified by the institution of deodands. But in this context the non-specialist like the present writer comes up against what appears to be an ingrained aversion on the part of students of English legal and constitutional history to accord Scripture any significant role in this history. Maitland, for example, was unable to suppress his antipathy towards those who detected scriptural influence in medieval law and practice, referring to such authorities as "bibliolaters."[36] At least part of the difficulty

is rooted in precisely the same set of circumstances that marked off the political development of England in the earlier Middle Ages from that of comparable lands in Western Europe in the same period. It focuses on the extraordinary power exercised by the English monarchs, arising from the Norman Conquest and its consequences. The distinctions which these developments created between continental feudalism on the one hand and English feudalism on the other had their counterpart also in the relationship between crown and church. The Norman English kings from the very first asserted, and for the most part were able to maintain, an independence from the ecclesiastical power of the papacy that contrasted sharply with the situation of the continental monarchs in their relations with the papacy. But it would not be correct to read into this a precocious expression of the "secularization" of political authority or of any recognition of the discreteness of the two realms of church and state. The theocratic idea was not one whit less strong in England than anywhere else in Europe in the earlier Middle Ages. From his own point of view the English king was, in fact as well as in theory, the vicar of God the Father, the incarnation of Christ, and the high priest at one and the same time. His anointment and consecration upon ascending the throne were visible tokens of his investment with these qualities. It was he, rather than the far-off Pope in Rome or the highest church dignitary in England, who mediated between the transcendent and the mundane, between the Lord in Heaven and the people comprising His earthly flock. And the people were overwhelmingly in accord with this view.[37]

The intellectual and spiritual climate of the time did not permit any cleavage between the mundane and the supernatural as regards events on earth. "Heaven, purgatory, or hell ranked equally with the world around them as the unavoidable experience of man."[38] It is superfluous to stress that the religious climate in the early Middle Ages was all-pervasive, but it might be helpful to remind ourselves that no

---

[35] Pollock and Maitland, *op. cit.*, 1: p. 79.

[36] *History of English Law* 2: p. 472 n. 3. The context is specifically that of the execution of animals in continental Europe and the possible bearing on this practice of the goring-ox laws of Exod. 21:28ff. As Maitland's text at that point shows, however, he shared the evolutionist (and mistaken) view of his time that the punishment of animals was a phenomenon known to "ancient

law" in general (and presumably to primitive law as well) so that, in his view, it would have been unnecessary to attribute the medieval (and later) European practice to the influence of biblical ideas. In his subsequent discussion of the deodands he goes so far as to declare that it represented a "sacral element" derived from a "heathenry" which "Christianity could not wholly suppress," largely because it was "in harmony with some of those strange old dooms that lie imbedded in the holy books of the Christian" (p. 474). The description "holy books of the Christian," that is, the Bible, implies a more specific if veiled allusion to the laws of the goring ox in Exodus. As I am attempting to demonstrate here, the deodand owes its inspiration precisely to that scriptural antecedent rather than to some imagined "ancient criminal law" or to "heathenry."

[37] The kings of England (and of France) were at that time also claiming miraculous powers of healing, claims which gained broad and "astonishingly tenacious" recognition; R. W. Southern, *The Making of the Middle Ages* (New Haven, 1965), p. 94.

[38] D. M. Stenton, *English Society in the Early Middle Ages* (Harmondsworth, 1959), p. 203.

opposing conception had as yet been propounded. There was no domain of social life which could be distinguished as "secular" and be sharply marked off from the remainder. Such distinctions or categorizations are our own and hence are an anachronistic intrusion into—and to that extent are a distortion of—the perceptions of the people during the period in question. The "temporal" was no less a part of the religious order of the world than was what may more narrowly be defined as "spiritual." Whether it was ecclesiastical or lay power that more immediately retained the authority over the large gray area lying between the extremities of the two realms, and where the precise border between these powers might be demarcated, were issues determined largely by material factors such as geography, military might, economics, and the personal equation—the magnetism and forcefulness of any given monarch or pope.

In short, the real basis for the rise of the deodand institution in England is to be sought in the assumption by the Norman and Angevin kings of the role of vicar of many transcendent concerns which elsewhere in the medieval world (and before them even in England) were within the jurisdiction of the Church. Foremost among these was the belief in the transcendent value of human life—a fundamental principle of the biblical world view. It was not merely a question of the belief in the eternity of the soul: the definition and supervision of that were gladly left to ecclesiastical authority. When, however, a human life had been taken, whether in circumstances such as would amount to murder or manslaughter, or even in the taking of the life of a convicted felon, the king annexed to himself the prerogative of representing the divine authority to which the corporate community believed itself to be ultimately answerable. The English kings in this manner attained the enviable position of representing the pinnacle of both the mundane and the transcendent structures, and in a quite literal sense enjoyed the tangible rewards of both possible worlds. The Bible confronted the contingency of (other than natural) human death by an interdiction against the conversion of such misfortunes to private or institutional profit; even the religious establishment was prohibited from turning any aspect of such an accident to its own advantage.[39] The English kings, however, did turn every such contingency into an occasion for imposing a forfeiture redounding to their own benefit, precisely on the rationale that the king is God's counterpart on earth and is therefore the proper legatee of those expiatory exactions which resulted from harms inflicted upon one human being by another, whether one person was only the unwitting instrument of the victim's death, or even whether the killer and the victim were one and the same person, that is, a suicide. It was in justification of the forfeiture for suicide that Sir Matthew Hale wrote in the late seventeenth century:

No man hath the absolute interest of himself, but 1. God almighty hath an interest and propriety in him, and therefore self-murder is a sin against God. 2. The king hath an interest in him, and therefore the inquisition in the case of self-murder is *felonicè & voluntariè seipsum interfecit & murderavit contra pacem domini regis.*[40]

It can hardly be doubted that the rationale as stated by Hale was identical with that which already prevailed in England in the early Middle Ages, in which period the forfeiture to the crown of the chattels of suicides is well attested. The same forfeiture was imposed on those who killed by mischance or in self-defense and who fled or sought sanctuary in churches or monasteries rather than present themselves to the mandatory inquests.[41] Most telling in this connection was the king's interest when a murder occurred and the killers remained unknown or unapprehended. In such instances the king exacted a fine, known as the *murdrum,* from the community in whose jurisdiction the murder had been committed. This was, in essence, a forfeiture imposed upon a community as an expiation for the otherwise unatoned killing; the amount of money assessed often constituted "a crushing penalty" upon the community in question.[42] While there was no biblical precedent for exacting the forfeiture of the chattels of suicides,[43] the notion that a community incurs some blame or "sin" if a murder was committed within its jurisdiction and the slayer remained unknown does have a biblical antecedent. The procedure decreed for such occurrences is described in Deut. 21:1–9: a young heifer is to be killed (not by normal sacrifice, but by having its neck broken) in the presence of the assembled elders of the community; under the direction of the priesthood the elders plead for divine absolution for "bloodshed" while declaring at the same time that none of them was responsible for the killing or had any knowledge of its circumstances.[44] Here, as in the case of the goring ox, we are confronted by an instance of expiation for guilt which was contracted without moral blame. Both kinds of case touch

---

[39] See above on the prohibition against human consumption of the carcass of the ox that was to be stoned and against the acceptance of "blood-money" by a victim's kin whether the death had been the result of mischance or intentional homicide (Num. 35:31).

[40] M. Hale, *Pleas of the Crown* 1 (ed. W. Stokes and E. Ingersoll; Philadelphia, 1847): p. 411.

[41] See N. Hurnard, *The King's Pardon for Homicide Before A.D. 1307* (Oxford, 1969), pp. viii ff.

[42] Pollock and Maitland, *op. cit.*, 2: p. 487. In its origin the term murder denoted only secret killings of this kind and only much later was it applied to intentional homicides generally.

[43] I shall return to this in more detail in the final section of this essay.

[44] For the full translation of the passage, see *Temple Law Quarterly, op. cit.*, p. 192.

upon transcendent concerns which, if not properly attended to by an appropriate expiation, are sensed as endangering the well-being of the community at-large. In the English parallel the same view prevails, seen from the perspective of the king. If a wrong was committed, its rectification was obligatory, in order to safeguard the integrity of the "king's peace." If a murderer remained unapprehended or unidentified, the "king's peace" had in effect been challenged successfully. This state of affairs could not be tolerated if the integrity of society was to be maintained, since the king was seen—or better, saw himself—as its embodiment. If those directly responsible for the deed remained unidentified, the most proximate instrument for reestablishing the balance of society was the local community. It remains immaterial to the essential rationale of expiation whether or not the *murdrum* fine imposed on the community implied any measure of "guilt" for having failed to apprehend the slayer, or for an implied dereliction in the maintenance of public order. The stress was rather on the king's overriding right to demand expiation and to be the beneficiary thereof, without regard to the circumstances which caused the malevolence. By our own standards there could be no rational justification for the exaction of deodands in most of the instances in which the institution was invoked. The justification of the *murdrum* fine similarly lay in the sphere of the quasi-religious and the transcendent; it had little or nothing to do with morality or justice as we perceive these concepts.

Perhaps the most "irrational" as well as to our modern sensitivities the most offensive of crown forfeitures for homicide was that imposed on persons who, by the merest mischance and without the slightest suggestion of negligent conduct, caused the death of another person. A good example is that of the laborer at work with a hatchet of which the head suddenly flies off, striking a passerby and causing his death.[45] According to Anglo-Saxon law a killing of this kind would have remained a civil matter, and the wrongful death would have been emended by the payment of a sum of money to the victim's survivors. At some time after the Norman Conquest such killings were lumped together with felonious homicides under the class of Crown Pleas—that is, they became cases for the King's Court—and were, in effect, treated as criminal cases. It became common for unfortunate slayers of this category to flee their locality, not out of fear of vengeance on the part of the victim's family, but because of the unpredictability of their treatment at the hands of the judicial system, from local juries of inquest up to the hearings of the justices in eyre. The immediate consequence was that the chattels of such innocent fugitives were forfeited to the king.[46]

At the beginning of the fourteenth century the pretense that the forfeiture was a penalty for the flight (rather than for the accidental killing) was dropped, and the forfeiture of chattels was imposed indiscriminately, whether the unfortunate slayer fled or stayed to face the inevitable inquest.[47] If the inquest found that the slayer was innocent, the king would often order the restitution of the chattels, but this extension of royal grace was vitiated by the requirement that the petitioner pay for it, at a price that sometimes approached the full market value of the chattels in question.[48] This practice, which would appear to flout even the most elementary standards of justice, nevertheless remained statutory until the nineteenth century. It was abolished only in 1828 with the start of the great and long overdue reform of the English penal law.[49] In the seventeenth century Hale was perplexed by this punishment of persons who were morally blameless, but concluded that it was imposed for the good reason of instilling in men a greater sense of carefulness in going about their work and "because the king hath lost his subject."[50] Up to the eighteenth century other English jurists, including Blackstone, held similar views. But Hale, in contrast to the other commentators, perceptively cited by way of support and analogy the law in Deut. 19:5–6 which not only required that a homicide by inadvertence (*per infortunium*) flee to a city of refuge, but also permitted the kin of the dead man, bent on vengeance, to slay the unfortunate fugitive with impunity if he could manage to overtake him before he reached the refuge city.[51]

It is clear in the biblical rule[52] that the rationale for the law affecting homicides by inadvertence had little if anything to do with instilling caution. It is rather the objective harm engendered in the world order by the shedding of human blood, however inadvertently or even unavoidably, that dictated the harsh consequences for the slayer. The cosmic order, not human justice, required that expiation be made. Although he was innocent by human standards, the society would sooner that the slayer alone bear the burden of expiation—by being left to the mercy of a blood-avenger if, for any reason, he does not reach sanctuary (or leaves its boundaries before the death of the high priest)—than expose the entire community to divine retribution. There is similarly in the realm of human justice no reason to search for the rationale behind the crown forfeiture of the chattels of slayers

---

[45] See *Ibid.*, p. 188.
[46] See Hurnard, *op. cit.*, chap. 5, pp. 131ff.

[47] *Ibid.*, pp. 147ff.
[48] *Ibid.*, p. 145.
[49] See J. F. Stephen, *A History of the Criminal Law of England*, 3 (London, 1883): pp. 76f.
[50] See *Temple Law Quarterly*, *op. cit.*, p. 186.
[51] For the full quotation from Hale, see *Temple Law Quarterly*, *op. cit.*, p. 186.
[52] Which is also stated in much the same terms in the Priestly version in Num. chap. 35.

by mischance. As Hale saw, the ancient analogy for that medieval English practice was the biblical one which he quoted. The justification of it was the same in both cases. The objective harm to the social order in the biblical instance was the violent death of an innocent human being, the supreme creation and the image of God. In the English example the harm is inherent in the fact that by the killing "the king hath lost his subject." The guilt of the unintentional slayer in either case is not "moral" but is inherent in the transcendent nature of the harm resulting from the unintended act. The measure by which this wrong is righted is entirely consistent with that evolved by the English king for other cases of wrongful death: it is atoned for (at least in part) by a pecuniary forfeiture.

The English deodand forfeiture is thus to be seen as forming part of a single pattern of royal judicial procedure that amounts to simple transformation of the biblical prescriptions for all manner of cases of wrongful death, including criminal homicide. Both biblical and early English law exclude wrongful death from the realm of civil actions and place it squarely in the domain of public wrongs. It makes no difference whether the death resulted from an unambiguous crime such as intentional homicide or manslaughter, or whether it was only a quasi-crime such as accidental death or death resulting from negligence. Biblical law excludes the possibility of converting any aspect of the resolution of such cases into a pecuniary consideration,[53] requiring in every instance a form of atonement: the destruction of the offending animal (the goring ox), the slaying of a heifer (the case of the unsolved murder), exile to the city of refuge (the accidental slayer), execution of the criminal himself (intentional homicide). In contrast the English kings transformed these expiations in every parallel case into pecuniary forfeitures or direct confiscation of chattels. Wherever possible they carried the biblical rationale of expiation to a point never contemplated in biblical or early Israelite law. Suicide, regarded by the church as a grave moral offense, was thus turned into a *de facto* criminal act, which provided the king with yet another occasion to exact a forfeiture of chattels, to the detriment of the suicide's next-of-kin. In biblical law and throughout biblical history, however, there is not the least suggestion that suicide was considered a moral wrong, much less a crime.[54] Also in line with this tendency was the institution of the king's pardon and the privilege of sanctuary, both of which were elaborated to a degree far beyond their analogues on the European continent where, to be sure, they were not altogether unknown. It would be unfair to say that the prospect of gaining revenue from such sources resulted in reducing all

criminal penalties to a *de facto* pecuniary standard. But the temptation to resort to this kind of penalty was at times sufficient to allow even criminal murderers to escape the penalty, by such avenues as asylum in a monastery or church, abjuration of the realm, or royal pardon (though the latter was not often brazenly granted to intentional killers). All of these alternatives to execution entailed for the criminal at the very least confiscation of chattels, escheat of lands (in the case of convicted murderers), as well as other pecuniary fees needed to secure the royal favor. As Maitland observed: "Such justice was a profitable source of revenue, of forfeitures, fines and amercements."[55]

To summarize succinctly, the deodands were the distinctively English reflex of the biblical law of the goring ox. They shared a common rationale, one based on a perception of the universe as a strict hierarchy, between the categories of which no breach can occur without dire consequences. The execution of homicidal animals in Europe represents the literal implementation of the biblical rule. For that very reason it reached a dead end with the coming of age of learning and enlightenment in the last two or three centuries, although we have seen that there have been odd survivals into even contemporary times. The deodand, on the other hand, was a transformation of the biblical rule resulting from the perception of the special nature of sovereignty and its exclusive prerogatives. It was in turn rendered obsolete, but only through yet a further transformation which rendered its underlying rationale more potent than it had ever been before. I will treat this last and still very vital reincarnation of the biblical goring ox in the third part of this study,[56] but first we must consider the evidence for the trial of animals in the United States.

XI. ANIMAL TRIALS IN THE UNITED STATES

I called attention earlier to the fact that during the Middle Ages and later animals and/or executions of homicidal animals occurred commonly in continental Europe, but that the practice appears never to have gained a foothold in England. There we find instead of the execution of homicidal domestic animals the institution of the deodand, by which animals as well as inanimate objects that had by their action caused the death of a human being became forfeit to the king, or rather, a sum of money equivalent to the value of the animal or thing became due to the king as deodand. These two lines of development would appear to be mutually exclusive. Before I suggest an explanation for this contrast I wish to point out that the institution of the deodand in its original form was

---

[53] With the exception of the goring-ox case, discussed earlier; in that case the owner of the animal could be charged with negligence.

[54] See *Temple Law Quarterly, op. cit.*, p. 183f.

[55] F. W. Maitland, *The Forms of Action at Common Law* (ed. A. H. Clayton and W. J. Whittaker; Cambridge, 1936), p. 12.

[56] *Temple Law Quarterly, op. cit.*, pp. 213ff.

never part of the law of any of the original colonies or of any of the states after the establishment of American independence. The omission of the English deodands from both the common and the statute laws in the United States appears to have been deliberate.[1] The notion that a disequilibrium in the society at large precipitated by a fatal accident caused by an animal or an instrument can be set aright by means of a pecuniary expiation to the king—for this is what the deodand procedure amounted to on the ideological level—was particularly repugnant to the Puritan colonists of New England. They saw themselves as a New Israel in which the duty of maintaining the sacred and pure condition of the community devolved in a palpable way upon each individual and not upon a quasi-High Priest—a mortal, if regal, being who pretended to have the transcendent authority to offer absolution for sins which lie wholly in the cosmic sphere by the crass mechanism of exacting an obligatory contribution to his private treasury.[2] Thus it was perfectly consistent for the colonists in New England to reject the deodand—as well as the related practices through which the English kings exercised the exclusive right of claiming as forfeitures all the property of convicted felons as well as of suicides,[3] while adhering to the letter of the biblical law by executing beasts together with persons who had used them in the crime of bestiality.[4]

The institution of the deodand is a concomitant of a particular view of sovereignty in which ultimate political authority is merged with transcendent sacred authority that was considerably more than symbolic, both being indivisible and incarnate in the person of the reigning monarch. This view was unacceptable to the New England Puritans, and the deodand and similar English royal prerogatives did therefore not take root in America. The distinguishing prerogative of sovereignty to enforce forfeitures *per se*, on the grounds that a harm to the body politic necessitates a corrective action without regard to the moral guilt or innocence of any particular individual, nevertheless was preserved. It assumed a form that was never invoked in those contexts which were characteristic for the imposition of the deodand, but that nevertheless

elaborated on the underlying rationale of that institution to a degree never before envisaged in the history of Western law. The final sections of this essay will be devoted to an investigation of this development.[5]

If the preceding analysis of the grounds for the absence of deodands in American legal tradition is valid, then we may return for a moment to an issue raised earlier: why did the institution of the deodand develop in England but remain unknown in continental Europe? The question is all the more insistent if we recall that the noxal surrender, which was one of the two main sources of the deodand was as well known in early European law as it was in England. The answer, I strongly suspect, lies precisely in the unique character which the English monarchy assumed beginning with the Norman Conquest, and which in significant measure is attributable directly to that conquest. The continental—particularly the French— experience of the fragmentization of what was *de facto* sovereign authority among a host of feudal barons was not duplicated in Norman England. The centralization of political authority, and the administrative structure designed to maintain it, was a firm social reality by the middle of the thirteenth century. The concept of the "King's Peace" was widely recognized and its enforcement was assured by the ever enlarging scope and corpus of criminal law, which lay directly within the royal jurisdiction under the rubric of the Pleas of the Crown. That itself was an innovation of Norman times which had the most profound consequences for the English legal system. The deodand and similar forfeitures to the crown's benefit were developed within this framework.[6] We already noted that the opposite was the case in France, and that an attempt made in Burgundy to institute a procedure analogous to the deodands proved abortive. The political realities in France could not support it.[7] The English monarch, in a word, began to weld a new social reality, the nation, with all that this entity implies today in terms of ineffable sacredness and transcendent significance. (Centuries were to elapse before parallel developments occurred in Europe.) The monarch was the living embodiment of this social reality, and the conflict with the church's claim to preeminence in all matters affecting the transcendent facets of man and society was early manifested in English history. It is a commonplace that the Reformation under—and by —Henry VIII was the resolution of a conflict primarily over ultimate sovereignty rather than over religious doctrine. A century later the English concluded that sovereignty incarnate and transcendent nationhood were equally incompatible, and consequently the monarchy was reduced to a mere visible

---

[1] See *Temple Law Quarterly, op. cit.*, p. 195 n. 77.

[2] This is not, of course, to discount other factors in the break with tradition, such as the sheer difficulty in the seventeenth century of maintaining over a three-thousand mile gulf of ocean that sense of the monarchic mystique which alone was capable of sustaining the credibility of the deodands institution up to the middle of the nineteenth century in England itself.

[3] See above, pp. 79 and 81.

[4] I have not come across references to punishments of domestic animals for having killed or injured persons in colonial America or in the earlier social history of the United States, such as those that I will cite below from more recent times. But while I should not be surprised if some instances of such a practice were to be found in local newspapers, gazettes, and the like, they are not likely to be found in legal sources, properly speaking.

[5] *Temple Law Quarterly, op cit.*, p. 227ff.

[6] See above, pp. 75ff and 80.

[7] See above, p. 68.

symbol of the sovereignty of the nation. The monarch became a focus for expression of the sense of identity with and pride in the nation in all its unique qualities. The New England Puritans found even the symbol inimicable to their sense of purpose; what is more, for them it was not even visible.[8]

Since the institution of the deodands was allowed no place in American law there was no official mechanism by means of which attacks by domestic animals against persons could be recognized as a *communal harm*—as distinct from a civil tort for which the owner of the animal could be sued for damages—other than by some solemn procedure ranging from the literal, as in medieval Europe, to the semi-serious and even the facetious. I called attention elsewhere to the biblical sense of hierarchy inherent in some American opinions expressed in the context of the conflicting interests of ecology and commercial expansion, which assert the invariable priority of human, or social, interests over those of the animal world, or of nature in general. Such views are by no means incompatible with the equally strong tendency towards the anthropomorphization of animals, particularly those that are seen as useful to man either economically or psychologically. The reverse of this coin, inevitably, is that the same animals—especially household pets, to whom some form of personality is imputed—will be viewed as near criminals should they commit an act that is injurious to man or to his interests. I have culled the following examples from relatively recent sources; I have made no attempt to ascertain how far back in American records similar evidence might be found.

From a decision of the Supreme Court of Tennessee:

This is a lawsuit arising out of the unlawful act of a disorderly mule. He was found loitering about the streets of Knoxville, without any apparent business, no visible means of support, and no evidence of ownership, except a yoke on his neck.[9]

The action in question was legally not one against the animal, but involved an attempt by the animal's owner to recover possession of the mule, which had been taken up by someone else under the provisions in the Tennessee Code governing the disposition of stray cattle and draft animals.[10] The court, obviously amused that such a case should have gone up on appeal, permitted itself a response in this unusually humorous vein, which nevertheless is significant from the standpoint of the issues that presently concern us. The court is transposing a legal issue revolving about a statute whose origins lay in the distant past

into a framework more readily comprehensible to a modern urban society: an analogy is drawn between the mule and a human vagrant, and the animal is treated as if it had been in violation of the laws relating to vagrancy. Although this is not an instance of the trial or punishment of an animal, it is a manifestation of a disposition to contemplate and judge animal behavior in human terms.

The animal most frequently encountered as alleged "defendant" in American legal proceedings is the dog. The dog is to be found "in the dock" not only for attacks upon persons, but also for the killing or injuring of livestock or poultry. All state codes can be found to devote a greater or lesser amount of space to laws governing the maintenance of dogs both from the aspect of the animal's own welfare and from that of the protection of persons and property—including other animals—against attacks and depradations by dogs. We will not be concerned here, of course, with the civil liability of dog owners and custodians for damages in respect of injuries or loss due to attacks by the animals, or even with various pecuniary penalties levied against them in connection with wrongful omissions as regards control of their dogs as defined by statute. The point at which a certain degree of ambiguity enters in connection with the identity of the defendant—whether it is the animal or its owner—occurs when the fate of the dog itself has been put in the balance, that is, when upon the establishment of certain facts as prescribed by statute the dog is to be destroyed. The ambiguity often is found not in the formal aspects of the proceeding, but rather in the verbal formulation of their import by the participants, sometimes not even excepting the pronouncement of the court. In other instances the ambiguity is resolved altogether: in such cases it is soon clear that the defendant is in fact the dog and not its owner.

One of the most protracted cases of this kind arose in Virginia as a result of the killing of a sheep by a dog in February, 1961. The Virginia statutes deal with this kind of occurrence in stringent terms: a warden is obliged to kill the dog on the spot and ordinary citizens have the right to do the same, with immunity guaranteed against suit for damages by the dog's owner.[11] In this instance, however, the dog escaped and the authorities subsequently sought to get possession of it from its owner, one Jim Laing, who was served with a warrant charging that he did "unlawfully possess one sheep killing dog."[12] Laing was tried and convicted on this count. He appealed to Circuit Court on the ground that there was no statute that made it unlawful for someone to possess a sheep-killing dog, but the conviction was affirmed. On appeal to the Virginia

---

[8] We could pose this question: Had television been available in the seventeenth century, would an independent republic have been founded in America in the eighteenth?

[9] Tenn. 407 (1899); *Mincey* v. *Bradburn.*

[10] Tenn. Code Ann. 44-1502ff. (1956) as reported in *Tenn. Law Review* 25 (1957–1958): pp. 480f.

[11] Code of Virginia Annotated 1950 (1973), §29–197.

[12] *Laing* v. *Commonwealth,* 203 Va. 682, 127, S.E. 2d. 143 (1962).

Supreme Court of Appeals Laing's conviction was reaffirmed by a four-to-three decision. The court nevertheless conceded that there was in fact no statute that made it a crime for someone to possess a sheep-killing dog, and that in consequence "the defendant's motion to dismiss (the charge) should have been sustained."[13] But the court went on to state that "the failure of the trial court to do so under the circumstances of this case[14] was harmless error."[15] This view was based on the actual proceeding in the trial court which did *not* in fact convict Laing of any crime: the verdict did not entail any sentence against him, but merely ordered that the dog be killed and required Laing to pay the cost of the proceeding.[16] The Supreme Court upheld this decision on the ground that "the only judgment in the case is against the dog and the defendant does not question here the . . . evidence of *the guilt of the dog*."[17] The court concluded by affirming that "there is no ground for reversing the judgment against the dog."[18] The dissenting justices pointed out that by this ruling "the court without notice or process converted a criminal proceeding against the owner of the dog into a civil proceeding for its forfeiture."[19] It seems to me that the dissenting minority's opinion has here isolated the most sensitive legal spot in the issue. It is one which we shall inspect more closely in the final part of this study when we turn to the rationale by means of which automobiles have been found "guilty" of offenses and therefore became subject to confiscation by the sovereignty. Two points are at issue: (1) Who or what *in fact* is the object of the prosecution in such cases, the owner of the dog or the dog itself? (2) By ordering the "execution" of the dog, is any punishment implied, whether of the dog or of its owner? For the time being we shall leave these questions unanswered.

Some clue as to the thinking of the court in *Laing* v. *Commonwealth* may be found in the language it used in a subsequent action which, in effect, recast the terms of the original warrant:

The purpose . . . is for the court to determine if the dog is a killer of livestock, and the warrant is designed to require

the owner or custodian, if known, to appear and make his defense in behalf of the dog, if he is so disposed.[20]

There is no implication of wrongdoing on the part of the owner of the dog; he is merely enjoined to make an appearance "at the hearing of evidence as to whether the dog was *guilty* of the depradations."[21] It would therefore appear that the guilt (or innocence) of the dog was the sole issue. There was no accusation against the owner, although that was implied by the original warrant. Our interest in this case is limited only to its value in illustrating boundary confusion as it affected a long sequence of actions in a single case. This confusion was not limited to the error—conceded by the Supreme Court of Virginia—perpetuated from the initiation of the proceedings through the first appeal, but persisted into the thinking of the Supreme Court itself. In its last decision in the case, after Laing had tried without success to bring his appeal to the United States Supreme Court, the Virginia Supreme Court unanimously affirmed Laing's conviction (in a lower court) and his sentence to four months' imprisonment (in addition to a fine)—for contempt of court, because he had persistently thwarted authorities in their attempts to gain custody of the dog.[22] The governor of Virginia, however, commuted Laing's sentence, and he was freed after having served only one week of it. This denouement was reported in the *New York Times* in these terms:

Jim Laing, who went to jail for his dog, got his freedom today, having served seven days of a contempt sentence of four months after he refused to yield his German shepherd, Ricky, for execution. Gov. . . . Harrison commuted Mr. Laing's sentence Monday. . . . After losing court appeals to save the dog, Mr. Laing refused to produce Ricky. He has since said he did not know where the dog was.[23]

It is not difficult to provide illustrations of the legal punishment of dogs which show less ambiguity over the question of who was the object of the punishment. The article by J. P. McNamara noted earlier[24] was prompted by a case in Virginia in 1927 similar to the one just described. It was reported in the local press of the time as one in which the Circuit Court of the county "imposed the death penalty upon a dog tried and convicted of sheep stealing."[25] Contrary to the case of Jim Laing and his dog, that earlier instance was apparently reported in a light vein. The following more recent item, dateline Chattanooga, Tenn., is reported in a similar light tone:

[13] *Laing* v. *Commonwealth*, 203 Va. 682, 127 S.E. 2d. 143 (1962).

[14] That is, that it was only a matter of the wording of the warrant, which should have addressed itself only to the objective of taking custody of the dog instead of charging the owner with a non-existent crime.

[15] *Laing* v. *Commonwealth*, 203 Va. 682, 127 S.E. 2d. 143 (1962).

[16] *Laing* v. *Commonwealth*, 203 Va. 682, 127 S.E. 2d. 143 (1962).

[17] *Laing* v. *Commonwealth*, 203 Va. 682, 127 S.E. 2d. 144 (1962), emphasis added.

[18] *Laing* v. *Commonwealth*, 203 Va. 682, 127 S.E. 2d. 144 (1962), interpreting the appeal as having been addressed to that initial decision.

[19] *Laing* v. *Commonwealth*, 203 Va. 682, 127 S.E. 2d. 144 (1962).

[20] *Laing* v. *Commonwealth*, 205 Va. 511, 137, S.E. 2d. 896 (1964).

[21] *Laing* v. *Commonwealth*, 203 Va. 682, 685, 1962 emphasis added.

[22] *Laing* v. *Commonwealth*, 205 Va. 511, 137 S.E. 2d. 896 (1964).

[23] Nov. 13, 1964, p. 18.

[24] See above, pp. 69f. n. 33.

[25] I owe this reference to L. Nader. I have not attempted to trace the record of the case in the law reports of the region.

A watchdog bit an Outlaw and wound up in jail.

The dog was sentenced to serve a 10-day term at the Chattanooga Humane Society for biting Police Detective H. R. Outlaw at a residence where the officer said he was investigating a burglary.

"I can't understand why the dog didn't get the man who broke into the house instead of me," Mr. Outlaw said.[26]

I will conclude this section with one further extended saga, all episodes of which were datelined New Canaan, Conn.:

NEW CANAAN DOG TO BE PUT ON TRIAL FOR HIS LIFE AS VICIOUS.

Duke, a seventy-pound German shepherd, will go on trial for his life before the Board of Selectmen on May 25. . . . [He was] the subject of "numerous" complaints . . . that he is vicious. . . .

The owner of the dog maintained Duke was not vicious. She said she would fight any attempt to have the animal destroyed and retained a lawyer to represent her at the hearings. . . .[27]

Duke, a seventy-pound German shepherd who attacked a woman here on April 7, was banished by the Board of Selectmen.

The board ordered the five year old animal to be confined to a licensed commercial kennel for "proper care and treatment." The owner's lawyer will appeal the ruling.

The sentence was handed down by the three-member board. . . . The animal did not appear.

The session was held under a provision of the state statutes that provides that the Selectmen may order the "restraint or disposal" of a dog considered a "nuisance" by reason of "vicious disposition."[28]

Finally:

NEW CANAAN GIVES EXILED DOG CHANCE TO START A NEW LIFE.

Duke, the German shepherd dog exiled from the town for biting too many citizens, has been given a conditional welcome home by the Board of Selectmen.

He was given a second chance today after the head of the West Redding Canine College, where Duke has been since May, told the Selectmen the dog had developed a new and much more kindly personality. . . .

Duke's owner . . . took the dog's case to the Court of Common Pleas, contending the sentence had been too harsh. The late Judge John T. Dwyer ruled the Selectmen had had a right to banish Duke, but urged them to review the case.

John Behan, director of the dog school, had given Duke a diploma with A's in special adjustment and has told the Selectmen that Duke is "a much more controlled dog and has undergone a change in personality and temperament."[29]

Let us now recall the statement of Kelsen with which I began this part of this study:

In primitive law, animals, even plants and other inanimate objects are often treated in the same way as human beings and are, in particular, punished. However, this must be seen in its connection with the animism of primitive man. He considers animals, plants, and inanimate objects as endowed with a "soul," inasmuch as he attributes human, and sometimes even superhuman, mental faculties to them. The fundamental difference between human and other beings, which is part of the outlook of civilized man, does not exist for primitive man.

Whether there is the merest grain of truth in this dictum, and whether, perhaps, the shoe may not be altogether on the other foot, may now be left for others to ponder.

---

[26] *New York Times*, Sept. 13, 1972, p. 23. Hospitality of a more attractive kind awaits the deserving law-abiding dog, as suggested by the following advertisement: "The Grooming Salon at PET LODGE, N.Y.'s Only Top-Rated Pet Hotel. You'll love the prices and the mid-week overnight package." *New York Times*, Jan. 19, 1972, p. 43.

[27] *New York Times*, May 12, 1960, p. 37.

[28] *New York Times*, May 26, 1969, p. 35. The "banishment" of the dog brings to mind a case reported from Russia around the end of the seventeenth century. According to von Amira, who included the case in his review of the evidence for the punishment

of animals ("Thierstrafen und thierprocesse," p. 573 n. 1, citing Carl Meiners, *Vergleichung des ältern und neurern Russlands* **2:** pp. 291), a court sentenced a pet goat to exile in Siberia for having butted a child down a flight of stairs; the family was required to contribute a kopeck a day for the goat's upkeep.

[29] *New York Times*, Sept. 23, 1960, p. 31.

Finkelstein used the vehicle of the goring ox laws to discuss the implications of ancient Mesopotamian and biblical legal and cosmological concepts, and to trace the impact of ancient attitudes, however transformed, on the Western world. He saw the scope of the discussion as reaching from the earliest expressions of the rules concerning the goring ox through modern legal attitudes, and he formulated his approach in those terms, as he indicated in the Introduction to this volume. He chose a tripartite presentation of the result of his investigations, and developed his project in that form.

The text of parts I and II appears above. They deal with the ancient Near Eastern and early European sources, and with the related ethnographical evidence. In part III, Finkelstein takes the discussion into the modern world, starting with the abolition of the deodand and culminating with the topics of damages for wrongful death, and forfeiture proceedings in this country. Finkelstein's purpose in this section was more to show a trend in the development of legal thought than to write a definitive legal history of the problems involved. Because he felt least at home with the later material,[1] he published a preliminary version of the third part first. His intention in doing so was to elicit the reactions of legal scholars, and possibly to develop his own interpretation of the material. However, Finkelstein's untimely death made it impossible for him to use the preliminary publication for this purpose, and it certainly is not within the province of an editor of posthumous material to make substantive changes in that material.

I was therefore faced with the choice of adhering to Finkelstein's original publication plan or omitting the third part. There were strong arguments both for and against including the third section under the circumstances, since all that could be done would be to edit the material to bring it into line with the rest of the work and to exclude the introductory explanatory material which is now covered in more detail in parts I and II of the study. However, given the scope of the problem, and the fact that the *Temple Law Quarterly* is not readily available to scholars not within reach of a law library,[2] I had hoped to present the entire work following Finkelstein's original plan as closely as possible.

Unfortunately the resulting manuscript was extremely long, and the value that would be gained from reprinting the third part here could not be considered to justify the added expense. Therefore the present volume includes only the first two sections of the work, while for the third part the original published version of the material must serve.[3] Anyone wishing to follow the odyssey of the ox to its conclusion in the twentieth century must do so in the original publication. For those who have not yet seen that work, it must be mentioned that the precedent of the goring ox is explicitly invoked until the present: the biblical rule is cited in many modern American forfeiture decisions. A recent one, which it is appropriate to mention here, is the United States Supreme Court decision in *Calero-Thompson* v. *Pearson Yacht Leasing Co.*,[4] which refers to Finkelstein's preliminary discussion of the topic among other authorities cited.

---

[1] See *Temple Law Quarterly*, *op. cit.*, p. 169.

[2] A limited number of paperbound offprints of the original version of part III still exist. These may be obtained, for a small handling charge, by writing to the editor at the Babylonian Section of the University Museum, 33rd and Spruce Streets, Philadelphia, Pa. 19104.

[3] However, to complete the set of citations which introduce the three parts of the work, I cite here that which was meant to introduce part III: "If an ox gore a man that he shall die, the ox shall be stoned, and his flesh shall not be eaten. . . . When this ancient concept is recalled, our understanding of the law of forfeiture of chattels is more easily understood."

[4] 416 U.S. 681, S.Ct. 2080 (1974).